Praise for

HOMESICK
AND HAPPY

"Every parent dreads letting children go. Partly, we dread it because we lack a clear road map of how and when to do it. *Homesick and Happy* changes that. It is a powerful and very accessible book that helps build maturity and resilience in our children—and in parents, as well! I highly recommend this book to every parent of a boy or girl who is ready to take the next step, and I equally recommend it for every young person ready to do the same."

—MICHAEL GURIAN, author of
The Wonder of Boys and *The Wonder of Girls*

"I am constantly asked how to help kids become more assertive, independent, and confident. Here is a compelling response: good old-fashioned summer camp. If you're on the fence about sending your child, or are too anxious to consider it, read this book now. Michael Thompson is back with a compelling argument for the brawn and bonds that only camp can give a child. You'll be signing yours up before you make it through the first chapter."

—RACHEL SIMMONS, former director of
Girls Leadership Institute Summer Camp
and author of *The Curse of the Good Girl*

"Michael Thompson understands children and their need for growth, exploration, and independence. And he also understands parents and their well-meaning, but often unreasonable, need to protect and shelter. With this deep understanding, a great sense of humor, and impeccable resources, he succeeds brilliantly in helping parents understand why children need time away from home and away from them . . . why children given the right opportunities at summer camp can rise above those minor bouts of homesickness and create the most extraordinary memories. And he also succeeds in generating just a touch of envy in the hearts of all those parents who read *Homesick and Happy* . . . for the great fun their kids are going to have."

—HARRIET LOWE, editor in chief, *Camping* magazine

"Parents and schools both play an important role in helping children on their developmental journey to adulthood. In *Homesick and Happy,* Michael Thompson has the courage to remind us that sometimes we parents and we educators must step back to leave space for the magic that can only come from downtime and from time away from us."

—PEG SMITH, CEO, American Camp Association

"If you are trying to decide if you should send your child to camp, you should read *Homesick and Happy*. It explains how camp provides the safe challenges away from home that all children need as they move toward adulthood. If you have been to camp, you will enjoy the trip back. If you did not go to camp, you will understand why your child should."

—ADAM N. WEINSTEIN, executive director,
American Camp Association,
New York and New Jersey

"Both a sublime elegy on the pleasures of camp and an indispensable guide to drawing the most from those indelible days, this unique book grips like a novel and instructs like an authoritative text. A man who loved and loves camp himself, Michael Thompson pours his heart into these pages, along with his unsurpassed wisdom about children and their parents. Full of practical advice and unforgettable anecdotes, this book is an instant classic."

—EDWARD M. HALLOWELL, MD

"Aaaah. I can almost hear the sighs of relief as parents read and absorb the message of *Homesick and Happy*. With his usual compassion and warmth, Michael Thompson helps parents let go of the imagined dangers that feed our anxieties, and avoid the real dangers of holding on to our children too tightly: timidity, fragility, lack of initiative, and risk-aversion. Children need adventures, and that means summer camp, school trips, overnights—time away from mom and dad. Children have known this since forever; Thompson makes that wisdom available to those of us who forgot it when we became parents."

—LAWRENCE J. COHEN, PhD, author *Playful Parenting*

HOMESICK
AND HAPPY

HOMESICK
AND HAPPY

How Time Away from Parents
Can Help a Child Grow

Michael Thompson, PhD

Ballantine Books Trade Paperbacks
New York

I am grateful to the many people who, through personal interviews, phone calls, emails, letters, books, and research have shared their stories, their expertise, and their insight in these pages. Names and personal characteristics of some camp staff, former campers, parents, and children have been changed to disguise them. In some instances, additional details have been changed for the same purpose. Any resulting resemblance to persons living or dead is entirely coincidental and unintentional.

A Ballantine Books Trade Paperback Original

Published in the United States by Ballantine Books,
an imprint of The Random House Publishing Group,
a division of Random House, Inc., New York.

BALLANTINE and colophon are registered trademarks
of Random House, Inc.

Library of Congress Cataloging-in-Publication Data
Thompson, Michael.
Homesick and happy : how time away from parents can help
a child grow / Michael Thompson.
p. cm.
Includes bibliographical references.
ISBN 978-0-345-52492-8 (pbk.)—ISBN 978-0-345-52493-5 (ebook)
1. Parental deprivation. 2. Parental overprotection.
3. Parent and child. 4. Self-confidence. I. Title.
BF723.P255T46 2012
155.4'192—dc23   2012004893

Printed in the United States of America

www.ballantinebooks.com

2 4 6 8 9 7 5 3 1

Book design by Karin Batten

To *camp counselors everywhere.*
You inspire children with your energy and creativity,
your devotion and your love.
You make an indelible difference in their lives.

CONTENTS

INTRODUCTION

A New York City Boy
Goes Back to Camp

How did I get here? It is 9:15 p.m. on October 30, the day before Halloween. Cold winds are blowing off Lake Champlain and I am shivering in the dark woods as I pull on a bathing suit, preparing to jump into that bone-chilling water. No one sane in Vermont is swimming at this time of year. I'm told the water is about fifty-two degrees, but that's warmer than the air temperature, which is in the high thirties, so even if I do manage to get myself into the water—and I have my doubts about whether I have the courage to do so—I know it is going to be truly freezing when I get out.

I don't like cold water; I haven't liked it for years. I'm sixty-three years old. This is really not my thing and, now that I consider it, it never really was. I'm a New York City boy. And this is a young man's game. I stupidly let myself be tricked into it by three men in their thirties.

An hour earlier, I was sitting on the ground around a camp-fire with Matt, Ben, and Neill, three outdoor educators. We were discussing the challenges they were devising for four boys, ages thirteen to seventeen, as part of an intense weekend mini-camp. While we were talking, the four boys for whom this weekend was designed were off in the woods, each one sitting alone, sep-arated from the others, without a flashlight. They were complet-ing the first of their formal "challenges" of that evening: experiencing their own thoughts in the dark and cold. The three counselors were talking about the ultimate challenge of the eve-ning: a swim in Lake Champlain. And then they looked at me, the author, the overweight psychologist with the white beard, the observer there to study children's camp experiences for the book he was writing.

"We want to let you know that when the boys get back from their solitary sit in the woods, we're going to challenge them to go into the lake," Matt said. "And we're all going to go in with them. We would never ask them to do something we wouldn't do. So we're going . . . all of us."

You didn't have to be a psychologist to see what was coming.

"We wanted to let you know, so you can choose either to head back to the inn or to stay."

Ah yes . . . the inn, less than a mile from this spot, containing people my age, my bed, a warm shower, a drink of scotch at the end of the evening, and a place where I could be surrounded by respectful adults who didn't challenge me, not like this anyway.

Our leader, Matt Kolan, six-foot-four and rail thin, with a dark black beard and beguiling smile, never said the actual words, "You can't stay to watch the boys swim and write about the experience unless you yourself are willing to go into the lake." He didn't have to. I heard the message. I was immediately uncomfortable and anxious.

"Let me think about it," I said. "I don't much like cold water and I think I'm a little old for that." They glanced away strategically, leaving me alone with my fear. There was no one to whom I could appeal.

And then Ben told his story. He had joined a group of "Polar Bear" swimmers in western Massachusetts who all cut through the ice to swim on New Year's Day. "And . . ." he said, "we had a seventy-year-old woman who did it. She was amazing."

Uh-oh. He got me. Ben was not only challenging my age, but my manhood. If a woman that age could go swimming through the ice, then surely a sixty-three-year-old man could jump into Lake Champlain in balmy October. I reluctantly surrendered, agreeing to join their swim, and stayed with the group.

When the boys walked out of the woods, using the campfire as their beacon, Matt continued with his plan to go around the circle and have the four men—they were kind enough to include me—tell the boys stories about their rite of passage or about overcoming some significant psychological obstacle on their way to adulthood. For the three young outdoorsmen, the stories were about challenges they had experienced in nature: stories of killing a deer, hypothermia and near death, and boredom and fear while alone in the woods. The teenagers were enthralled by the stories. All four boys were from privileged backgrounds and none of them had ever faced a prolonged experience in the wilderness. Indeed, these brief weekend mini-camps—this was the fourth in a series—probably constituted their most challenging times in nature away from their parents.

As the young men spoke, I had time to reflect about what I was going to say. Knowing that a terribly cold swim was minutes away, I was feeling very much like the anxious, soft, private-school boy that I had been growing up. Looking around the circle, I personally identified most with the youngest boy in the group, an anxious thirteen-year-old from a wealthy family who attended an independent school in Boston. I tried to pick a story from my life that would speak to him, because I could see his nervousness and I could feel my own. The cold, the setting, the upcoming challenge put me in touch with all of the fears I had faced in my life: childhood fears and grown-up fears, indoor and outdoor fears. Lord knows, there was no shortage of them.

Instead of talking to the boys about my few outdoor adventures—none of which could compete with the counselors' tales—I talked to them about the fear of flying that bedeviled me for years and how I eventually conquered it to become an author and school consultant who flies more than 100,000 miles per year. Hardly exciting stuff, but in my life, a significant achievement.

As soon as I finished, Matt uncurled his long legs and stood up. He told them that the moral he had taken from the four stories was that the key to any personal growth, the secret to finding one's courage, was to make a commitment and keep it. It didn't matter whether the commitment was to hunting a deer or flying on a plane or sitting alone in the woods for days on end. The key was commitment. He picked up a stick and traced a line in the forest floor, near enough to the campfire so that it was visible to all of us. He asked each boy to make a commitment to accept that evening's final challenge by stepping over the line. If they stepped over the line, they would be committing themselves to completing the challenge, but—and here was the rub—they had to do it without knowing what the challenge would be.

My guess was that these boys had been offered thousands of choices in their young lives, but not one like this. Like many American families, their parents practiced a kind of "democratic" parenting that honors a child's ability to negotiate and choose among alternatives from a young age. Commit to something unknown? Sight unseen? That was, I'm sure, an unusual experience for these boys. But their trust in their counselors won out over any fears they might have had. All four boys stepped over the line, I followed them and the three young men followed me. We were all going swimming. No more discussion.

Matt reached into a plastic container that had been sitting unnoticed in the dark and pulled out a bunch of identical blue bathing suits. He nodded toward the woods and encouraged us to find a private spot to change and then join him down by the edge of the lake, twenty yards away. As I changed into my suit, I quickly began to shiver in the wind. When I got to the water's edge, Ben, that rugged outdoorsman whose seventy-year-old-lady-swimming-through-the-ice story was responsible for getting me here, was so cold his teeth were chattering. We all huddled together and beat our arms against our chests, trying futilely to stay warm while waiting for the last member of the group to arrive. When he finally joined us, we all turned to face the frothy whitecaps that were rolling onto the shore.

There was nothing to be gained by further hesitation. I moved directly into the water up to mid-thigh and then threw myself forward, surrounded by men and boys running, hooting, and shouting. I don't remember much of the next few moments, but I do know that I didn't turn and sprint for my clothes as I had imagined I would. Instead, seconds after being in the water, we were all standing around the campfire laughing, our chests warmed by the flames, our exultant faces lit by the yellow light, and we weren't cold at all. We had done it. We had done it all together! For a second, we were the kings of the world. We had made a commitment and gone through with it. The boys were clearly triumphant. So was the old guy—and that would be me.

TWO THINGS MOTIVATED ME to write a book about camps and trips where children sleep away from their parents and accept unknown challenges from outdoor educators. One was my own childhood. The other, more immediate and important, was a growing body of troubling conversation with educators and parents.

Educators had been telling me for more than a decade that

they were having trouble organizing overnight school trips because more and more parents were refusing to let their children go away. Even though the fifth-grade Science Camp trip had been a fixture in the town for years, for example, parents needed more meetings, more reassurance than they had needed in the past. Schools told me that they had growing numbers of parents—very anxious parents—who announced that they would let their child go on the school trip only if they were chosen as chaperones. When schools agreed, the teachers reported that they ended up spending a good part of their time peeling the anxious parent away from his or her child so that the child could make some new friends and have some novel experiences. A fifth-grade homeroom teacher in Chicago described how the parents of some of her students now made appointments in advance of the traditional trip to review sheaves of largely unnecessary special instructions for the care and feeding of their ten-year-old children.

The complaints I was hearing from educators dovetailed with things that camp professionals were telling me. Parents were less willing than in the past to send children for a long session of four weeks or eight weeks. Some of the parental concerns were financial; after all, private camps are expensive. But I was hearing the same story from a wide variety of camps at different price levels: two weeks instead of four, one week instead of two. And even when parents were willing to have their children sleep away, they were often choosing to send their children to three one-week "skills camps" rather than to one longer community camp. Much of this was in service of parental ambition. A man in New York City told me about his son who, together with his best friend, had gone to a YMCA camp for two years. The man's son loved the camp and was going back, but his son's best friend wasn't returning. Not because the boy didn't love it; he did. But his father was sending him to an "elite" tennis camp. For many ambitious parents, the summer is for getting ahead. A YMCA camp that emphasizes choice, friendship, and spirituality? That's not going to get you on a varsity team.

I am witness to this same issue/phenomenon every summer at Belmont Hill, the boys' independent school where I serve as the supervising psychologist. The school runs an excellent summer school; however, many students are not there for the traditional reason: to make up work. Many of the students are there to take a course in the summer *before* they take the same level course at their local high school, thereby increasing their chances of getting an A in the "real" course. The parents of these children are not waiting for school districts to go to the twelve-month school year. Their children are in school for the academic year from August to June, and the parents are keeping their children at home and in school during the summer, sitting in classes and doing homework from late June to early August. Two underlying assumptions are at work here: The more academics the better, and children do not need a break from school and its endless evaluations. I disagree.

In his book *Outliers: The Story of Success*, Malcolm Gladwell praises the lifelong impact of parents who engage in what the sociologist Annette Lareau calls the "concerted cultivation" of their children. If you read *Outliers*, you are likely to conclude that the best parenting means constantly being with your children, talking to them, sending them to some academic program or another, and coaching them in leadership skills from earliest childhood. According to Gladwell, a nine-year-old boy named Alex had the skills to cross-examine his pediatrician during his wellness checkup because his family had "painstakingly taught" him how, ". . . nudging and prodding and encouraging him and showing him the rules of the game."

I get a bit exhausted just thinking about all that "nudging and prodding and encouraging," because I had exactly that kind of upbringing. I went to a private boys' school in New York City. I had guitar lessons (classical!) for years, as well as skating and dancing lessons. I sang in the choir (no talent), and went to the theater with my parents because my mother loved it so, and (happily) I did, too. I took drawing lessons at the Metropolitan Museum of Art (no talent) and, during our eighth-grade year, shared piano lessons (no talent) at Steinway Hall with a talented classmate. If ever there was a product of "concerted cultivation," I was it, at least during the academic year in New York.

But not in the summertime. In June, July, and August there was no summer school, no music lessons, no sports camps, no grades, no striving. We went to live with my grandparents in their rural home by a lake in Massachusetts. I was surrounded by first and second cousins, some older, many younger. Also aunts, uncles, and assorted other extended family and family friends. The kids hung out together all day; we saw the grown-ups only at night. We spent our time in the woods, inventing games, talking, sharing secrets, competing. No one watched us, except when we swam in the lake, and then not at all after we had passed the family swimming test, a hundred-yard swim I completed paddling alongside my aunt. (You weren't allowed to take the test with a parent beside you because the family wisdom was that you needed to do it on your own, without their pressure or their praise.)

Having passed the test, I took a rowboat or a canoe out alone almost every morning (no life jacket) to fish or catch painted turtles. I went to an Audubon day camp at the Moose Hill Bird Sanctuary in Sharon, Massachusetts, for two weeks every summer and gained an appreciation for birds, butterflies, spiders, and snakes that I have never lost. I can still sing the camp song. At fourteen, I was sent to Camp Keewaydin on Lake Temagami in Ontario for seven weeks. That was a life-changing summer for me. I experienced the power of being far away from my parents, being in the Canadian wilderness and mastering challenges that I had never imagined I could do, namely paddling for six hours a day and carrying an extremely heavy wood-canvas canoe over demanding portages. The next summer other interests led me elsewhere and I did not return. This book has given me a chance to revisit Keewaydin and its timeless challenges, and discover why some campers return year after year.

Like many of them, at age eighteen I graduated from high school, but even with a letter of admission to college in my pocket, I didn't feel like much of a man. Hungry for mentorship and a rite of passage that would take me across the threshold from boyhood to manhood, I signed up for a one-month course at Hurricane Island Outward Bound School in 1965, the first summer of its founding. I got exactly what I was looking for in that rugged outdoor challenge and the acknowledgment that I was now a young man, from mentors whom I truly respected. Then I put Outward Bound behind me to pursue my education and training to be a psychologist.

It was only after years as a practicing child psychologist and school consultant that I slowly realized how often I was drawing on my experiences at Camp Keewaydin and Outward Bound rather than on my training in child psychology. I began to believe that much of the "concerted cultivation" I was seeing was leaving young people emotionally fragile and overly dependent on guidance from their manager/advocate/coach parents. I could see that children are often capable of taking responsibility that their parents cannot imagine, and that many children do less well when their parents are watching or supervising them. It was also evident that self-esteem did not and does not come from your parents trying to "support your self-esteem," it comes from building skills. Finally, it was clear to me that many students who exhibited tremendous gains in character and confidence were finding that growth outside of school and away from their families. They were taking trips abroad, being camp counselors, taking care of small children. While politicians and parents became increasingly focused on test scores emerging from schools, I began to focus more on what was happening to children during the summers.

When I started out writing this book, I intended to write about a wide variety of away-from-home experiences: camps, to be sure, but also semesters abroad, overnight school trips, boarding school, any situation where children sleep away from their parents. However, as I interviewed children for the book, I began to zero in on what I call the "magic of camp" for three reasons: for the vast majority of children, their first away-from-home experience and the first experience of homesickness is usually at camp. (Very few eight-year-olds go to Spain for a semester.) It only made sense to go where the first-timers were.

Second, as I interviewed students who had gone to a variety of travel programs, I realized that such programs, while they always provide lifelong memories, are often hit-and-miss affairs and may just involve more school. I interviewed a group of seniors and juniors at a charter school in Cambridge just after their return from a ten-day trip to Guatemala. The students appreciated it, but many confided that it had not been the life-changing experience that the grown-ups kept predicting. While it gave some a dramatic change in their perspectives on poverty, it was just ho-hum for others. Many students reported that the most powerful aspect of their trip was working with younger children, which brings me back to camp.

As my research went on, I found myself less interested in writing about school-style experiences because the excitement and passionate voices of campers won me over. So many former campers talked about camp as having an impact not only on their worldview, but also on their characters, spirituality, and friendships, that I was gradually pulled further into the camp world. I wanted to go where the development was happening. In my book *The Pressured Child,* I said that being a school psychologist was like having front row seats on Broadway for the hit show *Child Development.* I began to realize that when it came to watching child development, the view from camp was every bit as powerful as that from school, and in some ways more powerful, because at camp children feel in charge of their own growth.

While researching this book, I visited nineteen camps; the majority of them were sleepover camps in the Northeast. I interviewed seventeen camp directors and numerous program directors. I talked to hundreds of counselors, either individually or in groups, and watched them in action with children. I observed hundreds of campers and interviewed many of them during meals or before campfires, interviews that spanned from one question to twenty questions. Close to seventy former campers and counselors filled out my detailed online questionnaire. I read histories of the American camp movement and reviewed the camp outcomes literature, including research by the American Camp Association. Throughout my research, my acknowledged bias was toward camps that appeared more interested in overall character development than just skill development, and camps where many campers returned year after year and eventually became counselors. I visited camps whose alumni told me their identities had been profoundly shaped by their camp experiences. That meant that I did not visit many one-week sports camps, relying instead on my memories of my athletic daughter's experience at her numerous soccer and tennis camps, and those of the many student athletes I have counseled.

I loved doing the research for this book because I loved going back to camp. Yes, I ate more corn dogs, waffles, and fudgesicles than any man in his sixties should eat; I endured a lot of mosquito bites and some smelly mildewed mattresses, but I survived.

Finishing this book, I had only a few regrets. I am sorry that I could not visit fifty camps, maybe even seventy. There was so much to see and learn, and it was a lot of fun. I am even glad I jumped into Lake Champlain in October. But because time was a factor—children are not in camp year-round and the deadline limited me to two summers—I had to narrow my list of camps that I could visit. I would like to have visited more specialty camps—religious camps, for instance—for a closer look at children's experiences in those settings. My biggest regret is that I would like to have written more about the partnerships that exist between public schools and camps. Experiential learning has a power that is unmatched. If schools could get more children and teachers out to camp, if we could get more children away from their parents for a while, if we could do more expeditionary learning, we would see some exciting growth and development. Perhaps that's the subject for another book.

For now, I invite you to sit back and enjoy this armchair travel adventure to the heart of children's camp experience. This is as close as you can get—or should get—to a fireside view of your child's camp experience for one simple reason: You are not supposed to be there. No parents should be there. That's the point of this book. Perhaps *Homesick and Happy* will remind you why it is so important that your child is at camp on his or her own, and why, if they're lucky, you are watching from a great distance.

Michael Thompson, PhD
Arlington, MA
October 2011

HOMESICK AND HAPPY

one

OFF THEY GO

Eight Things You Cannot Do
for Your Children

I HAVE WORKED FOR A DECADE as the consultant to a canoe tripping camp in northern Ontario. After the youngest campers, the eleven-year-old boys and girls, complete their first five-day canoe trip away from the main camp, they return to home base. The community holds a campfire in the evening where each child gets to tell his or her story about the journey. Because most of the older campers and their staff are "out on trip," there isn't a huge audience to listen to the youngsters' adventures. Nevertheless, after supper everyone walks out of the dining hall—there are no electric lights indoors—and gathers in a circle by the lakeshore. It is still daylight at seven o'clock in the evening and the water twinkles in the summer sun. Behind the assembled crowd are the simple wood cabins. To the right and to the left are the skinned log frames that cradle the canoes upside-down when they are out of the water, their green canvas bottoms facing up. It is a simple setting: the lake, the sun, the cabins, the canoes, and this small gathering of people, not much more.

Tradition requires that each staff person describes the journey his or her section has completed, where they went, on which lakes they paddled, and the distance of the portages they completed. Standing next to the head counselor is the guide, who is typically a few years younger, perhaps nineteen instead of twenty-three, and then ten campers in a ragged line. Some of the children are delighted to be in front of an audience; others are shy and uncomfortable. The counselors are dressed in the most beat-up outfits imaginable: ragged jeans and T-shirts are featured. Wearing new outdoor gear is not valued at this camp. A few are wearing checkered flannel shirts, which signal that they have been at the camp for ten years. Every head counselor introduces each camper by name and says something personal about that child, often a wry comment about a personality trait or a klutzy start that ended in a moment of mastery. Finally, each child gets to tell his or her own story.

Without fail, both boys and girls talk about all the worst stuff that happened to them. A boy will say, "We paddled in the rain for four hours and when we got to the campsite, we couldn't light a fire because the wood was so wet. We had to have a cold dinner."

One eleven-year-old girl described hiking along a portage with a pack bigger than anything she had ever carried in her life. She stepped into a sphagnum moss bog and as she struggled to get free, she got slowly sucked in until she was stuck in mud up to her waist. Her friends had to pull her out, muddy and wet. A second friend had to fish in the bog to recover her shoe.

A boy described being out on the lake when a thunderstorm broke out. They had to paddle frantically to get to shore, away from the threat of lightning. His group tried to tie a tarpaulin to four trees to shelter them but the wind was so strong that the tarp kept blowing away. In any case, the rain had been almost horizontal at that point and there was no way to stay dry. They slept in semiwet sleeping bags that night.

Another boy spoke about the hundreds of mosquitoes that surrounded his face and attacked his bare arms and legs on a swampy trail. He was wearing shorts at the campfire that evening and we could see the multitude of red bumps up and down his legs. (The parent in me wanted to shout, *Put on pants! It's dusk—don't you know that's when the mosquitoes come out?*)

SUMMER AFTER SUMMER, as I have listened to these campfire horror stories, I've been struck not by the particular discomforts recounted, but by how proud and happy these children seemed. They had just completed one of the scariest and most uncomfortable five-day trips of their lives, yet they looked triumphant, with big smiles, upright posture, and—from the boys—a bit of arm-pumping and self-congratulation. But this wasn't superficial bravado. They didn't hide their fears from the audience. They talked honestly about having been scared, having felt overwhelmed, and especially not being sure that they could do it. The girls often adopted a tone of: "I know this doesn't sound like a girl thing, but . . ." or "I never imagined myself in this predicament, but . . ." You could see their identities changing and their definition of what it meant to be young women expanding in the moment.

I am always very proud of these children. It is impossible not to be. And as I've listened, I've had two strong and contradictory thoughts: *I wish their parents could see them now,* so they could see the remarkable growth in these children in just five days, and, *I'm so glad that their parents aren't here.* Because I believe that the developmental leaps these children have achieved in a week would not have taken place if their parents had been present.

WONDERFUL THINGS CAN HAPPEN for children when they are away from their parents. I am deeply convinced that the presence of Mom and Dad does not always add value to a child's every experience. This remains true, in spite of the fact that this generation of parents, especially college-educated mothers, are spending more hours with their children than ever before.

For years I have been asking audiences of parents a deceptively simple question: "What was *the* sweetest moment of your childhood?" (Before you read on, take ten seconds and answer this for yourself. Don't dissect the question; just let your mind wander; a scene will come to mind.) I wait some moments so that audience members can come up with a memory, then I ask, "Please raise your hands if your parents were present when that sweetest memory took place." I have done this with thousands of people and the result never varies much. Around 20 percent of adults say that their parents were part of their sweetest memories; approximately 80 percent say that their parents weren't there. When audience members turn in their chairs to see the result, they laugh self-consciously. As parents we're hoping that what we're doing is laying a foundation of happy memories for our children. When we are confronted with the fact that our own best memories of childhood took place away from our parents, we are a bit confused. That's a slap in the face to dedicated parents. Or is it?

When I ask individuals who said their parents were present to speak about their happiest memories, they cite the moments that most parents work pretty hard to create: opening presents on Christmas morning, cooking Thanksgiving dinner surrounded by relatives, being together at the beach in the summer, having Mom or Dad read a favorite book at bedtime, playing cards or Monopoly, a family road trip.

When I ask for the sweetest moments without parents, 80 percent of adults tell variations on a similar story that always have the same four or five elements: The child is away from adult supervision, out-of-doors, with friends, facing a challenge and doing something a bit risky. Many people remember being out in the woods, building a tree house with buddies from the neighborhood. Others recall standing knee-deep in a stream following a big rainstorm, building a rock dam with friends. A woman remembered walking eight miles with her friends through an unknown town and along an unknown road after the mother of one of the girls failed to pick them up.

A Canadian colleague of mine remembers that, at twelve, he and his friends used to walk two hours from home to play at the construction site for the brand-new campus of Simon Fraser University. They roamed for hours in the dangerous construction site, playing hide-and-seek and various chase games on unfinished multistory buildings. Years later, as a young man in his twenties, he attended Simon Fraser as an undergraduate. He recalled looking out the window of the library and seeing a ledge along which he had walked when he was a boy when it had been a newly poured concrete wall, four stories aboveground. The sight and the memory scared him. What he had done was dangerous. Now the head of an international school in Africa, it was clear how proud he was of his boyhood accomplishments, even his risk taking, and how sad he felt that the children in his school no longer have the freedom to play the way he and his friends did.

One Indian woman volunteered that the sweetest moment of her childhood was when her parents allowed her to take a plane alone from India to the United States and change planes at Frankfurt Airport on her own. This was back in the day before airlines began requiring minors to be accompanied. She was nine years old.

The trust and confidence of her parents meant everything to her; she was giddy with the feelings of independence. When I asked her whether she had ever allowed her children to do the equivalent, she said yes. She and her husband had allowed their son to make the reverse of her childhood journey on his own, from America to India . . . at age twelve.

When I pointed out that she had waited three years longer to trust her child than her parents had, she acknowledged my point, but stated that we live in a scarier world. We can argue about whether this is true. Rates of violent crime are at historic lows in the United States. However, with the Internet, continuous online and broadcast news, and social media chatter, bad news travels fast and far, fueling parents' sense of constant catastrophic possibility. Naturally, parents feel they must protect their children more than they themselves were protected. That is the tension at the heart of this book: When and how do we learn to let go? And why is it so important that we do?

I believe that at many points in their children's lives, parents need to step aside, ask other adults to take over and even send their children away in order to help their offspring become loving, productive, moral, and independent young adults. For me, these four adjectives capture the central, universal goals of parenting. You want to raise a child who can both find love in this world and show love to others; you want a child who will make a contribution to society and who won't break laws or exploit others sexually or financially; and you need them to be someone who can live without you and not be a dependent burden on others. That's a reasonable description of what it means to be a responsible adult.

I believe that childhood requires an endpoint—children need to turn into adults—and parents need to have some images of adulthood in mind. My friend Bill Polk says that a parent's job is to raise children "who can leave you." The problem with that simple definition, of course, is the leaving part. When is the right moment to let go, or even push your child out of the nest? How

does a child learn to leave? There are actually many moments of letting go, from the time you release the hand of your toddler so that she can take a few steps on her own, to the day you wave good-bye to your son or daughter moving away to college or a life on their own.

In my work as a clinical psychologist and so-called "parenting expert," I have spoken with many parents who, out of the deepest love for their children, want only to do more—not less—for their children. They believe that the more time, energy, attention, and money they can devote to their child, the better. Indeed, if you were to boil down the thousands of parenting questions I am asked in a given year, their essence basically is: *What should I be doing for my child?* The question has infinite variations: "How can I help my child's self-confidence?" "How can I help my child make more friends?" "My daughter is a perfectionist. How can I help her to not be so hard on herself?" "How can I help my eight- and ten-year-old sons to stop fighting?" "How can I help my child do better in school?" "How can I motivate my tenth-grade son to get better grades?"

These can be tough questions to answer, because quite often the parent is not doing too little but is already doing too much. For example, moms who are spending an enormous amount of time trying to adjudicate their sons' disputes should probably just leave the room when they start fighting. Let them learn not to start something they cannot resolve. Parents who are trying to persuade an anxious and perfectionist daughter that things are going to be okay in life should not stay up until 1 A.M. keeping her company while she does her homework. Though some of these cases seem obvious to me, it feels harsh to scold caring parents by saying, "Don't do so much for your kids!"

I have tinkered with ways to make parents laugh at their tendency to overparent. I tease them. At parenting talks, I bend at the waist and rush frantically about the stage snatching invis-

ible items off the floor, doing an impression of a mother picking up her children's clothes, all the while complaining, "My children are so sloppy and irresponsible. I don't know why they never pick anything up." The audience laughs because they recognize immediately why the children don't pick up their clothes. Mom always will. The only price her children have to pay for letting their mother do all the cleaning is her anger, which is very familiar and not all that scary.

Parents ask me questions about more subtle problems: how they can help their child get over fears, or learn to take risks, or become more responsible. It often seems to me that no matter how loving the parents, they are not going to be able to help their child through this challenge. It is going to take someone else. Perhaps the child's friends will give him the courage to overcome fears or take risks. Or perhaps it will be an aunt or an uncle, a family friend, or a camp counselor who does that. Here's a paradox: a nineteen-year-old camp counselor—a stranger—is often better at getting children to pick up their clothes from the floor than a thirty-nine-year-old parent.

There are many times when my answer to a parenting question has been: Have you thought about sending your child to sleepaway camp? Have you considered that your child needs to be *away from you* to take this particular developmental leap? I ask because, in the final analysis, there are things we cannot do for our children, no matter how much we might want to. In order to successfully accomplish these tasks, to grow in the ways they need to grow, children have to do it on their own, and usually away from their parents, sometimes overnight, sometimes for days or weeks or even months.

In my conversations with parents, they are often surprised and relieved to learn that, developmentally speaking, there is a limit to what they can and should do for their children. More specifically, there are eight fundamental things that parents want to do for or give their children, but cannot:

1. We cannot make our children happy.
2. We cannot give our children high self-esteem.
3. We cannot make friends for our children or micro-manage their friendships.
4. We cannot successfully double as our child's agent, manager, and coach.
5. We cannot create the "second family" for which our child yearns in order to facilitate his or her own growth.
6. It is increasingly apparent that we parents cannot compete with or limit our children's total immersion in the online, digital, and social media realms.
7. We cannot keep our children perfectly safe, but we can drive them crazy trying.
8. We cannot make our children independent.

I understand from my conversations with parents over the years that they *wish* they could do all of these things. But let's take a closer look. I hope you will come to appreciate why, as parents, we cannot accomplish what are essentially our children's developmental tasks.

1. *We cannot make our children happy*

If there is one single sentence that parents say to me more than any other it is this: "I just want her [or him] to be happy." Moms and dads say this to convey a number of different thoughts. One is a disclaimer of parental ambition; they are saying that they don't have a specific goal in mind for their child. They don't need her to be a doctor or go to Harvard, they just want her "to be happy." The second is that they understand the bottom line in life is emotional, and while they do have specific goals for their child, they are going to love their child even if she fails to achieve those goals (play the violin, be a good athlete). The parents are going to be satisfied with happiness. The third idea is that parenting is confusing and overwhelming and it is really hard to anticipate the future for your child, but happiness seems like the catchall thing to wish for. Finally, parents are often saying, "I find it extremely difficult to bear my child's unhappiness. I am so empathically tuned in to her that my emotional state is linked to hers." This is captured in the parenting wisdom that so many mothers have shared with me: "A mother is only ever as happy as her least happy child."

What almost no parents ever say to me is the simple truth that I have tried to capture with the title of this book, namely: *My child is often happiest when he or she is away from home.* Although it can be tough for any individual child to be away from his or her parents, the vast majority of children often feel quite relieved and happy when they are away from home. Let's be honest: At different times in our childhood we felt happier away from home than we were in our house. Home was safe and familiar, but it was also filled with expectations and anxiety and the endless need on our parents' parts to protect and shape us . . . because they are parents.

Human beings are biologically programmed to protect and feed their young. We are not alone in that. The ability to care for our children is signature mammalian behavior, one of the things that make us the creatures that we are. Like other mammals, we keep our offspring with us until they are truly ready to go off on their own. What is uniquely human is that our children are so dependent for so long—longer than any other animal—and that we tend our children's emotional lives.

Parents and children have a sophisticated system of signaling one another when there are threats. When our children cry, we come running to find out if they are in danger; when their faces look sad, we wrap our arms around them to comfort them. We are equipped with neurons in our brains that mirror the emotional activity in their brains. We empathize with what they are feeling and we respond appropriately, and protectively. They possess the same "mirror neurons" that enable them to tune in to us and, ultimately, their friends' and later their own children's emotional lives. The empathic connection between parent and child is a fundamental part of our nature, instinctive and un-questioned.

But that's where things get complicated. It has been said that the single most important fact about the psychology of human beings is a period of prolonged dependence on parents, which typically spans at least eighteen and perhaps as long as twenty-five years. In the past two hundred years advances in medicine and certain cultural trends have dramatically expanded our ca-pacity to protect our children's health and provide material com-forts and enrichment opportunities far beyond the expectations of earlier generations. But how long, and to what extent, are we responsible for their emotional well-being? Does protecting a child mean protecting his or her feelings from threat or discom-fort at every moment? I certainly understand the wish. I hate to see my children unhappy, but I sometimes feel that middle-class and upper-middle-class parents—myself included—have more child-protection equipment available to them than they need, from oversupervision to ferocious advocacy.

Our hope is that we can protect our children from all bad feelings. But I don't think this is wise from a philosophical per-spective, since struggle and suffering are part of life. I also fail to see the wisdom from a child development perspective; children need to learn to manage their own feelings. Sometimes they have to get away from us and experience a little suffering in life, along with the full range of feelings in life—boredom, anger, giddiness, romance, et cetera—to get the hang of it on their own. As long as a parent is standing by watching, the child is going to inter-pret his or her experiences through the parents' reactions.

As a child, you don't know exactly what you truly feel unless you are away from your parents. Maybe your mother is standing by you saying, "Oh, I am so happy that you got the sixth-grade good citizenship award," but it didn't feel like a big deal to you and her reaction is confusing. Perhaps you are not as unhappy as your father is about your lack of playing time in Pop Warner football. Maybe you were okay with sitting on the bench. Can you tell him that? Probably not. You have to filter your feelings through the lens of his feelings. That's why children need to get away from their parents to discover what truly makes them happy. Children who go away to camp often report that only at camp can they "be themselves." As one eleven-year-old boy said: "Sometimes at home I feel pressured, but at camp I don't feel that people are judging me."

Away from home, children know what they hate and what they love, what makes them miserable and what makes them happy, because they are having the experience on their own. You don't have to share your camp feelings except by letter. No one else is interpreting the experience for you.

2. We cannot give our children high self-esteem

We not only want our children to be happy, we want them to have a consistently high level of self-esteem. I sometimes tease parents about determined efforts to boost their child's self-esteem. I remind them that children can never feel consistently self-confident because: 1. they are generally much shorter than everyone; 2. they have no money of their own; 3. they lack important skills; 4. people boss them around; 5. they have no car keys; and 6. they cannot escape. Moms and dads laugh at this reminder because, of course, it is all true. If you and I suffered from all of the above-mentioned deficiencies we would feel terrible. Teasing aside, it is also true that at times children do suffer emotionally, just from being children. They are overwhelmed by their sense of inadequacy and frustration. They are too small and too immature to achieve what they want to achieve. That's true of adults as well, but grown-ups are more accustomed to the reality that we cannot bend the world to our will and opinion. Children are still hoping that the world can be made perfect, so they protest and complain. Some feel like failures about what they cannot do and what they cannot change and may suffer from, what parents may perceive as "low self-esteem." Some may grow depressed.

I have seen frustrated children hit themselves in the head and even bang their head against the wall. Kids sometimes break things, insult people, and proclaim that they hate themselves. A friend of mine recently reported that her bright and conscientious daughter comes home miserable from high school every day complaining that it is "boring." Another friend is troubled by her third-grade son's fear of his teacher, a legendary tyrant at his school. Another is worried that her daughter's failure to make a competitive dance team will scar her for life. It is hard for these parents to watch their beloved children grapple with demoralizing school situations, especially when they see their children's bright potential. We all wish to save our children from feeling frustrated or inadequate; unfortunately, we just cannot manage it. Even if the high school did offer the bored student more challenging courses, or the fearful boy a different teacher, or if the aspiring dancer made the cut, the children might (like most of their peers) face problems with teachers whose personalities they didn't like, tensions with friends, or other disappointments in school or life. We need to remember that the journey through school—through life itself—is always stressful and that there are things in our children's lives we cannot fix. Nor should we necessarily rush to try. Some experience of failure and frustration is an essential part of a child's emotional education.

In my book *The Pressured Child,* I shadowed several high

school students whose significantly different abilities, challenges, and personalities might lead one to believe that they would suffer from problems in self-confidence. Not surprisingly, each child's fuller story showed the much more complex and often counterintuitive story of development—and self-esteem. Grades aside, because they often obscure more than they illuminate about a child's inner life, it is a child's experience of connection, recognition, and power that deeply shapes self-esteem. A parent who tries to orchestrate those things only confirms a doubtful child's sense of incompetence, and only becomes an obstacle to the child's genuine accomplishment.

The myth of the happy childhood and the goal of consistent self-esteem for kids have a powerful hold on today's parents, especially those who are financially secure, who have had unparalleled control over their children's lives and who are devoting themselves to being "great" parents. Research tells us that college-educated mothers are spending much more direct face time with their children than they used to, from eleven to twenty-one hours per week, almost double the number of hours that was typical twenty-five years ago, and parents are reading about parenting much more.

Fifty years or more of writings about psychotherapy and a growing body of research about post-traumatic stress disorder (PTSD) has changed the way we think about the resilience of our children. We know so much now about the ways in which children can be damaged for life: by sexual abuse, by constant belittling criticism from a parent, by an undiagnosed learning disability in school, by social isolation and bullying. Once you learn about all the possible threats to a child's emotional well-being it makes you want to protect them against emotional trauma to the nth degree. Once a parent reads that depressed children suffer from low self-esteem, he wants to be able to help his child achieve good self-esteem all the time. It isn't irrational for parents to ask about self-esteem. The impulse to protect all of your child's feelings is completely natural. The problem is that the ideal is unachievable, even undesirable.

You cannot, and you should not, make yourself responsible for your child's continual sense of self-confidence, for three reasons. First, children are often going to lack confidence just because they are children. Second, if you are constantly scaffolding your children's every experience at every moment, he or she will not truly learn to be competent. Third, and most important, self-esteem is not the engine of learning; it is the by-product of learning. Children don't learn because they feel good about themselves; they feel good because they have mastered something.

"He just gives up," parents say about their son who really wishes he were better at this sport or that game or special interest. Well, perhaps he needs to practice more or consider doing something else that comes more naturally to him. Learning to manage your sense of inadequacy is something all children need to do. We expect that with repeated experiences over time, children's skill levels will grow and they will gain mastery over their feelings of discouragement.

Not all bad or sad feelings are evidence of a child being traumatized. William Damon, a professor of psychology at Stanford University, addressed this issue in his book *Greater Expectations*. He believes that the public's knowledge of trauma and post-traumatic stress disorder has subtly undermined our appreciation of children's natural resilience. Instead of seeing our child on the edge of mastering a challenge, we see a child about to be overwhelmed whose self-respect will never recover, and, therefore, a child who needs our protection.

This is the story I am hearing from elementary school principals everywhere. Parents rush in to rescue their children from difficult but ordinary social situations, claiming that their sons and daughters are being bullied. Other parents worry that their children will be traumatized because they cannot master a skill, are getting disciplined by the school, or weren't chosen for a select team or class. If you get cut from a high school varsity team, it can be emotionally painful, a real bummer, but is that a lifelong trauma? If your parents believe you've been traumatized and become enraged at the varsity soccer coach, it makes it difficult for a child to recover.

Martin Seligman, the famed University of Pennsylvania psychologist and the father of positive psychology, argues that both American psychology and American parents head down a dead-end road when they became so invested in the maintenance of self-esteem. After promoting self-esteem for two decades we are seeing increased levels of depression and anxiety in our young people, not the higher levels of self-confidence for which we hoped. It turns out that telling children they are great and wonderful just doesn't help them all that much. It actually makes them suspicious of adults because they can see with their own eyes that they are not as good at doing some stuff as other children. Self-esteem comes from the repeated experiences of building skills and mastering more and more challenging situations. The term *developmentally appropriate* means that your child is being presented with challenges that are at the right level: not crushingly hard, not ridiculously easy, but developmentally just within his or her grasp. It will take a stretch, but he or she can do it.

Sometimes the greatest sense of mastery comes from succeeding in a situation where you have tasted defeat, been really upset, and then come back to triumph. If your child arrives at sleepaway camp and cannot pass the swim test that everyone else in the cabin passes on the first day, he or she is likely going to feel bad about it. No way around it. However, when the child manages to pass the swim test at the beginning of the second week— or whenever continued effort eventually leads to success—he or she is going to have a wonderful feeling of achievement, like nothing else.

Here's the hard part for parents: it is far more likely that the child will pass the swim test under the gaze of a nineteen-year-old counselor or a twenty-seven-year-old waterfront director than he or she would with you, especially on the confidence-shaking second or third try. When a child is anxious and frightened, it sets off a parent's anxious identification, and when the child then sees worry in the parent's face—or, worse yet, a forced cheerfulness that doesn't fool a child for a second—it makes the child even more anxious. Parental efforts to provide continual encouragement and scaffolding can also undermine a child's confidence.

It is a rare parent who can remain totally objective when their child is falling apart, confident that he or she will certainly feel better in a few minutes after passing the swim test. Because camp professionals have seen so many children look frightened, tremble, cry, and then succeed, they can manifest a sense of confidence that is tough for any parent to feel.

And here's the kicker: When a child accomplishes something away from her parents, she can be absolutely sure that she owns the accomplishment. When your parents are not there, you can be sure that no one else did it for you. In his gut a child thinks: *My mom didn't supervise it, my mom did not arrange it, I did just what all the other kids had to do. Therefore, I earned the self-confidence that comes with that achievement.*

3. We cannot make friends for our children
   or micromanage their friendships

Human beings are social animals. Our children are born with the ability to connect, to be kind, and to make friends. If you watch a baby sitting on his mother's lap, you may notice that he is utterly transfixed by the sight of another infant on another mother's lap who looks just like him. *Wham!* It is love at first sight. As soon as they are able to crawl they can choose a "friend" to sit near. They may not yet be old enough to talk or coordinate their play, but it is quite clear that children are powerfully attracted to each other. Researchers in day care settings have observed that children's moods are better when they are sitting near a child of their own choice; and if that is true at fourteen months, it is absolutely true when they are fourteen years old.

However, the two essential ingredients in friendship that we cannot arrange or actually teach our children directly are mutuality and reciprocity. Don't we teach them to share toys and take turns? Of course, but that is not the same as the mutuality that emerges within a friendship. It is your child's friend who reminds him forcefully not to be annoying, who says, "I don't want to do that anymore. We've played your game long enough." It is your daughter's fourth-grade friend whose feelings get hurt by your child and who says to her, "You're not my friend anymore," at which point your daughter cries and withdraws, or else she scrambles to reassure her friend that she is still her buddy.

The cues that children give one another are different from the ones that parents give, but they are often just as powerful. In short, it is children who teach one another to be friends. We can model friendship for them—mainly in our own adult friendships—and we can teach them some of the skills that they will need, but in the final analysis, friends teach each other friendship. Children experience themselves as inventing, or at least discovering, friendship on their own. The power, the satisfactions, and the joys that can come from it are all a child's creation. A girl's best friend is the best friend ever and her group is the original, never duplicated, most special group that ever was, because she and her friends made it so. No one gives their parents credit for their friendships, and almost never do children thank their parents for either knowing a lot about their friendships or saving them from bad friendships.

Everything about friendship and group membership has to be experienced. And what are the very best friendships of all? I would argue that they are the ones you truly make on your own, with another child whom you have found at school or in an after-school activity, someone with whom you have grown close just because you really liked each other. "Mom, I made a new friend," has to be one of the signature shouts of a child's independence because his mother doesn't yet know anything about the other child. As a parent you can support your children's friendships, you can give your children a place to play or hang out, you can order the pizza and surround their friendships with love, but you cannot micromanage the details of the friendship. If you try, it isn't your child's friendship.

4. We cannot successfully double as our child's agent, manager, and coach

One of the things that distinguishes the parents of this generation from prior generations is that they know more about child development and brain development than ever before. That's all to the good. What has not been helpful is that all of the knowledge has encouraged parents to think that they can, and must, manage all aspects of their child's growth.

Parenting always involves some aspects of coaching and managing, and sometimes those are the most appealing aspects of the job. Research shows that the fathers of teenage boys are happiest when they are in the role of coach (although this doesn't mean that their sons are happy about it). I understand the temptation to coach. My daughter, Joanna, played twelve seasons of varsity sports in high school, three sports every year for four years (clearly not cursed with either my lack of coordination or my fears). My completely unexpected role as the father of a good athlete gave me the opportunity to share the sidelines with other parents for more than a decade. I witnessed the over-invested, determined coaching parent in action and it was not a pretty sight. Watching manager-coach parents, it has always baffled me why they focus on such a narrow range of physical skills ("Why didn't you stick check him?") when the most important skills their children are going to need in the years to come, according to the Partnership for 21st Century Skills (a national organization that advocates for the readiness of every student), are teamwork, collaboration, creativity, responsibility, self-direction, and an ethical sense.

There's an appeal to being your child's teacher, and when you and your child share a natural gift—be it for sports, music, math or any other area of endeavor—it may seem logical to play coach. A few parents seem to be able to coach or manage their child's career to a high level right through adolescence. But I would argue that these cases are the exception, and, beyond professional accomplishment, often come at a heavy price to the parent-child relationship. At a certain point, as the child becomes both older and more accomplished, the stakes become higher and the parent's role as coach and manager begins to distort the parent-child relationship, or the parent-child relationship interferes with the coaching relationship. Parents already have so much power in their children's lives, to add the roles of coach and manager to that of parent is to tip the balance in a way that puts the child's mental health at risk.

Ambitious parents with athletically talented children might want to read *Open*, Andre Agassi's compelling memoir in which, among other things, he chronicles his father's obsession with making his children into tennis stars. He tells in excruciating detail the way their father destroyed the confidence of Andre's brother and sister by pushing them too hard, and how the father finally earned the undying hatred of his champion son. If tennis does not speak to you, then I recommend Fred Waitzkin's *Searching for Bobby Fisher*. Waitzkin, a writer for *Sports Illustrated,* unexpectedly fathered a chess prodigy and wrote a wonderful reflection about the perils of managing his son's chess career—until he had the wisdom to step aside.

Chess, the violin, baseball, or golf, the sport or instrument or talent doesn't matter. If a parent wants to manage his or her child's way to success, it is important to remember that it has the potential to enrich the parent-child bond, and to burden it; and there is always a risk that the level of parental involvement may poison the enterprise for a child. I will never forget a boy I saw in psychotherapy, a varsity basketball player who quit the team in the fall of his senior year just to punish his sports-mad father. "That's all he cares about in my life," the boy said.

No matter what a child's talents or aspirations, the wise parent, sooner rather than later, turns the job of coach and manager over to a trusted other.

5. We cannot give our child the "second family" they need

Even in the most wonderful family, as children grow up there are developmental tensions and conflicts that cannot be resolved. There may be a temperamental mismatch between one parent and child, one sibling who requires more care, or one child who is driven to push the envelope of family structure, thereby driving everyone crazy.

Teens in particular have a strong drive for independence. Think of how crucial a driver's license is to a sixteen-year-old's sense of identity and maturity. Adolescents often experience their parents as unable to acknowledge their grown-up status and push against the old rules. Most families struggle to open up space for their teenager's growing autonomy. There isn't a teen in the world who has not had the furious feeling—at least for a moment—that he or she was really meant to be raised by some different, better family where there would be more recognition for his or her maturity. There isn't a mom and dad who hasn't, in the middle of a fight, wished his or her child were living elsewhere. My wife and I have an old sign tacked up in our kitchen that reads:

TEENAGERS.
Tired of being harassed by your stupid parents?
ACT NOW.
Move out. Get a job.
Pay your bills while you still know everything.

Now that we have a married daughter and a son in college, the sign makes us nostalgic. We would like to have our children back in the house more, but there were certainly times in their teenage years when their presence was almost unbearable. What helps the tension when teenagers and parents are fed up with each other? The answer is often a second family. In his book *The Second Family,* Ron Taffel writes that the peer group typically serves that function for adolescents. He is right, and teens need friends. The problem is that adolescents are more apt to engage in risk-taking behaviors with a group of peers than they are alone. Beyond that, what every parent should hope for is that their child has a close, confiding relationship with another adult outside the family who respects the child's gifts, provides a different model of a caring adult, and exercises a nonjudgmental restraining influence.

Many adolescents adopt a friend's house as their base of operations or adopt someone else's mom or dad as their backup parent. Many children develop a powerful relationship with a coach or aunt or grandparent. These relationships are less tension-filled than the relationship with their own parent. The wise parent is glad when this happens; the unwise parent feels jilted and sulks. The wise parent understands that the child not only feels that his maturity may be more recognized outside of the house, but knows that her child is probably more mature in the presence of that other parental figure. If a teen admires another parent or coach, it will bring out the best in him or her.

Of course, our first families sometimes do bring out the best in us, but more often they happen to bring out the worst in us, too. We are needier and whinier with our moms and dads, brothers and sisters than we are with almost anyone else. That eighteen-year period of prolonged human dependence that I mentioned earlier in this chapter makes family relationships so intense, with such strong feelings of love, anger, disappointment, and yearning, that Sigmund Freud called it the "family romance." Most of us spend a good part of our psychological lives trying to figure out our relationships with our parents, and we wonder if our parents ever really saw us for who we were.

In adolescence, one of the first steps in the creation of an adult identity is to find a mentor or adopt another family that makes us feel understood. I have seen that happen between families in the same neighborhoods, on town sports teams, in schools, and especially in settings where a child is far away from his or her parents. It is a bit easier for children to show high levels of respect and even love for that second family when their parents are not around because there is always a bit of disloyalty to one's own family involved in the selection of a second family. That is why a child's parents cannot pick a mentor or second family for their own children. The child has to choose that person or family on his or her own because psychologically it involves a move away.

6. *We cannot compete with our child's electronic world*

We are living in the midst of an accelerating technological revolution that is changing the habits of both parents and children and childrearing itself. CNN reported that half of the mothers who own smart phones hand the phone to their children under the age of two to keep them occupied when they are in a restaurant or store. Many smart phones have apps specifically designed for younger children. When PBS released its iPad app in 2010 that gives children easy access to one thousand streaming PBS videos and games, it reported in a survey that 70 percent of parents said their children used their parents' iPads; 40 percent said their children used their iPads at least once per day. Parents had an average of eight apps on their iPads specifically for their kids and they praised the educational value of these applications. These users are largely children under the age of six; after seven, the use of electronic devices increases dramatically. By the time they are in their mid-teens, American children are spending fifty-three hours per week in front of screens: television, social networking sites, cell phones, and video games. The Kaiser Family Foundation reports that there was more change in children's usage of electronic media in the two years from 2008 to 2010 than there had been in the previous thirty years. By the time this book is published, many more changes will have intensified the relationship between children and technology.

I'll talk more specifically about children and electronics in the camp setting in the next chapter, but overall the impact of technology on society is a subject so vast I cannot, as a psychologist, do an adequate job of either describing it or analyzing it. It is also a moving target and the results are not in yet on how it will change our brains and behavior. What I can say is that parents ask me all the time what to do about the intensity of their child's attachment to electronic devices. Their children appear to be more interested in their cell phones than they are in family dinner or almost anything else. They tell me that their children no longer want to play outside, that boys, especially, cannot get friends to come over to the house unless the group can play online or other screen games. They ask me whether they should allow their eleven-year-old to have a Facebook account (Facebook recommends thirteen as the minimum age), whether playing violent screen games will make their teenage sons violent, or whether they should be reading their middle-school daughter's text messages to make sure that she isn't involved in online bullying or social advances from strangers.

The parents who ask me these questions are clearly worried about the impact of technology on their children's brain development, values, and social interactions and capabilities. Parents rightly fear that their children are losing the creative, imaginative play of childhood that parents once enjoyed as children. They wish very much that they could limit their children's use of electronics. In spite of their hopes and fears about what might be happening to their children's lives, most parents find it very hard to limit their children's access to technology for four reasons: These devices are new and unknown. Most parents do not have a model from their own childhood about how to set limits and boundaries on things like cell phones. Many of these devices have an educational purpose (try contradicting your high school student's contention that he or she is "... doing my homework!" on the laptop). And electronic devices are increasingly necessary to our lives and they are psychologically addictive.

Research suggests that all of us—children *and* adults—are spending equal amounts of time in front of lit-up screens. The oldest axiom in parenting is that children will do what we do, not what we say. They watch us, and they are never fooled. Our children model themselves on our addictions, our rationalizations, our materialism, and our willingness to buy them all we can afford to buy them. They may even come to think that material things, especially electronics, are the best expression of parental love. "Don't you love me?" their beautiful faces ask, "Won't you buy me a cell phone?"

In the last five years, the only place I haven't seen children using cell phones is sleepaway camp. It is so unusual to see a group of twelve-year-olds without handheld electronic devices that seeing them that way at camp is startling. At most camps, the children have turned in their cell phones and there are no computers for them to use. And they thrive. They are happy and they are proud of themselves. The lesson of living simply is one that children need to learn, and one that parents with a house full of gadgets are having trouble teaching.

7. *We cannot keep our children perfectly safe,*
   but we can drive them crazy trying

For the last fifty years a great many Americans have migrated away from crowded cities with high crime rates to raise their children in "safe" suburbs with good neighborhood schools. But somewhere along the way we lost our internal sense of safety. We don't trust our neighbors or the streets; we worry constantly about strangers and pedophiles. We watch cable television and are now acutely aware of all the terrible things that can happen to children. We no longer trust that our kids will be all right.

One mother of three children ages eleven, eight, and seven told me that her family lives only three blocks from their elementary school. "I know I should let my kids walk, but I just can't," she said. The intense guilt in her voice signaled that she believed she was depriving her children of some important childhood experience. She continued, "I've always driven my children to school. I can't stop doing it, even though I know I should."

Why does she feel so guilty? After all, she's only doing what most American parents are doing. She is keeping her children safe by driving right to the door of the school, and then picking them up at the same door at the end of the day, and she has plenty of company. Forty years ago, 41 percent of children in the United States walked to school; now only 13 percent of children do so. Forty years ago, 87 percent of children who lived within a mile of school walked or biked to school alone. Now, it seems, even children who still walk to school have a parent at their side, and, if they are permitted, some parents walk them all the way to the classroom.

The fact that most American children no longer walk to school is only one symptom of our hyper-vigilance. In his book *The Power of Play*, David Elkind cites studies that children have lost ten to twelve hours of independent play per week over the last twenty years. American children are not biking to school, they are not roaming in the woods; often, they are not even playing in their backyards. They are sitting indoors, watching television or playing on the computers, close by their parents. If they are outside, it is in adult-organized team sports.

Much of that loss of free play is due to our worry about their safety, or our assumption that time spent with us or supervised by other parents is always preferable to time they might spend alone.

What have children gotten in return for their loss of outside free time? The answer might be parental attention. Tara Parker-Pope, the health reporter for *The New York Times*, writes that before 1995 mothers spent an average of about twelve hours per week attending to the needs of their children, and by 2007 that number had almost doubled. College-educated women are leading this trend at 21.2 hours per week, but less educated women are increasingly tending their kids, too, up to 15.9 hours per week. Educated fathers are also increasing the amount of time they spend with their children, from 4.5 hours per week prior to

1995 to 9.6 hours per week; high school–educated men are spending 6.8 hours per week, up from 3.7, according to Betsey Stevenson and Dan Sacks at the University of Pennsylvania. When you combine these statistics with the fact that the divorce rate is dropping, it is clear that children are getting more of their parents together and separately than they did in the 1970s, '80s, and '90s. It could be said that we are living in a Golden Age of Parental Attention. With experts like Malcolm Gladwell, the author of *Outliers,* urging them on, parents who are financially able to do so are doing everything in their power to raise "cultivated" children. Often they are also raising overprotected children.

As someone who makes his living writing parenting books and running parent workshops, I can hardly afford to criticize mothers and fathers who are trying to do a really good job of raising their children, and who are consulting experts to get it right. Yet all this parental attention makes me a bit uneasy. I am not sure that it serves children well. At some point, the effort to provide safety becomes a constant bath of parental anxiety, and too much parental attention starts to suffocate a child's capacity for independence.

8. *We cannot make our children independent*

In *Stand by Me,* the Rob Reiner movie based on a Stephen King short story, four thirteen-year-old boys, all close friends, lie to their parents about the adventure they have impulsively planned. They grab their sleeping bags and a bit of money and head out along the railroad tracks for an overnight hike to find the body of a boy who was reportedly hit by a train but who has not yet been found. The boys crave the adventure and the possibility of local fame by finding the corpse. In the rugged hunt, two of them almost die themselves. In one unforgettable scene, two of the boys are trapped on a railroad bridge by an oncoming train bearing down on them. The characters in the film believe that their two-day adventure was the peak experience of their boyhoods, their "sweetest moment" as friends.

In the magical film *Hugo,* the young Hugo says it succinctly when his friend questions the wisdom of their sleuthing. "We could get into trouble," she says. To which Hugo smiles and replies, "That's how you know it's an adventure!"

Not all children need a high-risk action adventure to develop independence, though almost all have to do something daring—perhaps something that their parents wouldn't approve of—in order to feel independent. In our society today there are fewer and fewer "journeys to manhood," as Bret Stephenson describes in *From Boys to Men,* and of course the same is true for young women. Some seek out different kinds of challenges to test themselves, improvising their own rites of passage. At times the challenge arrives unbidden in a family or community crisis. Sometimes children move easily into a growing sense of independence and sometimes a worried parent blocks the way.

At a morning coffee in an international school in Prague, a mother stood up and told the following story about her exchange with her fifteen-year-old son. He came to her one Friday afternoon and said, "Mom, I want to go out with my friends and walk around Prague tonight." His wish—call it a request—started the following conversation.

"Where are you going to go?" she inquired.

"We're just going to walk around the city," he replied, probably a bit annoyed with his mother who surely should know that Prague is one of the safest walking cities in the world. Everybody walks in Prague.

"But where?" she persisted.

"I don't know. We're just going to walk."

"What are you going to do?" she asked, shifting her question slightly.

"Nothing."

"What do you mean, nothing?"

"I told you—we're going to walk."

"Are you going to drink?" she persisted.

"Mom," he replied, increasingly annoyed, "if I want to drink in Prague, I could do that anytime." Was his mother so naive that she didn't know how easy it is to get alcohol in the Czech Republic? Had it not occurred to her that he drank when he wished at friends' homes?

"Are you going to go to clubs?"

"No, Mom."

"Well, if you aren't going to clubs, where are you going?" Now she was doubling back to her original question.

His growing exasperation suddenly turned into a steely tone. "Mom, I'm not going out with my friends tonight."

Surprised by this sudden change, but a bit relieved and then guilty, she asked, "You're not?" And then, "Why not?"

"Mom," he said, "you're just not psychologically ready for me to go."

Embarrassed, she had come to my parenting coffee to ask me, "Did I do the right thing?" Like any good psychologist, I began to ask her questions about whether her son had earned her mistrust, whether he had a bad track record, whether his friends were pretty reliable and good students. Before I had finished, she reflected, "I think I'm just anxious. I probably should have let him go."

A SWIMMING COACH IN MASSACHUSETTS remarked to me that she's worried about kids today. Her tenth-grade swimmers show up at competitive meets without their goggles and excuse it by

saying, "My mom must not have put them in my gym bag."
When fifteen-year-olds cannot remember their goggles, is it because they are incredibly disorganized, or because their mother
is doing their remembering for them? The swim coach, whom I
was interviewing about her children's camp experience, recalls
that she sent her disorganized twelve-year-old son off to a camp
where he had to go out on trips. She imagines he left a trail of
socks, T-shirts, and underwear through the woods. "I'm sure he
arrived back at the base camp with only one sock and no underwear, but then he learned. After that he probably kept track of
his clothes."

Every child has to practice being independent and every parent has to practice letting his or her child be independent. Independence is like high jumping. You can't clear the bar from a
standing position. You have to run and jump and sometimes fail,
then move the bar up and run and jump again. Over and over.
As the parent, you have to watch them do it; you wince when
they hit the bar, but you cannot do it for them and, unlike the
SATs, you can't arrange to have a tutor suddenly make it happen. Only the child can do it.

Once you accept the idea that you cannot *make* your children independent; once you accept the reality that you have to
let them try things and fail, once you relieve yourself of the responsibility of preparing your son or daughter completely for
the outside world (as if anyone is ever fully prepared for the
world), when he or she steps out the door into the big city, you
will be in a much better position to appreciate what does happen
to them when they are away from you, and what they make happen for themselves. Oh, there will be scary moments; they will
take some risks and they will learn some lessons the hard way.
That's going to happen, but they will also test and internalize
their fundamental values, and grow morally stronger as a result.
They will become more productive than you could ever have

imagined when you saw them spending hours on Facebook and *not* doing their homework on a Sunday afternoon. They will also meet people who love them, friends and mentors whose love they will return in the fullest measure. It will bring tears to your eyes to see how much your child can be loved and how powerfully she can return that love.

Finally, and maybe painfully, they will have a lot of sweet moments without you there to see them happen. If you believe that your job is to raise your children so they can leave you, there is only one way to know whether you have done your job: to let them go and watch from a distance as they grow into independence.

two

A LOST WORLD
OF FAMILY TIME

THE FIRST TIME I drove up to Vermont to do a staff training for a camp, I was looking for a challenge, some novelty, a change of scenery. I never imagined that seeing a camp would change my worldview. It did. Slowly but surely, my experiences there changed the way I thought about contemporary children and the lives they lead.

During subsequent visits to that camp and to other traditional sleepover camps, I began to feel that I had discovered a lost world, a place where the rules of modern life are suspended, where both children and adults behave quite differently than they do in their suburban homes and schools. It took me a long time to put words to what I was seeing because it was counterintuitive. Even though I was watching campers and counselors, what I was actually seeing played out was family life from an earlier era: Time slowed down, love was expressed in old-fashioned ways, levels of intimacy and trust existed between older children and younger children that are impossible to find in schools. I felt as if I had entered a time machine and gone back at least several decades.

Let's take one small example: writing letters. Where else in the modern world do people write letters every week and wait eagerly to receive them from others? Camp is the only place I know where that is true. During election cycles, politicians and pundits often bemoan the loss of family values. What I discovered by visiting camps is that family values are alive and well, lived by campers, counselors, and staff who treat one another like family. Of all the organizations that serve children, camps come closest to re-creating elements of family. Once, sitting around a campfire with a group of counselors talking about the meaning of camp, one young man declared: "Camp is my family. This is my family."

This child's statement, this idea, may be a bit painful to a parent's ear. We all want to create this feeling for our children at home, but often cannot because of other circumstances or priorities in our lives: two careers, homework, academics, town sports, church activities, and a focus on skill building of all kinds. Divorce may have complicated the home front. Camps create a natural time machine that evokes an earlier time and a different kind of family than we have today. That lost world of family time includes: an electronics-free world, family-style dining, intimacy between older "siblings" and younger "siblings," a multigenerational community, meaningful daily rituals, and a place where time slows down. Let's take a closer look.

An Electronics-Free World

Sleepover camps are one of the last places on earth that are largely electronics free. Electronic gadgets have become such a ubiquitous part of everyone's life that it is almost weird—in a good way—to experience being around children and adults who aren't constantly connected. American children spend an average of fifty-three hours per week on computers, cell phone, or video games. That's more than two days per week. Some of that screen time is devoted to schoolwork; much more is devoted to social networking and gaming. School corridors are now filled with kids on laptops. Getting children's attention, or negotiating with children whose faces are bent over a cell phone is now a fact of school life. When the school counselor and I start our discussion group for children of divorce, the so-called family group at Belmont Hill School, she and I have to remind the boys to put their cell phones away. Sometimes, much to our annoyance, two boys will slip them out of their pockets and text side remarks to each other during a session, the modern version that we dislike of passing notes in a class. However, this kind of texting isn't that much different from what happens at home. Siblings text each other from room to room. Kids text us with questions from another part of the house: "When is dinner ready?" or "Can I go out later?"

On the bulletin board of my office is a cartoon by Alex Gregory that appeared in *The New Yorker* magazine a few years ago, just a week before Thanksgiving. It portrays the modern family at Thanksgiving dinner. The cartoonist pictures the interior of the house, with the dining table in the background, stacked with food. No one is sitting at the table. Everyone is in the living room engaged by some electronic gadget. The father is sitting in the center of the couch, drinking a can of beer and holding a turkey leg in his hand, while watching (presumably) football on the television in the near foreground. To his left is his wife, the mother of the family, holding a plate of food in her hand while she talks on her cell phone. On the other side of Dad is a young teen girl texting on her cell phone while her plate balances on the arm of the couch. Her brother is sitting on the floor eating, his earphones encircling his head and his iPod close by his side. The baby sits drinking a bottle, watching television. Behind the couch, Grandma holds a bowl while talking on a landline phone, and Grandpa films the entire scene using a digital video camera. Ouch! For anyone who has ever looked up from television to survey their own brood at home—as I have done—only to find every single member staring at a large or small screen, the cartoon is a painful reminder of the grip that electronics have on us.

When you spend time at a sleepover camp, at first you cannot appreciate how different it is from school and home. Gradually you see it. At camp, watching people—other children and adults—is the main form of visual recreation. Children come out of the dining hall talking to each other and their attention stays fixed on one another. Boys continue to talk as they wander over to the tetherball or basketball court. Girls emerge with their arms draped over each other's shoulders and around each other's waists. They continue to talk and, most charmingly, to sing spontaneously as they make their way back to their cabins. The picture is so heartwarming and natural that it takes some reflection to realize what is missing, namely the tendency of teenagers who are emerging from a meal or a school building to immediately reach for their phones and begin texting.

According to surveys done by Pew Research and the Nielsen Company, the average teenager sends fifty to eighty texts per day. Researchers estimate that they send and receive an average total of 3,339 texts per month, which takes up about an hour and thirty-five minutes per day of waking time (actually, a fair amount comes out of sleeping time). At sleepaway camp, camp-ers send an average of zero texts per day. Into the space created flows a bunch of old-fashioned human behaviors: eye-to-eye contact, physical affection, spontaneous running and jumping, or simple wandering. It is really wonderful to see a twelve-year-old girl wandering alone down a gravel path kicking small stones or twirling a wildflower in her hands. She's neither here nor there, not in the dining hall, not in her tent, not competing, and certainly not needing to be in touch by cell phone. She is simply living in the moment, warmed by the sun, thinking her own thoughts, feeling sad or happy, off in her own imagination. When was the last time you saw your child walking outside that way?

When I ask camp staff whether kids experience withdrawal symptoms from leaving their electronic gadgets at home, they tell me no. Many children express some reservations about liv-ing without electronics but, according to one counselor, most children are relieved to be away from the constant pressure of keeping up socially online. Facebook creates a compulsion to check and recheck so that you are on the cutting edge, so you have heard the latest. Many teens have expressed to me the fear of falling behind in the flow of information between their friends. It would be disloyal for teens to criticize the Internet in conver-sations with adults; they never want to give us an excuse to limit their activities, but I know from college students that many have had to grapple with their social networking compulsion as if it were an addiction that threatens to take over their lives. The cyber-world threatens to engulf their personal world.

Camp solves that problem. The size and intimacy of camp create a community where campers are with their cabin mates throughout the day. They are going to run into everyone at least three times a day, at mealtime, and the rest of the day they are doing many of the same activities. Since no one is getting a lot of information from outside the camp environment, the stories that campers have to share are anecdotes about what has happened at camp, not what is new on YouTube. The conversation changes from, "Have you seen [the latest video posted online]?" or "Have you heard [the latest rumor making the texting rounds]?" to "Did you see?" and "Did you hear?" anecdotes about camp life.

One older sister, an assistant counselor of sixteen at Camp Champions in Texas, told me that she and her younger brother, who is fifteen, grow closer when they are at camp. She said that although they love each other and are best friends at home, they experience their closeness in a different way at camp. Several factors work in their favor. They live on separated sides—boys and girls—of a coed camp and participate in different activities during the day. They don't sit together at night because the dining hall has separate tables for boys and girls. Where do they get a chance to talk? My guess is that unlike home, where all of the downtime is filled by the Internet, at camp there is more open downtime, after breakfast, after lunch, before dinner, before lights-out ends the camp day for everyone at the same time. Brother and sister are also motivated to talk to each other because at camp they have a shared network whereas online they have separate networks. Sitting at one camp's evening Torchlight ceremony, I saw the younger brother receive the honor of being a torchlighter. His sister was immediately up and out of the stands, giving her younger brother a prolonged hug in front of three hundred other children—something that comes more naturally in a camp setting than in almost any other place in a child's life.

The elimination of electronics simply opens up a huge amount of space for children to relate to each other, and to adults. Much of that, of course, takes place at mealtime. Even though many camps serve children cafeteria-style, there are others that have family-style meals.

Extended Family–Style Dinner—and a musical!

Fifteen minutes before breakfast at YMCA Camp Becket for Boys, the cavernous dining hall comes to life. While the kitchen staff cooks the scrambled eggs and sausage that will soon be devoured by hungry boys, each table is being set by an individual boy assigned for that week to wait on his cabin's table. The boys, ranging in age from eight to fifteen, have straggled in from their cabins; some look pulled together, others are still stumbling and spacey, but they all soon get to work, retrieving the forks, knives, and spoons from the bins and setting the circular tables that will seat an entire cabin of boys and their counselors. As the younger boys receive spontaneous help from older boys, the newer campers get instructions from the two counselors who are supervising. But this is a large dining hall, with more than thirty tables that will seat close to three hundred boys. Two counselors cannot really cover the territory. So the picture here is not of men forcing, or even overseeing, reluctant boys to do an unpleasant task, but rather of boys rising to a challenge alongside other boys. One suspects that many of these boys do not set the table at home with the same focus and enthusiasm as they do at camp; at camp you are doing it for your cabin.

The face-to-face, around-the-table, home-cooked family dinner has been gradually dying out in America. The average American family spends 45 percent of its food budget on restaurant food or take-out food. As suburban parents rush from elementary school to music lessons or to Little League or perhaps to an after-school education program and then to the high school to pick up a varsity athlete or a debater, the prepared sit-down dinner has become a casualty. Many dinners are eaten from take-out containers, if not at the fast-food restaurant itself. But even when dinners are prepared and eaten at home, very often everyone is looking at the television. Sixty-six percent of Americans eat dinner while watching TV. Once again, this element of the camp experience feels like stepping into a time machine; the TV-free traditional camp meals evoke an era that predates even most parents and grandparents today.

At every camp with a religious affiliation, every meal begins with bowed heads and a formal grace. Even in secular camps I have noticed that there is a moment of grace, a song of gratitude for the food, for the bounty of the earth, or a song that expresses the solidarity of the community. Then everyone sits down together, waiting for the call from the kitchen that it is their turn; when it comes, the assigned waiters hop up enthusiastically, returning moments later with the platters. At a camp like YMCA Chimney Corners, the counselor serves all the girls in her cabin, lifting the lasagna or grilled cheese sandwich from the large platter onto each girl's plate, who hands it to the camper sitting next to her. The girls pass these plates down the line, to the last one at the table, often asking, "Do you want this?" because they have grown aware of each other's allergies as well as their dietary likes and dislikes. They know if someone in their cabin is a vegetarian and won't eat meat lasagna; they know if someone despises carrots. They know because they have been eating alongside one another for the entire camp session. Camps offer more choice than they did in the old days (in my day); there is usually a salad bar now, but in family-style camps, there are just a few shared foods and a communal style of serving them for at least two courses, the entrée and dessert.

This kind of dining is fundamentally different from sitting at the kitchen counter and having your mother make breakfast for you. It is also a dramatic departure from the school cafeteria, where each child has his or her own tray and proceeds through a line, picking items from a variety of steam tables where servers load the plates and (with a few exceptions) gradually become invisible to the masses of kids whom they serve daily. Perhaps unlike home, children sit at tables occupied by other children. At camps that serve food family-style, the person putting your chicken patty on your plate is known to you, she asks you if you want one, she looks you in the eye, and then when you complain that you don't like chicken patties, she says, "Well, that's what there is for dinner tonight. Do you want to go to the salad bar?"

This kind of dining is inefficient. It requires a lot of dishes, it limits the number of possible choices, and it means *you can't always get what you want.* But for the modern child from a small family (the average size of the American family is 2.2 children), other than holidays like Thanksgiving, Christmas, or the Seder, camp is as close as they get to the extended family table, especially to what it would be like to eat at a family table with a pack of brothers or sisters. At a table where one grown-up is serving and there isn't an endless supply of food, eating becomes an intensely personal, interpersonal, and communal experience. It can, at times, be competitive. I have seen campers compete ferociously for the extra ice cream sandwich casually rejected by the one rare boy who doesn't love that winning combination of soggy chocolate crust and artificial vanilla flavor. As the boys start to shout, "It's mine!" and "I asked first!" it becomes the job of the counselor to play King Solomon and settle the matter by declaring, "No fighting, guys. Pick a number between one and ten; the boy who guesses right gets the extra ice cream sandwich." It can also be cooperative. I have seen boys redistribute the different flavors of the Popsicles that the counselor handed down the line randomly. They make sure that the campers who like grape get grape, and the campers who like cherry flavor get cherry, giving the one orange pop to the boy who shrugs his shoulders indicating that he is flexible on the matter.

All the elements of family-style eating: setting the table or cleaning up, the expectations for waiters to do a good job for their table, the limited menu, the counselor at the end of the table urging you to eat the things you might not eat at home, all of these have a powerful psychological impact on campers. The twin realities that you can't manipulate your mother into making something else for you if you don't like what's being served, and the certain knowledge that you cannot graze later by going to the refrigerator or, if you're a teenager, you cannot order some pizza later, have an impact.

Family-style dining teaches patience, respect, cooperation, and skills. A communal table creates both personal flexibility and powerful shared meanings, just as Thanksgiving and a Seder do. The counselors, who may be twenty or twenty-one, play the traditional roles of parents; the children act as one another's siblings. The novelty of eating with others at camp expands a child's awareness of eating itself; learning about one another's food quirks throws your own fears into perspective. Does a child want to be the only kid in the cabin who doesn't eat a generally popular item? When children see other kids their age eating stuff they've never been willing to try at home, and they know there is no Plan B, they may be willing to try the very thing their mother has been unable to get them to eat for years.

Terri, a mother we'll hear more from in Chapter Four, sent two picky eaters to camp: her ten-year-old, Richard, to Mishawaka, and her eight-year-old, Blake, to Buckskin. When Blake went off to camp, he would eat only about fifteen things, fewer than the average boy his age. For years he had resisted his mother's efforts to get him to broaden his choices, and the two had fought about this many times. He had worn her down, the way all children wear down their parents. At home, you have to pick your battles. Camp changes the dynamic.

For Blake, who is rigid and fearful about trying new foods, the food stakes were much higher than for his brother. Since he had fought about food with his mother over the years, he was invested in not eating certain things. What happened when he got to Camp Buckskin? He didn't eat for the first two days. Then the camp nurse told him that he "had to eat." According to his mom, "The rest is history." When his parents picked him up from camp, he gave his mom an epic hug and a big smile. Then he said, "Guess what, Mom? I eat fluffy eggs now." Since camp, his parents have witnessed him eat twenty foods that he had never eaten before.

In camps that I visited where the meals were cafeteria-style, the counselors ate at the same tables with the children in their cabin. The attention they paid to younger children during meal-times was unusual, making it seem as if every child had an older brother or sister there. During and after every meal there were collective chants, songs, and table-slamming games. On the girls' side of the dining hall at a coed camp, six girls would stand on benches and lead everyone in song for the last ten minutes of the meal. I visited Camp Carolina in May, before the campers arrived. At every meal there were spontaneous eruptions of songs or call-and-response rhymes; most notable were the complex, rhythmic hand-and-elbow table-pounding sequences that the veteran counselors were teaching the new arrivals, so they would all have mastered them by the time the children arrived in a week's time. The ritual banging and shouting in camp dining halls is part of a collective eating experience that pulls everyone in. I once visited a camp where the director introduced me as a visitor. Three hundred boys immediately began to sing a traditional greeting to visitors, accompanied by dish-rattling stomping on the floor: "Mich-ael Thomp-son" Stomp . . . stomp . . . stomp-stomp-stomp. It is one of the most heartwarming greetings I have ever received in any community.

It is a stretch to call this family-style dining. Most families cannot muster six hundred feet pounding on the floor. But camps manage to re-create at almost every meal, a festive, silly, and affectionate spirit of a large family enjoying a holiday meal. At a

girls' camp I watched the director get up to make announcements at the end of the meal. Her own administrative staff, gathered around a circular table, interrupted her announcement
repeatedly, drowning her out with shouts whenever she said a
particular word. It took her a while to realize that the word she
was saying that would bring down the house every time was *the*.
These interruptions were perfect silliness, affectionate and anti-
authoritarian, the way families behave when the rules are relaxed on big occasions.

Seasonal Siblings: Older "Brothers" and "Sisters" Taking Care of Younger Ones

The most remarkable thing about camp is the sense of family
created by the relationship between big kids and little kids. With
the exception of a babysitting situation there is no other place in
modern American life that I can think of where twelve-year-olds
get to watch nineteen-year-olds so closely, and where sixteen- to
twenty-one-year-olds really pay attention to twelve-year-olds.
The power of these interactions and the intimacy of these relationships cannot be underestimated. They don't occur in schools
because age separation is at the core of the design of elementary,
middle, and high schools. Separated age cohorts, which make it
easier for teachers to target educational material at different developmental levels, have an unhappy downside. Younger children do not get to see and identify with older children and young
adults. Of course, teachers and coaches serve as role models, but
a forty-five-year-old teacher, no matter how gifted, is not as effective as a twenty-year-old in connecting with children. Also, a
child is not going home with her teacher, but she is living with
her camp counselor all day and every night.

I talked with a middle-aged woman, Linda, whose memories

of camp were focused on her counselor, Blondie. She does not remember the counselor's real name, but she recalls following Blondie around, adoring her, wanting to be *just like her*. It was only as an adult that Linda realized that her counselor had filled a vacuum in her life created by her older sister's departure for college. The youngest of five children, Linda had been eight when her only sister, ten years older, left home. "My sister had a very steady personality; my mother's moods changed rapidly," Linda reported. "Blondie had a steady personality like my sister and I was really attracted to that kind of energy." At camp she learned new things that she never forgot (for example, that Queen Anne's lace was the name of an unusual, white wild-flower), but what she really recalls is the intense attachment to her counselor.

It isn't just children who are missing older siblings who are susceptible to adoring their counselors as if they were older sisters and brothers. These affectionate camper-counselor attachments are on display at every camp. At the Sunday morning service at a YMCA boys' camp, every single boy who stood up to speak at the service was accompanied by his counselor, who stood with his arm around the boy's shoulder, in front of the entire camp. The visual message was that every boy had an older brother, every boy was being looked after, and the looks on the boys' faces signaled how meaningful it was to each of them. Sitting at that chapel service was another moment when I wished that the parents could be there to see their children, and I was so glad that they were not.

I BELIEVE ALL YOUNGER CHILDREN have an emotional soft spot for older kids. Being cared for by older children or young adults is more exciting for them than the parental care with which they are so familiar. When a teenager or a young adult takes care of you, you can take more liberties and it feels like more of a part-

nership. When I visit camps, I see boys hanging on to their counselors, jumping on them, or challenging them to wrestle just as
they would with older brothers. One day I watched a young
male counselor get boys to take risks in the water, or forget
about their anxieties, by playing a wild form of water polo with
them. When he was holding the ball, his campers would physically jump on him so hard that he would wear his skateboarding
helmet in the water. It was certainly a quirky look, but in the
boys' eyes, it just made him cooler because he was willing to risk
being uncool. Counselors can literally assume a different posture with children than an older staff person would. I have seen
young men lying stretched out on a campfire bench next to a
homesick boy while listening to him cry about missing his mom.

Little boys and little girls hold their counselors' hands, they
sit in their laps. At a camp in Texas I observed a homesick girl
from Mexico who was attached to her young woman counselor,
always holding her hand, or being carried on her hip. The little
girl, maybe six years old, looked frightened of her new
surroundings—her English was not very good—but she had
found an anchor. She was constantly staring into her counselor's
face for confidence and for guidance as to how she should inter-
pret events. If you walk around any camp, you will see boys and
girls fascinated by their counselors because these young adults
are both their caregivers and their developmental road map to
the future.

Campers are smitten with how cool their counselors are,
how knowledgeable and physically capable, beautiful, and—
let's be honest—sexy they are. The bodies that the counselors
have now are the bodies the campers will have in just a few
years. In her book, *Children's Nature*, a history of the American
summer camp, Leslie Paris quotes a camper named Lydia
Stoopenkoff, born in New York in 1930 to a working-class family, who wrote that she and her girlfriends had a crush on her

male counselor, Donat. "When he wore his bathing suit we would fall apart . . . we would giggle if anyone would refer to his 'secret package.'" Lydia was twelve at the time and her reaction was perfectly normal.

When a child models himself after his counselors, it has the power to shape his self-image. Mark Jeffers, a handsome and physically strong young man from New York who is now a camp counselor himself, went to Camp Keewaydin when he was fourteen. He describes himself as having been an "obnoxious, fat, messy, lazy kid who started fights with everyone" and didn't like the way he looked. Over a period of years Mark turned himself into a skilled canoe tripper and worked himself into shape. He was influenced by his counselors, both by their confidence and the sight of their "super strong . . . tanned" bodies. Their ease in taking off their clothes and going into the water inspired him to want to look better himself.

We have to acknowledge both the intimacy and partnership between older children and younger children who live together in cabins seven days a week, twenty-four hours a day. They are visually and emotionally exposed to one another. Children are constantly changing clothes when they are at camp, in and out of bathing suits, in and out of pajamas, in and out of wet clothes after a thunderstorm. Though campers can turn their backs when they change, over the course of a week or a month their counselors and fellow campers are occasionally going to see them naked and they will see others in the buff. This represents a change in the life of a child who has been seen naked only by his or her family, and often not past the age when they take over dressing themselves. Except for born exhibitionists (there are some kids totally at ease from the get-go), this is a little scary, but managing one's own body and privacy, or lack of privacy, is an important step on the way to independence.

Catherine Steiner-Adair, a psychologist and school consultant, and once an enthusiastic camper at a girls' camp in Maine, reports that the only award she ever won at camp was the Mad Dipper, given for regular morning skinny-dipping: "Camp taught me body acceptance. Seeing fifty to a hundred girls dropping their towels and jumping, screaming, into the lake . . . seeing all the different kinds of bodies, every size, every color . . . gave me such comfort in my own naked skin."

For small children sleeping away from home there is the issue of bedwetting, of course. It is the counselors who have to help younger children get out of clothes if they have had an accident. It is going to be a twenty-year-old who comforts your son who is ashamed and distressed about his failure to get completely through the night. I remember one camp village director who told boys he was conducting "sand checks" at inspection time, a face-saving story that allowed him to verify whether the beds that the boys said were dry were, indeed, dry. Boys who are ashamed about wetting the bed sometimes lie. At camp they learn that other boys have the same difficulties and that the big boys don't get upset about it the way parents sometimes do.

Why would parents who have taught their children modesty and have talked to them about inappropriate touching want to have someone outside the family see their children naked or have them see other children naked? Why would you want nineteen-year-olds helping your children with bedwetting, attacks of diarrhea, or getting their first period? The answer is simple: It is part of independence from parents. At some point in childhood or adolescence every child has to take his or her naked body and all the issues of modesty, bodily care, and sexuality out into a world of strangers. When it comes to people seeing their body and helping them care for it, most children go through a sequence of: parents, pediatricians and medical personnel, friends (at sleepovers), athletic teammates, and, finally, sexual partners. Children who have no siblings, who cannot do sleepovers, or who don't play on teams may never have these experiences.

Children who go to sleepover camp, by contrast, have lived in a family-style situation where they have learned to care for their bodies under the loving supervision of young adults. I see this as a transitional step from the privacy of the family to the high-risk situation of a sexual encounter. It is good, I think, for children to experience their own body in the presence of others, and to see the bodies of others in a nonsexual context.

Shannon Donovan-Monti, the director of YMCA Chimney Corners for Girls, said that many of her intermediate girls get their period during the summer session. "I actually think this is a great place to get your period for the first time. It normalizes it. They are freer to talk about it. And they are curious about it . . . and the staff can tell their stories about getting their period."

Shannon remembers that when she first got her period and asked her mother, "How long does it last?" her mother replied mordantly, "About thirty years." Most twelve-year-old girls might find that explanation somewhat troubling, and perhaps most mothers do a better job than Shannon's did, but there is no doubt in my mind that talking to other girls and counselors who have just recently gone through the experience is like talking to comforting older sisters. Shannon says that being present for girls who are getting their period for the first time is "such an honor." She recalled that one day when "a little girl and her friend came into my office and said, 'I just got my period for the first time,' I started to cry." When women campers say, as many do, that their camp director or camp director's wife was "like a mother to all of us," they mean she was like their very own mother, only sometimes better.

Four Generations at Camp

You don't see a lot of gray heads at camps, but there are a few, and when a community ranges in age from young children to grandparents, it is a special experience for children. Sometimes it can feel as if there are three generations in the dining room: the little kids, the big kids—teens and counselors—the middle-aged folks—usually the directors, nurses, and some long-serving staff—and finally, singing the same songs, enjoying the same activities, and eating the same food is the grandparental generation. Because we are such a mobile country (Americans move, on average, every five years) many of our children do not live near their grandparents. Outside of religious gatherings, many American children do not often spend time in any three-generational setting. (You could argue that schools are three-generational settings, but my experience in schools suggests there are only two generations: kids and teachers, who are all deemed "old.") Camps particularly, and especially private camps, can provide kids a multi-generational experience.

When I visited Camp Wabun on Lake Temagami some years ago, many campers and counselors told me how meaningful it was to them that one family owned the camp. The grandfather of the director, Dick Lewis, had been one of the founders of Wabun in 1933, and Dick's father had worked there as well. Many in the community said they wished that Dick Lewis's son, Jason, or his daughter, Jessica, would take over the camp when he stepped down. When, in an interview a couple of years later, I suggested to Dick that the many generations of his family were something of a draw for campers, he dismissed the notion out of hand, saying people came to the camp for "adventure" and to "jump off the cliffs at Bear Island." However, he went on to say that the idea of four generations was important to him. His grandfather, a POW in World War II and a lifelong teacher, had nurtured Wabun through tough times and he was his grandson's hero. No doubt Dick's grandfather has been featured in many of the campfire talks that Dick has given over the years, and former Wabun campers have feelings of admiration for a man they never met, the hero of one of their heroes. When Dick shared that he had decided to retire because Jason and Jessica had called him to ask whether they could take over the camp, he had tears in his eyes. Happy ones.

It isn't just the presence of older people, however, that produces the family feeling. From the campers' point of view, it is that older, *much* older, people, continue to love what the campers are currently loving. And campers are meeting the older men and women who were once mentors to their counselors. In school, a child almost never meets her teacher's teacher, but at camp it is quite common to meet your counselor's counselor. That helps barriers between the generations fall away, or more accurately, it connects the generations, with all the members of the community holding on to the same strong rope: their love of camp.

Johanna Liskowsky-Doak, whose friendship with her Camp Downer friends will be the subject of a later chapter, wrote me to say that if I wanted to understand the Camp Downer community, I should know that a longtime employee of the camp named Paul had recently passed away. When he entered hospice care, a former camp staff member posted the news on Facebook and:

> As soon as the word was out, the response from other former staff was unbelievable! People flew in from the west coast, others contacted each other for the first time in years all through this facebook page, and many people visited Paul in hospice who may not have otherwise noticed. The company that visited

him brought him camp music on cd's for him to listen to, they told camp stories and had mini-reunions with him and surrounded him with the Camp Downer spirit leading right up to his final day. It is an amazing story and tribute to the power of the camp relationships and how long lasting they are . . . his family was so happy with the outpouring of love and happiness he had in the end.

Johanna and her four friends talked about the possibility that a serious illness could strike one of them and concluded, "It is reassuring knowing that the Camp Downer family is always with you." Camps seem to know what to do for the young and the old, in life and in death, because good camps live by ritual celebrations of the life cycle—the camp life cycle: passing the swimming test, jumping off the thirty-foot diving tower, or jumping your horse over a high jump for the first time.

Ceremony and rituals such as campfires work when they tap into both the needs of people to feel part of the community and the psychological longings and anxieties of each individual present. When you go to a wedding, for example, you go to wish the couple well and give them a good send-off, but everyone present is thinking about their own relationships, whether they have love in their life, and every couple is reaffirming their love for each other . . . or not. The ceremony works at the communal level, the couples level, and the individual level. The same is true for the campfire. The community is celebrating itself and feelings of belonging. All of the camp songs, the familiarity, and the collective voices make a child feel part of something bigger . . . a family. But many, indeed most, of the skits speak to the anxieties of each child about being little in a world with cooler and more grown-up kids, about being away from parents, about sometimes feeling confused or stupid or unskilled. Actually, that is the underlying theme of almost every camp skit, and every child can identify. But there is always redemption or forgiveness or laughter at the end, and we all share in it. That is the reason I love campfires; they are never mean, there is always forgiveness, even for the most inept skits.

Down Time

The most striking "lost world" aspects of summer camps are nap time and free time. During these openings in the camp day, time slows down to a crawl and children appear to be moving in slow motion. At some camps breakfast can finish at 8:30 and the first official activities of the morning don't start until 10:15. Children wander back from breakfast to their cabins to prepare for inspection, pick up brooms, start to make their beds, talk with their friends, go to the bathroom, wander around, talk some more, coax one another to complete a job, and joke with their counselors, who joke with them or grow exasperated with them. They all move slowly. This unscheduled downtime is, perhaps, the most important time of the camp day because the stakes are so low and the sense of time is so vast.

I am aware that camp brochures and Web sites advertise the fun activities and all of the skills that children are going to develop at camp. That is understandable from a marketing point of view and skills are good things, but after all, children cultivate their talents in school and in after-school programs. Camp offers a profound change of pace, a sense of time profoundly different from either school or the scheduled family. When I go to camps, I see children sitting in circles on the ground, I see pairs of friends walking from the dining hall to their tents holding hands or sitting on each other's laps or with their arms wrapped around each other. They walk down and check on the horses; a few teens may pull out guitars and sing. There is time for friendship to develop.

Most camps also have an enforced after-lunch rest time or

nap time for as long as ninety minutes. Ostensibly, this is for the children to rest between the intense activities of the morning and the afternoon. In truth, most children do not sleep during rest time, but their counselors sure do. Many times I have seen a cabin with every child quietly awake while a twenty-two-year-old man or woman sleeps heavily on his or her bed. Being with children from seven A.M. to ten P.M. is demanding and, at times, stressful for counselors. They need a break so they can maintain their patience later in the day. Also, because their social lives with their peers have mostly taken place late at night, camp staff are often a bit sleep deprived. They need the catch-up time.

Kids understand this, and they accept the required rest time with good grace. It gives them a chance to listen to music (in camps that allow iPods), write letters home, play cards, and read books. If one of the sweetest sights in a school day is nap time for preschoolers or kindergartners, the sight of three hundred campers—as old as fourteen or fifteen—lying on their bunks entertaining themselves quietly without much grown-up intervention is quite extraordinary. It throws the modern child back on his or her own imagination and ingenuity. It feels like childhood from a long time ago.

The busyness and technology of the twenty-first century sometimes seems like a vast conspiracy against having an inner life. Camps and nature restore a bit of the balance. Enforced rest time with its requirements for quiet or silence gives children time to be with themselves. Bill Polk, the former headmaster of the Groton School, an independent school in Massachusetts, writes that:

In periods of silence the imagination roams, the mind digests, fragments find connections and a larger context comes into focus. In periods of silence you find your center, your peace. In periods of silence you find places where you come to understand that the most significant mysteries of life are not to be resolved but to be experienced.

To some, children may seem incapable of that kind of reflection, but I assure you they are not. They cannot always put it into words, but I have seen many children return from camp "centered" and with exactly the sense of peace that Polk describes.

Camp Rituals: Sober, Silly, and Special

Many years ago, when my wife and I spent a week hiking with friends at Cold River Camp, an Appalachian Mountain Club family camp in the White Mountains, there was much conversation about a much-loved couple in their late seventies, longtime regulars at the camp, who had decided that the next day was going to be the last hike they would ever make up North and South Bald Face Mountains. All the regulars at Cold River had hiked the Bald Face Mountains and many had done it in group hikes led by these two classic, white-haired, rail-thin New Englanders. Their declaration that it was to be their last hike hit everyone hard. In an after-dinner announcement we learned that they were going to do it together by themselves and take a half bottle of champagne to toast each other at the top. We weren't invited, but we applauded and celebrated them. The next day we all climbed different mountains in our groups, but every hiker at Cold River community was thinking about that couple and their ritual last hike to the top of the mountain. I had never met those people before that week at Cold River, but I can never forget them because of the ritual celebration with which the camp surrounded them.

The great genius of camp is the creation of ritual. From the moment you arrive at camp, there are ways of doing things, rules about the waterfront, how to enter the dining hall and get your plates, ways to clean up the cabin, and safety procedures on the high-ropes course. All of these are essential for order and safety, and these rules fall into categories of control that are well known to children from school. There is, however, another layer of rules and traditions at camp: plaques and flags, totems, feathers and bells, funny announcements, wacky traditions, skits, and, of course, communal songs. Much of this business is silly, a lot of it is made up or stolen from other cultures, much of it from Native American tradition; yet in a very short time it assumes huge importance in the children's lives. Children crave ritual; they need it to guide them and help them harness their feelings. Camp is trying to fill that unspoken need.

America is a country of immigrants, an extraordinary cultural mix. I think our greatest strength is our diversity, and one of our greatest weaknesses is a lack of shared rituals. What rituals do children have in school? The Pledge of Allegiance in the morning, the prom, Homecoming weekend, and high school graduation can sometimes be a pretty impoverished collection of experiences, and they leave many children out. Families create rituals, and children find them deeply reassuring. "We always do this on Thanksgiving," they say, or, "We always have this at Easter." Modern family life is dominated by working parents (one or two), town sports, homework, schedules, logistics, and television. Ritual celebrations get crowded out. Many families find meaningful ritual in their churches and temples; other families do not. For children, church rituals often require them to adapt to an adult set of rules.

Camps, by contrast, create rituals designed for kids that meet their needs. Campfires, for example, are an unabashed celebration of community, designed to make everyone feel that they belong. They are highly predictable; that's the magic of them. We all know the same songs, the same cheers, the same dances, we all know which funny counselors will make dumb jokes and which ones will dress up in something unexpected. At a day's end program at Camp Champions, in Marble Arch, Texas, everyone knows that the torch lighters will bring the torches at a certain moment and the camp directors will tell the kids how great they are. And the kids agree, and they hope to be like the camp directors when they get older.

One takes one's own family for granted; family rituals can be annoying and stale. Kids roll their eyes when Dad starts to tell timeworn family tales or jokes, and they may cultivate a studied disregard toward other family traditions imposed on them. Because you experience camp only for a week or two in the summer, or perhaps for one long session, the camp family seems fresh and you are very grateful to be part of it. Everyone says they love camp, but what they really love is the power and freshness of their own renewed feelings of belonging, of caring. Children are experiencing gratitude for having a place, which transfers back to their families when they rejoin them. I have talked to many parents who reported that their children were more loving and respectful when they returned from camp than they had been before they went. That's a common observation. Their children have practiced being loving toward the camp community all summer and their usual ennui and cynicism has been swept away.

Camps create traditions, both silly and serious, and so vivid that children never forget them. Linda, the camper who loved her counselor Blondie, was raised a Catholic and did not hear much gospel music in her family's church. She can still picture where she was sitting and how she felt when she first sang "Swing Low, Sweet Chariot" at her Scout camp. I have seen camp directors ask for song requests just as the songbooks are being passed out. Children shout out titles or sometimes even page numbers before the songbooks reach their hands. They

know them by heart. The familiar words warm the bonds between them; they laugh in anticipation of funny lines and wrap
their arms around one another when they come to the highly
emotional lines. They sway back and forth, tears in their eyes,
radiating love.

I've described camp as a lost world of family, but in truth this
kind of time and ritual has rarely been as consistently present in
family life as it is at camp. While most families are very loving,
they are also complicated by expectations, worry, and disappointments so complex that children cannot unravel the threads
of them. (That's what psychotherapists do.) Camp rituals celebrate the challenges of childhood and allow for the open expression of love in very clear, uncomplicated ways: love of Nature,
love of community, love for one another. The rituals of camp
open up the channels of feeling in children and they are accessible because they are handed down through an oral tradition. No
child is left out.

Camp rituals are almost never about family, yet they help
children reach down into their most powerful loving feelings,
where they discover gratitude for both community and family,
and help them to express that love. I have never heard children
talk about love as much as I have heard at camp.

My two favorite camp rituals, both of which evoke the image
of family time more powerfully than almost anything else, are
reading aloud to children in their cabins and singing a lullaby to
campers at bedtime. In many camps, after showers have been
taken, teeth have been brushed, and campers are in their pajamas, counselors read aloud in their cabin. They typically read
from one book, an ongoing story night after night, serialized
over a two-week or one-month session. Staff do this for eight- to
ten-year-olds, but they also do it for fourteen- and fifteen-year-
olds. For every individual child, the counselor steps into the
shoes of the parent who read to him or her when that child was

little. For some it is the first time. For the digital generation, this read-aloud experience is an extraordinary journey to the past, linking children to all previous generations of human beings who were calmed at bedtime by the spoken word.

I have been to camps where a bugle playing "Taps" signals the end of the day. Even though I never served in the armed services, that tune always moves me. No question the tune speaks to the heart of children. The camp ritual that touched me most deeply, however, was singing to children. When I volunteered to be a visiting staff member for a week at Camp Keewaydin on Lake Dunmore in Vermont, I was recruited to sing a lullaby with other staff in the middle of a circle of dark cabins just minutes after lights out. The lyrics were adapted to the camp, but the tune was one that mothers have sung to their children for more than one hundred years. In the dark, with some strong and some uncertain voices, six men sang the Brahms's Lullaby to twelve- and thirteen-year-old boys in their bunks, who received it without cynicism.

three

A FIRE IN MY STOMACH

THE WORLD'S LEADING EXPERT on the subject of homesickness at overnight camps is also the psychologist for a boarding school, Phillips Exeter Academy. All summer and throughout the academic year, Chris Thurber, an optimistic and high-energy man in his early forties, is surrounded by young people who are living away from their parents. During the academic year he counsels teenage girls and boys who live in dorms; in the summertime he serves as a camp counselor for boys and as a mentor for future generations of counselors. He has also done extensive research on the distress that children experience being away from their parents, studying how severe it is and how long it lasts. The story Thurber tells, the story that most homesick campers live out, is a story of psychological pain followed by happiness and triumph.

"Do you want to hear an interview with one of the boys in my study?" Thurber once asked me. Before the yes was out of my mouth, he pushed the button on his laptop computer. His book-lined office was immediately filled with the sound of a camper's voice, struggling to talk between sobs and gulps of air. "I miss my mom and dad," the ten-year-old boy tells Thurber. "I want to go home. I don't want to stay. . . . I just want to go home." The voice is so determined, the pain so raw, and the wish to get home so intense, it brings tears to my eyes. It seems like a crime against nature for that boy to be separated from his mom and dad. For just a second, I am suffused with feelings of homesickness. I know that wretched feeling. I think every human being does. There are times when you are so filled with yearning, so desperate about being away from the people you love that you miss everything: the house that has sheltered you, your room, your pillow, your favorite dinner that your mom makes, the pet that you hug every day. You miss it so much that in that moment you think you are going to die. That's homesickness.

Knowing of my interest in the emotional lives of boys, Thurber pointed out that this highly expressive recording puts the lie to people's beliefs that you cannot get boys to open up emotionally. Some boys may successfully hide their feelings, but not the boy in this recording. He is an open book, or rather, an open wound. He has thrown any feelings of shame or guarded-ness out the window; he is willing to expose himself totally in order to persuade someone, anyone, to *take him home*. The parent in me wants to grab my car keys, pop him into the backseat, and ask for his address, just to stop his pain. Hearing that level of pain, it is astonishing to think that a camp counselor, just a college student of nineteen or twenty, could maintain his own equilibrium and comfort a boy who was in that much distress.

Chris tells me that it was his personal experience of being a camp counselor who couldn't reassure a boy that made him want to do research into homesickness. As a young cabin leader, only seventeen years old, Chris was in charge of a cabin of eleven- and twelve-year-olds at YMCA Camp Belknap in New Hampshire. He had been a camper there himself, worked his way up to senior camper at fourteen, and into the post of junior leader the following summer. At sixteen, he became a leader-in-training for numerous cabins, spending a week in each, working with campers of different ages, and apprenticing under cabin leaders with different styles. At seventeen he was chosen for the serious honor of being a cabin leader himself.

He reports that he was really serious about his training. He wanted to do well. But like all camp staff twenty-five years ago, Chris was given only cursory training in working with homesick children. "We were given commonplace advice about homesickness," he remembers. "Keep kids busy." Was that the extent of the training? "We were told that if you get them through the first days, they'll be fine."

Armed with that wisdom, Thurber dove into the camp season. One day, in the second week of the second session, he and his campers were down at the waterfront for swim period. It was, according to Chris, "a postcard perfect sunny day" and he was feeling as if, as a first-year cabin leader, he had hit his stride. "It was nowhere near as hard as I imagined." At forty-three, Chris exudes confidence and a practical, let's-get-this-done attitude. It is not difficult to imagine him as a confident, even cocky, young man. Little did he know that he was about to get taken down a peg by a homesick boy. After the boys swam, there was a ten-minute leaders' swim and then the bugle blew signaling the end of the swim period. Chris walked up with the other cabin leaders through a two-hundred-year-old stand of white pine trees, then he veered off to head for the "Middlers," to meet up with his cabin group. That's when he spied a boy sitting in the classic position of despair: legs pulled up, arms wrapped around the legs, and head buried between his knees so that no one could see his face. Chris walked closer and recognized one of his campers named Caleb.

"Caleb, the bugle has blown. It's time to get back to the cabin," he told him. The boy looked up; he had been crying, his eyes were bloodshot and his face was wet from tears. Chris made the assessment that he didn't need to get right back to his cabin; in any case, it was just a couple of hundred yards away. He could keep an eye on it. He sat down next to the boy and put his arm around his shoulders, ready to do his counselor magic. Chris remembered, "He was going to tell me what was wrong, I was going to solve his problem, and then we were going to go back to the cabin and get ready for lunch."

"I'm feeling homesick . . . really, really homesick," said the miserable camper.

"Well, lots of people miss home when they are away at camp," intoned the reassuring cabin leader. "You need to stay busy and don't stress about it because homesickness usually goes away after the first few days at camp."

Caleb looked into Chris's eyes with a puzzled look and then he used his counselor's nickname. "Thurbs," he said, "I've been busy all morning. This is the first time I've sat down . . . and it's day ten."

The boy's homesickness hadn't gone away. His case wasn't fitting the profile; the bromides with which his counselor had been equipped were not going to work. Thurber reports that his mind went blank. He sat there feeling helpless and paralyzed. Caleb waited for some moments, then he looked up again and wisely observed: "Thurbs, you don't really know how to help me, do you?"

From that moment on, "Thurbs" has dedicated himself to understanding homesickness and to educating counselors, campers, and parents on how to handle the different phases of this completely normal but sometimes extraordinarily painful childhood experience. With the exception of some researchers in England who looked at boarding schools, homesickness had not been a subject much explored by psychologists for one simple reason: It is not a mental illness. Homesick children aren't usually taken to hospitals, medical doctors, or therapists. The distress of homesickness has traditionally been treated by camp directors and counselors, or sometimes by parents who drive up to the camp and take their child home. Campers are seen by medical personnel at camps, of course, because many express their homesickness as a stomachache or an emotional meltdown over a small cut or a twisted ankle. Sometimes their distress can be cured by a short talk and the application of a Band-Aid, hardly the level of distress that requires the attention of a serious mental health professional. It didn't seem like a topic that a respectable graduate student in clinical psychology should spend his time studying.

On Chris's first day of graduate school at UCLA, he attended a lunch for the new doctoral students at which each student was invited to talk about the research questions that interested him or her. Many students talked at length about the studies they wanted to conduct; he waited until the end, when he briefly described his desire to do research in autism. At that point, the chairman of the department thanked the students for talking about future research on subjects that they loved. Suddenly, the thought hit Chris Thurber that he didn't love the idea of autism research. What he really loved was camp YMCA Belknap. The idea of missing camp in order to do "serious" psychological research saddened him. So he went to two professors and asked whether he could study the phenomenology of homesickness. They gave their blessings and he headed back to camp after his first year in graduate school. When he returned to Los Angeles, he had with him six cardboard boxes with enough data for three doctoral dissertations. His professors ended up being his coauthors on nearly a dozen scholarly articles on homesickness.

What Chris Thurber and collaborators have found now informs the way camp professionals think about homesickness. His discoveries have been very helpful to parents who are sending children off to any away-from-home experience. His research has also helped nurses and doctors deal more effectively with homesickness in children who have to be kept in the hospital for surgery or serious illness. Recently, he has turned his lens on the issue of homesickness in college freshmen. Though proud eighteen-year-olds may not want to call what they are feeling homesickness, some suffer from the same constellation of yearning, sadness, and preoccupation with home that overwhelms some younger campers, and it can cause some freshmen to pack their bags and leave college.

The formal definition of homesickness is, "the distress or impairment caused by an actual or anticipated separation from home. It is characterized by acute longing and preoccupying thoughts of home and attachment objects." ("Attachment objects" is the awkward psychological term for both the people and the things you love—your mom, your dog, and your teddy bear.) Homesickness has been a theme throughout the ages in epic literature, music, and memoir; it was described in ancient times by the Greek physician Hippocrates. He thought it was caused by a surfeit of black bile in the blood. By 1768, physicians clearly recognized that it was caused by emotional disturbance.

At its most acute, homesickness has features in common with the psychiatric diagnosis of separation anxiety disorder, the name we use to describe the extreme clinginess and overwhelming fear that a few children experience when their parents are about to leave them. The difference between the two is that homesickness is not as chronic or as debilitating as separation anxiety disorder, which can affect almost everything in a child's life. Also, separation anxiety occurs *before* the separation; homesickness, by definition, starts after the separation from parents.

Homesickness can also, at times, have elements of both anxiety and depression. Because homesickness can look like other psychological disorders, and because it has been a mystery why some children seem to suffer so much from it while the vast majority of kids have mild cases, researchers have struggled to come up with theories to explain it. Some have speculated that it is caused by overprotective parenting, or neglectful parenting, or an insecure attachment to parents. Others write that it is a reaction to novelty or unfamiliarity. In an attempt to capture the back-and-forth phenomenon of children enjoying themselves far from home and then suddenly feeling terrible, Freud and his followers speculated that young people feel nervous, guilty, and homesick when they enjoy the separation from their families so much that they temporarily forget about them. Homesickness, then, is an unconscious attack of guilt. Many of these explanations are overcomplicated, or too pathological; none of them are data based.

HOMESICKNESS IS NOT a psychiatric illness. It is not a disorder. It is the natural, inevitable consequence of leaving home. Every child is going to feel it, more or less, sooner or later. Every adult has had to face it and overcome it at some point in life; perhaps when sleeping over at Grandma and Grandpa's house, perhaps when it was time to leave for college. If you cannot master it, you cannot leave home. My son, Will, a twenty-year-old college student who experienced some significant homesickness when he first went to overnight camp, observed succinctly, "If you can't sleep away from home, you are going to have to sleep at your parents' house for the rest of your life."

At overnight camps, in boarding schools, and especially in pediatric hospitals, homesickness is a routine phenomenon. What is commonplace for camp administrators, however, is never routine for the child because he or she is usually experiencing these feelings for the first time. When the level of distress is high, it can have a completely demoralizing effect on a child, as it did on Caleb. It can also have a devastating effect on his or her parent, if the parents are in empathic contact with a child's feelings.

I remember going to dinner years ago with friends who had just sent their eleven-year-old son, Tim, off to sleepaway camp for the first time. They arrived at the restaurant holding the first letter they had received from him, and it was totally devastating. He didn't want to stay, he hated everything, he was really unhappy, and he was excruciatingly articulate about it. He may have been only eleven, but Tim, the son of a psychologist and a journalist, was both psychologically sophisticated and a good writer and he knew how to use words to turn the knife in his parents' hearts. Holding his letter in their hands, it was very difficult for them to believe that he could be all right at camp.

My wife and I—both of us mental health professionals—spent a good part of the dinner drawing on our conventional knowledge, trying to reassure them, telling them that his homesickness would pass. It was a pretty good bet that our advice was accurate, but how could we know that for sure? That was the problem. It is also the problem with sending a child away. If he or she is unhappy, the parents are not there to evaluate the level of his or her distress. All that our friends had was Tim's letter, which they kept reading and rereading, in hopes of finding a silver lining that wasn't there.

What is the conventional knowledge about homesickness

that my wife and I were drawing upon that night? What do most people think they know about it? We're all experts to a certain degree because it is hard to forget the feelings of yearning and helplessness, and the weeping that accompanied those feelings. Most of us believe that most campers feel it and get over it in time, except a very few who don't and have to go home. We know that most parents get over the empathic pain they feel when their children are away—I call it "childsickness"—unless they don't so they keep their children home the next summer. We trust that the vast majority of camp directors can distinguish between the slightly homesick and the severely distressed— except when they miss it. There's the rub. Every parent thinks: *That could be my child in continual distress and not getting care. Can I be sure that the staff at camp will recognize if my child is seriously homesick and will know what to do if he is in significant distress? Will anyone else know how to comfort her the way I can?*

When I told Doug Stone, a writer, business consultant, and coauthor of *Difficult Conversations,* that I was writing a book about homesickness, he said, "You have to talk to me before you write that book. I was incredibly homesick. I never got over it, and my sister and brother were just like me. We joke that we have the homesick gene. I was miserable every day of camp. It never got better. And everything the camp personnel told me was more or less wrong. They kept saying that it would go away and it didn't."

The camp finally arranged for Doug's parents to come up and fetch him after three weeks of misery. He never returned to overnight camp. His camp story is the realization of a parent's worst fear for their child. What was striking to me is that in his fifties, Stone had almost no way of explaining why his home- sickness was so severe. It remained a painful memory in his life for which he had no explanation other than, "the homesick gene."

Thurber's research would have been helpful to Doug Stone's family and to his camp administrators. He has given parents and camp professionals an objective way to think about homesickness, with a research basis. Thurber's findings also offer great reassurance for both parents and children. He has provided answers to five questions, the first three of which I will discuss in this chapter, the latter two in the following chapter.

Who becomes homesick?

What percentage of children become severely homesick?

What predisposes children to homesickness?

What can parents do to prevent or lessen homesickness?

What can staff do to comfort a homesick child and
   diminish his or her distress?

Who Becomes Homesick?

The short answer is that we all do. Campers get homesick, so do soldiers in the Dutch Army, college women in Japan, and students in English boarding schools. All of the studies from 1943 to the present day show that the vast majority of both children and adults develop feelings of yearning and preoccupations with aspects of home when they are away. Thurber found that 97 percent of children in sleepover camps experience at least some mild homesick feelings, if not full-blown homesickness. What about the remaining 3 percent, those who report no homesick feelings whatsoever? Chris Thurber suggests that they were not answering the question honestly, or that they cannot recognize those feelings in themselves. His conclusion is that homesickness is universal but not always recognizable.

After interviewing many campers myself, I know that there are a number who report proudly that they were never homesick, "not for a second," but that appears to be the story they tell in retrospect. What they mean is that on balance, camp was terrific and their homesick feelings didn't register in their memory. If, however, they had filled out a questionnaire every evening at camp, or someone had interviewed them before breakfast or after lunch each day, a researcher would certainly have caught them in the midst of some fleeting homesick feelings. I believe that counselors intuitively comfort or distract homesick children the moment they see a camper with a sad face, often even before the camper has had much time to articulate the feelings. When I do camp staff trainings, I often ask counselors to remember their own homesickness feelings and they all have such memories. Some still do feel a little homesick, even while they are on the job that they love.

Homesickness is not related to how far geographically you are away from home—attending a camp only fifty miles instead of one thousand miles away from home may not make much of a difference—nor is it related to whether a family has money or not, or to gender. Boys and girls get homesick at almost the same rate. Girls are more likely to turn to their counselors for help with homesick feelings, while boys tend to internalize their feelings and put a good face on things. Most campers, both boys and girls, try to appear brave in the face of homesickness, letting down their guard only at night or at downtimes by crying in their pillows, or crying alone in the woods, like Caleb was doing when Thurbs found him.

Mild homesickness shows up in a variety of ways. The child with the classic pattern of homesickness comes to camp and finds him- or herself homesick in the first one or two or three days, after which the yearning lifts, returning only at moments and in milder form. Other campers become immediately engaged; they have fun for the first two or three days, only to find that homesickness hits them a bit later. Veteran long-term campers may find they experience no homesickness whatsoever up until the midseason visit from parents, after which they sink into thoughts of home.

There are many things that can make a difference in homesickness, both positive and negative. A physical injury or an asthma attack can precipitate powerful feelings of helplessness and homesickness. Camp nurses see this all the time. Letters from home can momentarily cause yearnings to flare up, though in the long run letters are absolutely the most effective antidote for homesickness because the camper can read and reread them and feel connected to home without the parent actually being present, which might cause an unraveling. Even more important is the letter that the child writes to the parent, because the simple act of expressing the homesickness and mailing it off to the parent means that the child has made a mental connection.

A helpful talk with a counselor almost always helps relieve homesickness, especially if the counselor listens well and can bear the child's feelings of sadness. It can even be a counselor who is a stranger. When I was visiting a camp last year, the camp director had me sit down with Suzanne, a girl whom I did not know, to speak with her about her low-level but chronic case of homesickness. Suzanne said that she had not discussed homesickness before she went to camp because she didn't expect to feel it, nor did her mother, who had attended that same camp when she was a girl. "I think she thought I would get over it fast," said the girl, who was still pretty sad on her ninth day of camp. I asked her to describe when and how her homesickness came over her, and she replied: "A lot in the morning. I wake up randomly at a time, at six-thirty this morning. Yesterday I started to cry. . . . I just kind of see her face and my bed and my cat. . . . Yeah, I feel lonely."

Suzanne's mother wrote me an email saying that my brief talk with Suzanne had been very helpful to her. I don't believe that I did anything special. I just talked with her directly about her homesickness, listened to her describe it in detail, and thanked her for her honesty. What I didn't do was try to jolly her out of her sadness.

HAVING YOUR SIBLING at boarding school or at camp with you does not reduce the likelihood of homesickness. It may even increase it. I have talked to a number of former campers who said that they were enjoying camp a lot but that they had a younger sibling at camp who was suffering from painful homesickness. On occasion, camp administrators had enlisted the older brother or sister to help with a younger sibling's homesickness. Most older brothers and sisters felt that they had not been helpful; their presence didn't fulfill the younger sibling's need to see the parent. Suzanne said that her older brother had gone to a camp, a psychological (mind-body-spirit) kind of camp at The Omega Institute where they "walk on hot coals . . . and sit in a sweat lodge." Her brother advised her to just "forget you have a home." It was not advice she could follow. She couldn't stop thinking about home.

From stories I have been told, children of camp staff and administrators often suffer from a lot of homesickness when they are living in a cabin only two hundred yards or so from where their parents are. Campers who visually see their parents but from whom they are separated by camp rules can feel tantalized, even tormented, by the closeness. When they go away from camp on an overnight trip, they often experience a second wave of homesickness because they are now really away from home. Chris Thurber said he had observed this phenomenon in staff members' children. It has affected his thinking about how to help his older son go off to camp. He and his wife took a leave of absence from camp when their older son attended for the first time.

WHAT IS, PERHAPS, MOST FASCINATING and not at all intuitive, is that homesickness is not directly related to age. Younger campers are only more likely to experience severe homesickness than older campers because they haven't had enough life experience. That is, the typical eight-year-old has had less opportunity to practice being away from home than a twelve-year-old, and a younger child might cry more openly than the older child, but the crucial variable in homesickness is not age, it is *experience being away from home*. If an eight-year-old has had more sleepovers than a twelve-year-old, it is the older child who is at risk for homesickness. Conquering homesickness requires practice.

What Percentage of Children Become Severely Homesick?

Thurber's research has shown that there are different levels of homesickness in children at camp. The vast majority of campers experience some homesickness or mild homesick feelings. Only 19 percent of children at overnight camps experience significant distress in connection with their homesickness. They may have a case of homesickness that lasts for the entire camp session. Only 7 percent, or one in fourteen campers, have a case of homesickness that lasts for the entire session of camp and gets worse the longer camp lasts. Vanessa, a fourteen-year-old girl at a summer arts camp, Buck's Rock, was one of them. Vanessa was legendary for the depth and intensity of the homesickness she experienced during her *third summer away*, at the age of twelve. She described how it felt to miss home: "I felt like I had a fire in my stomach and it was burning. People told me that I should get distracted and that would help me, but I just wanted to get my tears out."

I asked if she was crying all day. "Not all day," she reported. "There were breaks in there." Then she gave me a big smile and said, "I was really homesick."

Her first experience of homesickness was at another sleep-away camp when she was ten. The level of her suffering that first year was a surprise to her because she thought of herself as an independent little girl. She suffered through a two-week session and was afraid to go back, but decided she could do it and returned. The depth of her homesickness the second year was a surprise to both Vanessa and her parents. It led them to make that unfortunate parent-child bargain that never works: rescue. Vanessa explains why.

> When I was little I was very independent. But when I got older I was really attached to my parents. I shouldn't have been at the camp; I shouldn't have been at the camp *then*. . . . I was scared to go back my second year and everyone told me it would be fine. I was waiting for the bus saying everything is going to be fine, but when I saw the bus I burst into tears. Then my parents said if I was still homesick when I called in a week they would come and get me so I had no reason to get over my homesickness. So I wasn't in the mind-set that I have to be happy.

That winter, Vanessa and her parents decided that it had been a mistake to have taken her home early from camp, and that she should try a new camp, Buck's Rock, with an agreed-upon pledge that they would not bring her home early under any circumstances. She and they were determined that she would stay for the four-week session.

Once again, the homesickness hit her like a sledgehammer. Because Buck's Rock's governing philosophy is choice for children, the director gave her the option of talking to her parents on the phone and having them come up to visit her. The visits were a disaster. They ended in tantrums. Vanessa would promise her parents that she didn't need to come home, she just wanted to see them and that would make everything better, so they drove up, a number of times. The visits would go well enough until they would prepare to leave, at which point Vanessa would beg them to take her with them. They would remind her of this mistake from the previous summer and say no. That's when she would erupt: "Every time they told me that, I wanted to punch them in the face and kick them in the guts. They made me miserable. I would sit on the ground and hold on to their legs."

She and the camp director, Laura, discussed these upsetting visits and decided that Vanessa's parents shouldn't come up anymore. It seemed a sane and reasonable decision, and Vanessa's homesickness started to lift. She felt much better. But she had a dance recital coming up and was talking with the staff about whether or not her parents should come up to watch her. That's when she learned that her mother had to have surgery and couldn't come under any circumstances. Vanessa began to unravel: "There was a subconscious thing that *I couldn't see her.* And then I couldn't see her because she couldn't make the car ride up. And that really freaked me out. I had finally gotten over my homesickness and two days later it comes back and hits me in the face. . . . There was something in my guts and it scared the hell out of me. I don't know what it was but it terrified me."

For a while, she was back to square one. "How did things turn out?" I asked her.

"Well, I'm here," she replied, and we both laughed. She continued: "I waited it out. I was a four-weeker. I decided I wanted to keep trying. I had seen my mom, and I was still homesick, but I extended to six weeks."

What gave Vanessa the ability to sign up for two additional weeks of camp when she was still feeling so homesick? The answer is courage, and the inner desire to beat homesickness. She is not alone. Thurber and his colleagues report that while a majority of children don't return to the summer camp at which they experienced serious homesickness, 56 percent end up going to some overnight camp program in a following year. Is that because their parents force them, or do they make that free choice? And if they do, why would they choose to return to camp after they had been so miserable? The answer is simple: Children want to be independent, and they realize that they cannot be truly independent until they beat homesickness, even when they have a painful case of it.

Children also come to realize that their parents, by definition, cannot really comfort them when they are homesick. Talking to parents may give temporary relief, but often when a child is finished talking to his or her parents, the homesick feelings return. That is what Vanessa learned during her painful visits with her parents. That is why camps have traditionally not allowed phone calls in the opening weeks of camp, if at all.

In the best of circumstances, a homesick camper can use her hard-won growth to counsel a younger child suffering from homesickness. I have met many camp counselors who themselves suffered from pretty severe homesickness as campers, yet returned to the camp year after year, gradually mastering the pain of it, and ultimately used their experience to help younger campers making the transition from at-home child to sleepaway camper.

Vanessa closed out her interview by telling me that she was using her experience to help a new Buck's Rock camper with her bad case of homesickness. She knew the girl's brother from school. One day she saw the new camper sitting at a picnic table with a counselor. The scene was intensely familiar and she recognized herself: "I knew where she was sitting, I knew the time of day: That was me."

So Vanessa sat down with the counselor, who gracefully turned the unhappy girl over to her. Vanessa started "telling jokes, funny stories about home," and humorously reminded the girl that she wouldn't want to be home with her brother. Then she walked her to a camp dance, and later promised she would come and tuck the new girl in at night, because she recalled that that was what the camp director, Laura, had done for her when her homesickness was most acute.

I asked Vanessa if beating homesickness was the biggest personal victory of her life. Her answer was frank, and not at all triumphant: "I'm only fourteen. If it had only been one year [of severe homesickness], maybe I'd be prouder. . . . My pride is important. It was just something that was there and I learned to do it. Yes, it was a fight and it was a struggle, but there are just parts of it that I'm trying to forget."

If Vanessa doesn't sound victorious, I should note that I attended a rehearsal that afternoon in preparation for the final dance concert of the year. She was happy, focused, involved with friends, and had some challenging lead roles in the dance recital. Like the other younger girls, she was focused on being as good as her counselors, the college-age dance majors who choreographed the pieces. Vanessa was focused on growing up, becoming a more competent artist, and having fun.

What Predisposes Children to Homesickness?

If you are the parent of a child who is going off to camp, I am sure you wish you could know in advance if your child might be homesick. Though there is no foolproof way to tell, no psychological crystal ball, there are some things we do know.

There are some types of children whom we know struggle in sleepover camp; as we see elsewhere in this chapter, Thurber and his colleagues identified a collection of factors that predict with a good degree of accuracy what type of child is likely to be homesick. However, it is difficult to predict with confidence to what degree any particular child will be homesick. Some children take themselves out of the equation. We imagine that camps are not likely to see the pool of catastrophically homesick children. For those children, the idea of sleeping away from home is so unbearable that neither the kids nor the parents can entertain the thought of camp. But if a child is willing to fill out her portion of a camp application form; that is, if she is willing to risk going away, the only way you can know for sure whether she will be homesick is by putting her on the bus or dropping her off, walking away, and waiting to see what happens (though there are things you can do to prevent homesickness that will be discussed in the next chapter).

I have heard many stories of pretty anxious children who, after a period of adjustment, have come to love camp. I have also been told tales of reasonably confident children who got clobbered by homesickness, much to their own surprise. If you are frustrated by my inability to predict the future for a specific child, all I can say is that the child's history is the best guide to what might happen at camp. An extroverted child who has loved staying in after-school programs since the age of five, or who has no difficulty making friends, is a good bet for overnight camp. Many families have told me about having a six-year-old, with elder siblings at camp, who begged to attend camp for three years before the family said yes, and when the younger sibling finally got to go to camp, he or she loved it.

On the other hand, children who have a bit of Eeyore in them, who tend to see the glass as half empty and overfocus on the possibility of homesickness are what Thurber calls *homesick disposed*. Such children are more likely to feel the sadness and yearning when they do go away. Sending a pessimistic child who has struggled in new social situations to camp might be a high-risk proposition, unless, of course, the child really wants to try it. What is impressive to me is how many such children battle through their own negative mind-set to become successful at camp. Indeed, the vast majority do, which is why predicting success for campers can be difficult.

Common sense suggests that children who are more anxious or tend toward depressive feelings will become more homesick than others, but surprisingly Thurber did not find a correlation between the child's pre-separation levels of depression and anxiety and the levels of homesickness. What he did discover—no surprise—was that children who have never had much practice being away from home or children who were forced to go to camp against their will were more likely to experience homesickness. The director of a girls' camp once told me that she had two sisters at her camp who were desperately unhappy; both reported that they had been sent to camp against their will. The girls were so homesick that she and the team of counselors concluded that they really should not remain at camp.

This was such an unusual conclusion for the staff—counselors love camp and always try to make it work for kids—that from the director's point of view the decision was absolutely definitive and the phone call to the parents merely the next step. She had never had a mother say no to such a request. But in this case, the jet-setting mother simply replied that she and her husband had decided that the girls should stay at camp. The parents had paid their money and they weren't coming to get their daughters. I don't remember the exact words of the mother as quoted to me by the director, but they were something to the effect of, "This is our summer to focus on Gerald" (or whatever the brother's name was). It was clear that this wasn't a family that could handle three children for the summer; the girls weren't welcome at home. The director called her staff together and informed them that the parents didn't really want these girls home. As a group, the staff made a pledge to make it the best possible summer that they could for the girls and they poured on the love. They did a pretty good job of making the girls as comfortable as possible; there were more happy moments than sad ones for them.

The children who are most at risk for homesickness and general misery at camp are those who lack social skills and have had trouble making friends in school. I am not talking about the shy child who may struggle but who often can be drawn into camp life sufficiently to manage the separation and gain from it. The toughest cases that counselors present to me every summer are those of friendless children who come into the cabin expecting nothing good from their peers and are arrogant, impulsive, quarrelsome, or just plain unhappy. This child is one that counselors come to see as one with a chip on his shoulder. They try to sabotage games or they go on strike, sitting on the ground and making every transition into a power struggle. I recognize that these children are "rejected-aggressive" children; they are also known as provocative victims or victim-bullies. They are stuck at the bottom of the social hierarchy in their schools. Having experienced a lot of social rejection, and never having had close friends, they come into every situation picturing rejection, and they meet the imagined attacks with their own hostility. Their only psychological defense is a nonstop offense against their peers and authority. Such campers can be a real burden. Sadly, and in spite of the sometimes heroic efforts of their counselors to win them over, many of them succeed in destroying any possibility of happiness at camp by conducting a war against every activity. In the end, the camp director has to choose between the remote chance of success for that individual camper—camp directors don't give up easily—and the happiness of the group, because the relentless unhappiness of one member can start to affect everyone in his or her cabin.

Finally, as Thurber points out in his research, there are children who cannot deal with certain aspects of camp, whether as a result of negative past experiences, or sometimes the novelty of camp. The new social structure, new sensory experiences, new routines, new food, and new activities can cause cascading anxiety in children. This is especially true for children who are temperamentally inhibited, who take a long time to return to their physiological baseline when immersed in novel environments. These might include children like the author Doug Stone, whose distress never lifted and only deepened during three weeks of camp, and whose family finally came to get him. Maybe he was one of those children who may have elevated levels of cortisol, the stress hormone, or whose physiological reactions to novel situations may simply be more elevated than those of other children. The novelty that makes most children light up with excitement is stressful for these children.

Children with anxiety disorders are at greater risk for homesickness than average children, usually because they become more physiologically aroused in strange situations and that can manifest itself in panic attacks. The fight-or-flight response in anxious children is almost always decided in favor of, *I gotta get out of here,* and if they cannot flee, they become overwhelmed with anxiety.

Camp people certainly do recognize anxiety in children, but they always hope they can make them feel safe, so they do not often talk in terms of anxiety disorders. What they say instead is that some children "just aren't campers." By that they mean that some children can never be comfortable at camp and nothing that the counselors and staff can do is going to make them comfortable.

Any parent of a child who suffers panic attacks or debilitating anxiety episodes moves quickly past euphemisms to the painful reality of their child's experience and their own parental concerns over his or her well-being in the camp setting. I often think that the families of children with anxiety disorders wisely choose not to send them to sleepover camp, but no one has a choice about school trips. Most children do not want to opt out of school trips in advance, no matter how anxious they feel, because they do not want to humiliate themselves in front of their friends. But if the panic attacks come, they are humiliated in another way, because their parents have to come get them. The child who goes is showing a certain kind of courage and may, in fact, find just enough of it to complete the trip and gain the satisfaction of that accomplishment. The child who opts out may be ready to take that step the next time the opportunity arises.

I am not suggesting that we should assess which children will find camp easy and send them off and keep children who might find it challenging at home. It is the very challenge of camp that makes it such a life-changing experience for so many children.

Children have a lot more courage and resilience than we give them credit for. When it comes to homesickness they understand that their own independence and maturity are at stake. While the research finds that 7 percent of children suffer from a high level of chronic homesickness that never lifts for the entire two-week session of camp, suggesting that many of these children *could* be sent home, less than 1 percent of children leave camp because of homesickness. Kids want to stick it out. They want to be successful.

Also, in most cases, coming home early is like kicking the can of conquering homesickness down the developmental road. The child knows that he or she failed to do it this year and will have to do it another year. The youngster may experience a lot of fear and uncertainty for months before getting a crack at conquering homesickness again. I know from my work as a school consultant that children who are unable to remain with a school group on an overnight trip often carry negative feelings about themselves for a long time. Teachers and chaperones do everything in their power to persuade parents to let their children go on school trips so that they are not left behind developmentally. They also do everything in their power to keep a child with the group in order to prevent the hit to a child's self-respect that comes from being unable to do what all the other children can do.

Does the fact that we cannot predict the level of a child's homesickness with certainty mean we should never send children off to camp? Obviously not. Does the fact that 7 percent of children develop a chronic case of homesickness mean we should protect them from these experiences by sending them home? No. There are many children who have mastered both their homesickness and their fear of homesickness on school trips and camp experiences.

Caleb, the boy at the beginning of this chapter who was still suffering homesickness on the tenth day of camp and the source of inspiration for Chris Thurber's research, returned to YMCA Camp Belknap the next year and for several more years thereafter. Vanessa battled her homesickness for three years at two camps before she beat it; she was back for a fourth year when I interviewed her, enjoying her dancing and her friends.

four

HOMESICK AND HAPPY

TOM'S MOTHER WAS CONCERNED that her son might experience some homesickness at overnight camp. She was pretty sure that he would be okay, but she couldn't be absolutely sure. I offered to talk with him in April, three months before his first big trip away from home. Tom, a handsome ten-year-old boy with a winning, sweet smile, readily admitted that he was afraid he would miss home a lot. Then he added that his "biggest worry is being worried." Why was he so worried? He had not done well on an attempt to stay at his grandparents' home in Rhode Island a year before. He viewed that attempt to sleep away from home as his failure and it had shaken his confidence in himself. He continued: "I was eight and a half or nine. I was pretty scared. On the way there I was pretty much shaking. Toward the night it got harder. I went to bed and I felt totally alone. I was supposed to be there for a week, but I wimped out after a day."

His grandparents had been intending to send him to a nearby nature camp during the days. His homesickness scuttled that plan. I asked why he had used the self-denigrating phrase "wimped out." He explained that he didn't think in those terms at the time, but that he felt that way now. Looking back he has contempt for his younger, more frightened self. By comparison, he pointed out that his younger cousin, George, had been able to go to their grandparents for the full week.

Tom was now getting psychologically ready to go away for a whole month, to a sleepaway camp where a session of four weeks, as he put it, "is the lowest you can go." He said he was going because his dad had been a camper and his mother had talked him into it. He was both hopeful and apprehensive. When I followed up with questions about his worries, Tom told me that he was scared of spiders and snakes, and had memories of incidents when lightning knocked out the electricity on a summer vacation, and being alone in the dark.

You might call Tom a worrier, but he is also just young and inexperienced at being away from home. On the plus side, Tom had an upbeat view of what was possible at camp because his father had been an Outward Bound instructor and Tom and his family had vacationed together at a family camp on a lake in New Hampshire for many summers. At the family camp he and his friends enjoyed spending many hours playing away from his parents. "It's not that I don't want to be with my parents," he said, "but I find one of the highlights is that we can do whatever we want there." His optimism about what could happen when he was away from his parents was certainly a very good sign.

When parents try to assess their child's readiness for camp, they struggle to distinguish between what is normal anxiety about being away from home for the first time and what are symptoms of an anxiety that might presage a terrible experience. Children with separation and attachment problems may be at risk for higher levels of homesickness, as are youngsters with the homesick disposition that I discussed in the previous chapter. However, in some cases it can be hard to predict homesickness because separation problems do not always emerge before the leave-taking. It is the actual separation from Mom and Dad that triggers the psychological alarm system. Because of the failed sleepover at his grandparents' house, Tom was afraid that he might be one of those boys. How could he know differently?

I checked back with Tom eight days before he left for camp. I asked him if he was still nervous. "Yeah, I am a little nervous. I think about it every other night. The thoughts come just after I get into bed." But Tom was coaching himself, reminding himself that there was a break halfway through the month, and that he would get to see his parents then. He had the exact date in mind, "Saturday the twenty-fourth." He was also focused on having a friend to go with who might be feeling some of what he was feeling. "His name is Rory; he's really funny and he's nice. He's a lot like me. He probably fears the same thing and he probably fears it a little less."

It was going to be a first-time experience for his friend as well. When I asked Tom if he was worried about getting upset at camp, possibly crying in public or in front of his friend, he said that his friend Rory would be sympathetic, but that neither of them would ever talk about something as emotional as that. Tom says that if he were to talk about camp with his friend, "It wouldn't have been about how scared we were going to be; it would have been about how much fun we were going to have and what sports we were going to do."

I asked him whether he had had another sleepover since I saw him and he said that he had. "Yes, it went fine. I went over to friends' houses, they're twins. We had a lot of fun." Then he reflected, "Come to think of it, that's what's going to happen at camp!" This assertion sounded like 80 percent optimism and 20 percent uncertainty. It was just a little forced, and I couldn't tell whether he really believed it, or wanted to believe it, but I could hear that he was trying to focus on what might be great about camp, an effective self-coaching technique that would reduce his risk of being seriously homesick when he got there. Clearly, he was in much better shape for camp than he had been two months earlier.

Tom wasn't looking for his parents to fix things and somehow eliminate any worries about homesickness. He took those steps himself. But his parents also took reasonable, responsible steps to do what they could to help him prepare psychologically for the time away.

What Can Parents Do to Prevent or Lessen Homesickness?

There are a number of things that parents can do to help their children get ready for trips away from home, and to prepare for dealing with homesickness. Some are a matter of attitude; others are quite practical and concrete.

The first and most important thing that parents can do is to have confidence in the child's ability to manage the challenge of being away, and to have faith in the child's ability to beat homesickness. In other words, parents have to do their own psychological work in preparation for their child's departure. Camp directors tell me that many parents tell them, "She's ready to go. *I'm the one* who isn't ready." As an ironic comment, or as self-preparation for the departure of a child, that's okay. If what a parent means is: *I'm really going to miss her,* that's fine, as long as it is tempered by the deeper conviction that both child and parent are going to be all right.

Our children know us intimately; they read our faces, our voices, and our moods better than anybody else in the world because we have been the center of their universe since they were born. If the thought of your child being away is unbearable to you, it is going to be very hard for him or her to make the transition to camp. Why? If a child looks into the face of a parent and sees real doubt, it will inflame the child's own doubts. My work with school-phobic children, kids who cannot get themselves to school, has convinced me that there is always a parent-child worry cycle at work: The child's anxiety has sparked the parent's worry, then the sight of the parent's worry reignites the child's anxiety, and off they go together into an upward spiral of growing panic.

As a parent, if you cannot come to feel confident that your child is ready for camp, you need to talk at length with the camp director about the issues, or perhaps with other parents who have sent their children to camp. Camp directors are, naturally, camp enthusiasts; they also need to fill their beds. It is, perhaps, understandable that parents are sometimes skeptical about their advice. A nervous mother and father are perhaps more likely to trust the experience and perspective of close friends who have sent their children to camp, or even an expert. But the fact remains that camp directors have almost certainly seen more homesick children than any other type of expert whom parents might consult, far more than most psychiatrists and psychologists; and other parents, no matter how trustworthy, have only their own children's experiences to go by. Tom's mother availed herself of both and felt reassured by her talk with her son's camp director and her conversations with satisfied parents whose children loved the camp that Tom was going to attend. She, like Tom, was less nervous about him in July than she had been in April. It seemed as if things would go well for him, and they did.

The second thing that parents can do is talk with their children about the possibility of homesickness. Because Tom had already experienced an acute attack of homesickness, and because he was so openly worried that he might crash and burn at camp, his parents had no choice but to discuss it with him. But what if you have a child who doesn't bring the subject up on his or her own? Many parents imagine that talking about it will fan the fires of worry, so they do not discuss it. If you avoid the topic of homesickness, you are ensuring that your child won't know how or what you think about it, or whether *you* ever experienced it in childhood. Most important, he won't know whether you believe that he is capable of getting over it. Without knowledge of what her parents think about homesickness, a ten-year-old girl may believe that she is uniquely cursed, that only she is so weak or incapable. She may feel ashamed and smother her cries in her pillow at night, imagining that her parents never faced and overcame homesickness.

Though it seems obvious to say so, children do not have a lot of life experience. They need you to help them anticipate both their pain and their strengths. So you can say, "You will probably feel a bit homesick when you go to camp. Most kids do, but they get over it in time if they try hard to deal with it head-on and put some effort into coping." And then you can point to the silver lining of these sometimes painful feelings. "Feeling homesick just means that you have a home worth missing, a place where people love you. It is the most natural thing in the world to feel homesickness." Then, if it is true, you might say, "And I felt homesick the first time I went away from home for two weeks. It is part of going to camp."

This kind of normalizing conversation reassures a child that what she or he is likely to feel has been felt before and is survivable. It might give the child a cognitive weapon to use in a flash of momentary despair. *This isn't just stupid, pointless pain,* a camper can think. *It is evidence that I come from a loving home.* Whether she can hold on to that thought when in the grip of homesickness is uncertain, but perhaps a counselor will repeat the thought and revive the memory of the parents' words in her mind.

Third, parents can arrange for their children to practice being away. If you are going to send a child off to camp, you should encourage her to have that practice weekend with a friend, an aunt, or her grandparents. When I met with Tom in July, he had succeeded in his overnight stay at the twins' house, and that victory had superseded the earlier failure at his grandparents' home. It does not take a lot of success to change a child's negative opinion of himself. With this one victory in hand, Tom was no longer the kid who had "wimped out," rather he was a child who had succeeded at a sleepover. Neither parental reassurance ("You're going to be fine") nor parental optimism ("I'm sure camp will be fun") are going to be anywhere near as effective as a child's own achievements in persuading himself that he is ready.

Chris Thurber also recommends that parents teach their children about different periods of time. For a child of eight or nine or even ten, the idea of a two-week session or a one-month session can seem like forever. Telling her that camp won't feel that long is pointless. Using a calendar to count out two weeks by checking off the dates every week, or comparing it to a winter vacation in the recent past, will help the child grasp the stretches of time. Tom illustrated this by focusing on the midseason visit from his parents. If a month seemed very long to him—and it did—the idea of just two weeks until his parents visit at midseason was a huge comfort. Having that mental control, being able to think about time in segments is enormously helpful to children.

Finally, Thurber's research suggests that campers who feel more in control of the process suffer less from homesickness, so it is good to involve the child in choosing the camp, getting to know the camp, and shopping and packing for camp. But how much control do you have to give a child over the camp decision? Do you not send a child to camp until he has decided to go to camp on his own? Do you have to let the decision be the child's? Can you send a child off to camp when he or she hasn't expressed any interest, or feels nervous about it? Yes, you can, if you handle it correctly.

Terri, the mother in Chapter Two who spoke about her son Blake, the picky eater, and her husband, Sam, made the decision to send their three children (ages twelve, ten, and eight) to camp without having been campers themselves. Until they started doing research on the Internet, they didn't actually know that much about overnight summer camps. Terri had spent her summers by the ocean on the South Shore of Massachusetts where she grew up. Sam's parents sent him from suburban Chicago to his grandparents' farm in Nebraska for a few weeks each summer. The rest of the summer he played with children in the neighborhood. "It was kind of a camp in and of itself," he recalls. But for children today, including his, he says, "It's not like that now." He was worried that eight-year-old Blake would spend the summer sitting in front of the television. Blake had been diagnosed with attention deficit/hyperactivity disorder (ADHD); he struggled at school and had had trouble making friends. With no neighborhood friendship group, it was not only likely that he would fall into "the usual trap of screen time," as his father put it, it was inevitable. Sam couldn't stand the idea of his son spending the summer staring at a screen.

He convinced Terri that they should consider a camp for Blake. Then he began to do research online, starting with the search words *ADHD* and *boys' camps*. Soon he was introduced to a world of summer camps he had never known. After bringing Terri into the online search, they found a camp they both felt was right for him; Buckskin, a camp in Minnesota, described its mission to serve children with ADHD, learning disabilities, and Asperger's syndrome, as well as adopted children who face a variety of challenges.

When they talked, Sam and Terri were clear about one thing:

They weren't going to send Blake off to camp and keep their other two children home. That wouldn't be fair. Besides, if camp was going to be good for Blake, it very likely would be good to great for Amber and Richard. "We are not the type of parents who want to get rid of their kids, quite the opposite," Terri told me. "It was hard to let them go, but we wanted them to have great experiences."

They asked the director of Buckskin where he would send his children to camp if they didn't have special needs. He recommended Camp Mishawaka, a coed activities camp in Grand Rapids, Minnesota. They checked it out and it looked perfect. They took Amber, age twelve, aside and informed her that they were going to send her to Camp Mishawaka. She cried and, like any self-respecting twelve-year-old, was furious that they hadn't consulted her first. Her father began a lobbying campaign to win her over. He told her how much fun camp was likely to be, and showed her the camp Web site, where they studied the photos and watched the video. Amber had had a tough year with the sixth-grade girls in her school, and the fresh start with a new group of girls that her father promised her held some appeal for her.

Sam was a bit Machiavellian in the way he went about getting his children to camp—something that isn't always advisable—but when it came to Amber, he knew her well and understood that camp was going to be just her kind of challenge. He knew that she would initially oppose him, because she is a spirited early-adolescent girl. He also understood that she would rise to the challenge of camp for the same reason: She is a spirited early-adolescent girl.

Once she was on board, they notified the two boys that they, too, were going to camp. Blake was enthusiastic. Richard cried. He had never been away from home and he, too, was a fussy eater who stuck religiously to his favorite foods. He figured out right away that sleepover camp meant new foods. As a small kid for his age, Richard was also afraid of being bullied by bigger boys. Sam and Terri were reassured by the Mishawaka philosophy that Richard would be safe there.

In the weeks leading up to the departure for camp, they had several conversations about homesickness with the children. Sam told them that he had been homesick when he had gone to his grandparents' farm in Nebraska for several weeks in the summer. They assured the kids that homesickness would pass. Terri was confident that each child heard that message. Blake's camp started first. The whole family drove up to Ely, Minnesota, to drop him off. Here is Terri's description of the drop-off.

> Leaving Blake at camp was one of the hardest things I've ever had to do. As we approached the camp, Blake said his stomach felt sick. To break the tension, I had him jump out of the car and I took his picture by the camp sign at the entrance. . . . [At the parking lot] Blake then grabbed Sam's leg and clung to it. As we stood together on the steps of the porch he grabbed both of our legs.

Knowing how hard it would be for Blake to stand in line, Terri sent the family to walk around the camp with him, while she went to register. They met up again at the cabin, where, she admits sheepishly, "being a mom," she was ready to unpack Blake's gear and "get him all set up," but was surprised by the counselor who made it clear to her that he was going to help Blake unpack. He explained that it was camp tradition, part of Blake's transition from dependence on his parents to a trusting relationship with the counselor. Terri was stunned; she looked at Sam and could see that he was starting to tear up but was trying to hold it together. "I knew I had to do the same," she tells me, describing how she summoned up her courage, looked her son in the eye, and gave him a little pep talk about being a good friend and using his manners. "I'll miss you," he said earnestly, and gave her a loving kiss good-bye. At that moment, she recalls: "It was all I could do not to lose it and start bawling my eyes out. I held back the tears and gave him a smile and a final thumbs-up and walked away. Just outside the cabin, the tears came streaming down."

Sam got the van and when Terri got in, she was crying quietly, trying not to upset her two older children, both of whom would be heading for their camp within a week. "I controlled my crying," she wrote to me, "but I really wanted to let it out. I could have sobbed profusely."

The family had a long, quiet car ride to a hotel in Duluth, Minnesota, where they stopped for the night before driving home to Chicago. They missed Blake's presence, his constant energy. With his ADHD, he is the "spice" of the family. Terri focused her thoughts on how brave Blake had been. She remembered that before he had said, "I'll miss you," he'd said, "It'll be okay, Mom," and nodded his head as if to reassure her.

REMEMBER THAT BLAKE is eight years old, and that he didn't choose to go to camp. It was his parents' idea. But like his mom, he, too, had summoned up his courage at the moment of separation. Just minutes after clinging desperately to their legs, he was trying to reassure his parents that he would make good on their choice of camp for him. Blake was doing what all healthy children do when faced with the challenge of separation. He was reaching down inside to find his inner strength, and found it, at least at that moment. Though I don't have any description of the next few hours, I imagine that Blake accepted his counselor's help in unpacking his items, and watched other boys say good-bye to their parents. After all the grown-ups were gone, his cabin members no doubt formed a circle and learned one another's names, then played a game outdoors, perhaps took a swim, and then went off to dinner. At some point that evening, perhaps right after dinner or maybe at bedtime, the homesickness hit Blake pretty hard. His first two letters, in a boyish scrawl, read as follows:

LETTER #1: I'm feeling homesick. I really want to go home. Please pick me up.
Blake.

LETTER #2: I'm in pain and really homesick. Please come and get me ☹
Blake.

Because Sam works from a home office, he intercepted the letters and made the tricky decision to not show them to Terri because he was sure she would be consumed by worry if she read them. Instead, he suggested that they call the camp director to check on Blake's progress. The camp director told them honestly that Blake was battling homesickness and was having problems with unfamiliar foods (Terri imagined him starving to death), but he told them that he thought Blake was turning the corner and adjusting to camp. It was only after they heard a good report from the camp director that Sam showed Terri those two letters. She reports that after reading them she did a "face plant" of despair on the dining room table.

Terri and Sam were sending Blake letters, but before he could react to their letters, they received three more. It appeared that he had given up on his mom coming to rescue him and was focusing his efforts on his dad, at first pleading and then demanding, but he also let his mother know how he felt.

LETTER #3: Dear Dad, I'm sending you this because I'm really sad I'm here. I miss home really much. Please pick me up. ☹

LETTER #4: Dad, I hate it here. Take me home.
Blake

LETTER #5: Mom, I HATE IT HERE!
Blake

After ten days, they finally received the letter they had been hoping to get:

LETTER #6: Dear Mom and Dad, I am kind of hungry for junk food. Can you send me a big bag of chocolate chip cookies. I would like to share them with my counselors and cabin mates. 13 of us total. We will eat them on cabin unity day (Sat. and Sun.). Thank you if you give me the cookies. I'm trying new foods.
Blake (also send new stamps)

Blake was clearly identified with his cabin, he wanted to share his cookies with his peers, he was anticipating upcoming events on the schedule. Terri felt these were good signs. Blake had never really felt part of a group at school. He was also asking for stamps, which suggested that at some psychological level, he was ready to stay. He knew he would be writing more letters.

MEANWHILE, TERRI AND SAM launched Richard and Amber off to their camp. In the airport, when they were standing around with a large group of parents whose children were headed for Camp Mishawaka, two bigger boys aged twelve or thirteen walked up to Richard and introduced themselves. They welcomed him to the camp and offered to help him in any way, encouraging him to come to them if he had any questions about camp life. Two big boys (potential bodyguards!) being kind and helpful to their son who feared bullies! Sam and Terri could see that Richard was won over. So were they. Richard wrote his first card to them from the plane:

> Dear Mom and Dad, I am on the plane right now! Turns out we got first class so we get a free pillow, blanket and drinks and food! Its pretty fun on the plane and cool as well. Your camper, Richard.

Eager to embrace his new status and independence, he signed the card "Your camper." His second card, written in haste and filled with exclamation points, let them know that their son, the notoriously picky eater at home, was trying new things:

> Dear Mom and Dad, I am having a great time! I tried spagetti! I kinda like it my counselor remy encouraged me to try it! I doing fine with the food I am eating! And I ate a chicken patty! No bun though but I enjoyed it! I am very good at this game called gah gah I love it it's a lot of fun. I think I wanna come next year! —Richard

Amber's first card was equally enthusiastic. She reported that "I love my cabin," and she wrote the names of the other six girls. In her second letter she gave detailed descriptions ("Let me tell you about my cabin") of the other girls' backgrounds and personalities, with a special focus on a girl from the Dominican Republic who had clearly captured her imagination. She reported having passed her riding and swim tests ("the lake is SO COLD") and claimed she had the "awesomest counselor ever." Later she reported that she was going to a time-honored ritual group swim, "which is like a bath in the lake." "We wear swimsuits, though!" she reassured her parents.

Terri and Sam tell me that Amber is already thinking of being an assistant counselor at the camp. She has seen her future and it is camp! Although the camp tuitions aren't easy on their family budget, they say they want Blake to be in a camp with boys who share his struggles, and with whom he may make friends. And if their three-child camp experiment was originally about getting Blake away from screens and into a situation where he might be able to make friends more easily than he does at school, it was a runaway success for Richard and Amber. They are going back, for sure. Sam said, "Even if Blake only has a mediocre time, we're hoping that if Richard and Amber talk enthusiastically about camp, it will persuade him to want to go back."

Sam and Terri's story about sending their children off to camp, along with Tom's successful first-time camp experience, illustrate a number of supportive things that parents can do when sending children off to camp. It helps kids when adults speak frankly to them about their nervousness, acknowledge the possibility of homesickness (even the likelihood of significant homesickness in a child who is very worried), provide brief camp homesickness stories from their own lives (or comparable stories, like Sam's Nebraska farm experience), help them think about the stretches of time, and involve children in the choice of and preparations for camp. Most important, these parents showed confidence in the child's ability to make the transition to camp and were willing to trust the camp personnel to do what was needed for their child after they left. The important part, sometimes the hardest thing, as Terri described it, is to be brave enough to leave a child when you know that your departure is going to cause him or her real pain and sadness, or to be able to bear his significant distress at a distance. Ultimately, that requires you to trust strangers to look after your child.

What Can Staff Do to Comfort a Homesick Child and Diminish His or Her Distress?

Let's look, for a moment, at what camp staff can do to help children, because many have asked me, and it may be reassuring to you to see all that camp staff are doing to help a homesick child. And some of the things camp staff do may be helpful to you when you find yourself in tough moments or conversations with your own child.

The single most effective thing that camp counselors can do for children who suffer from homesick feelings is to do what they do best, namely to have fun with kids and create a socially safe environment where children can make friends. The traditional wisdom that you can cure homesickness by distracting them with games, contests, skits, or singing—the traditional staples of camp—is correct. According to Chris Thurber's research, the vast majority of children report very high levels of happiness at camp, rating their experience an eight or nine on a ten-point satisfaction scale. You may recall that 97 percent of children experience at least some occasional homesick feelings at camp, so the fact that the majority of children are giving camp extremely high marks suggests that the ordinary camp program is sufficiently entertaining, comforting, and distracting to meet the emotional needs of most children. Camp is fun, and the vast majority of campers are what the paradoxical title of this book promises: homesick *and* happy.

The true magic of camp, however, does not reside in the daily program of camp events; it lies in the relationship between children and other children, and between children and their counselors. Children who have been cared for all of their lives by "old" parents in their thirties and forties, or by "ancient" teachers moving through their forties and fifties, are delighted by the novelty of sharing adventures—and their pain—with their peers and being cared for by appealing young adults in their late teens and early twenties. Any parent who has ever seen how much more effective a friend can be in calming her child under some circumstances, or who has seen her children's devotion to their teenage babysitter, can imagine what it feels like to a ten-year-old child to find their camp filled with an army of friends and teenage babysitters.

I interviewed two girls at YMCA Camp Chimney Corners who were helping each other with their homesickness and who were also getting help from their assistant counselor. Both girls were surprised they felt as homesick as they did the second year, given that they were one-year veterans. They had come for the two-week session when they were nine. Sitting in one chair for our interview, they were happily mushed together, constantly touching, always listening to and supporting each other. They were practically finishing each other's sentence as they described their homesickness.

"You just feel kind of sad," Livvy said. "You don't want to talk to anyone else."

"I just wanted to be alone in my bed," Julia said. "I haven't actually cried at night. I normally cry after lunch or after dinner."

Did they get homesick at any other times? Yes, during siesta time, when they had a lot of time to think and read letters from home. I asked whether the letters were helpful. Julia had a mixed reaction because there were so many of them. "It's ridiculous," she said. "There are seventeen to twenty letters." So, her parents' efforts to help seemed a bit extreme to her, the number of letters implying, perhaps, a vote of no confidence from far away. Her friend was right there.

They tried to support each other, and mostly it worked.

"We were both still a little homesick but it was better because we both tried to focus on having fun and it was fine," Livvy said. "I still comfort her when she's homesick."

Julia, who is suffering more, knows that her homesickness is sometimes a burden to her friend, and she is aware that because of the contagion effect she cannot always be a comfort to Livvy. "It is hard to comfort someone when they're homesick because that makes me homesick," she observed. She doesn't want to overwhelm Livvy, so she looks to the assistant counselor for support: "I found Talia helpful because she could be more focused on me than the rest of the cabin."

Talia said all the right things, and encouraged her to focus on the good things, which helped, according to Julia. Once, when she was in the grip of great sadness, Shannon, the director, told her, "There's nothing I can do now . . . [but] maybe if you stay sad, you can call home in a few days." This backup plan to reach her mother had a paradoxical effect on Julia. "Knowing I was able to call her in a day or two made me not want to call her," she noted.

As Julia's experience reveals, having a young adult pay attention to you when you are young and homesick can feel wonderful. However, a large quantity of attention is not enough; the quality of attention is important. It is not enough for a counselor to listen to a child and offer generic platitudes: "Lots of kids feel homesick, but they get over it. You'll be fine in a few days." Indeed, too-fast and superficial reassurance can be confusing for a child who knows it isn't going deep enough, but does not know how to educate the counselor to do better.

If, however, the counselor is trained to do a few straightforward things with a homesick child, it can be enormously effective. The counselor has to make some time to listen, she has to ask some questions about what the child misses to empathize with the homesickness, and she needs to normalize the child's emotions. In other words, she has to acknowledge the pain of the yearnings and bear them alongside the child. That means saying, "Boy, I can see you are really missing home. I can see that it really hurts you. That's tough."

This is counterintuitive for most of us. Young people and adults alike see someone in pain and reflexively want to offer quick reassurances. After all, it is hard to sit in the presence of someone else's pain. It makes you feel a bit helpless and sometimes seriously incompetent. No one likes that feeling. Furthermore, most people are afraid that if they delve into a child's pain, asking for further details, it will cause the child greater pain. Finally, if you start to ask a crying child to talk about what makes him or her sad, you cannot be sure how long the process is going to take. So if a camp counselor has a group of children waiting in the cabin, as Thurbs did, or the group is in transition from activity A to activity B, it may feel ill-advised to invite a child to talk more. Things cannot always be brought to a complete stop. In my experience, if you make empathic contact with a child and say something that truly acknowledges the child's pain, then it can be relatively easy to say, "I really want to talk to you about this, but we've got to get up to the dining hall. Do you think you can talk more about this after dinner?"

After dinner, or when there is more time, the counselor needs to ask the camper some questions about what the child misses and listen to some of the child's stories. If a child feels that his or her homesickness is seen and acknowledged, that will be of significant help to most children. It cannot be done in a rush, though it doesn't have to turn into a one-hour therapy session every time, and for some children it really must not because a too-long session will unwind them. There is also a fairness principle at work; all the campers need the counselor's time.

A quick check-in helps most campers with mild homesickness, and sometimes a group discussion can do the trick: a group conversation at bedtime, for example. One counselor said that when her whole group of girls was showing signs of homesickness, she had them all describe their bedrooms to one another and to her, in minute detail. She also described her own room at home. The girls felt enormously comforted by the extended opportunity to share these details of home. Other counselors, usually young men, tell me that they had the whole group describe their favorite meals. To paraphrase the axiom about an army marching on its stomach, it turns out that one way to boy campers' hearts is through imagining what they wish they had in their stomachs.

For campers who are experiencing above-average levels of homesickness, it is important to help them think through what they themselves have found helpful. Did the letter from home help when it first arrived? Perhaps the child could read it again, or read it out loud to you. Are there things that a child wants to say to his mom and dad? You can suggest that he write another letter, or even, if he is crying, take some dictation. Write down his or her thoughts. I learned from my psychotherapy practice that it is enormously helpful to a child to say what he wishes he could say to his parents with you listening. Write it down and hand him the piece of paper when he is finished. Perhaps he or she can later put those thoughts in a letter, or maybe not. But having expressed them out loud will help.

But what about the one in five campers who experience significant distress? And what about that 7 percent whose homesickness gets more severe as the session goes on? What can younger counselors do for a seriously homesick camper? Naturally, most new and younger counselors will turn to the village leader, the scout leader, or the camp director for the simple reason that they have more time and more experience handling tough cases. That's what the seventeen-year-old Thurbs did when Caleb accused him of lacking expertise.

For children in significant distress, it can be comforting to feel that they are in the hands of someone older and wiser. A gray-headed person may be able to speak with the authority of a parent, or be able to speak to a child about a phone call that he or she had with the parent about the situation. It is enormously comforting to children to know that the people who are taking care of them are communicating their situation to their parents. For many children that is sufficient to give them the courage to stay at camp.

In those rare instances when a child's homesickness is completely debilitating, it is the camp director who is best positioned to make the decision that a child is too homesick to stay. No one likes the idea of the shortened session. As much as the child wants to go home, he or she doesn't want to feel like a failure in front of peers who are able to remain at camp. Parents of a camper who has to leave camp early often feel like failures as well. Why is their child not capable of making it away from home? Did they cultivate excessive anxiety or dependence in their son or daughter? I don't think so. It just doesn't always work out that first or second summer.

When you consider that 99 percent of children succeed at camp, when you reflect on the fact that a majority of the most homesick children return to some sleepaway camp the following year, you have to admire the courage of children. They understand intuitively that leaving home is a challenge they have to master sooner or later. Even a failed first attempt is worthy of respect. That is why a shortened stay should always be treated as a significant achievement by camp staff and parents. A child should always have a chance to say a warm and dignified goodbye to his or her peers, and should always hear the respect of staff who have witnessed the child's efforts to master homesickness. You never know: The child who struggles with homesickness and has to leave camp at thirteen may thrive during a college sophomore year in Italy or Guatemala. The biggest mistake we can make is to count children out. Their development always surprises us.

ing, too late to charge the battery, and a child would be stuck, immobile, and unable to participate for one precious day of camp.

On the first day I visited Camp for All, the counselors and administrative staff, including Kurt, were wearing bright yellow T-shirts that read: LABELS ARE FOR JARS NOT FOR PEOPLE. Other shirts displayed a motto attributed to Scott Hamilton, the Olympic figure skater: THE ONLY DISABILITY IN LIFE IS A BAD ATTITUDE. But not everyone or everything at the camp was quite so earnest. The eight members of this week's medical staff were all wearing baseball hats decorated with head boppers, pom-poms, and sparkly spray. One counselor, a tall, thin young man well over six feet tall, was wearing a cone-shaped, purple party hat that hit the door jamb every time he walked through a doorway. His shirt proclaimed: TRIUMPH IS JUST "TRY" WITH AN EXTRA "UMPH." Indeed, it may take a lot of "Umph" for special needs children to go to camp. It also requires something extra of their parents and caregivers.

Sending a child with special needs off to camp is a psychological journey for both parent and child. If it is emotionally difficult for most parents to send a child away to an ordinary sleepaway camp, imagine the anxiety of sending off a child who suffers from a life-threatening illness. Imagine sending your son or daughter to participate in archery and canoeing when they spend their lives in a wheelchair, and have little upper-body strength. How can she possibly pull back the bow to launch the arrow? Can she do it? Will she be humiliated if she cannot? And what about canoeing? Wouldn't you be afraid that the canoe would tip over and she would drown? Horseback riding? How could she stay upright? And what about a high-ropes course? There is no way. Imagine your child sharing a cabin with other children when she or he has to be catheterized to urinate. If the centerpiece of your daily routine is making sure that your HIV-positive child gets all the medications she needs to protect her from transitioning to full-blown AIDS, how could you relinquish control and hand it over to a camp? The answer is that maybe you could if there was a camp specifically designed to meet the needs of such children.

Camp for All is a "barrier free" camp in Burton, Texas, which partners with many other nonprofit organizations to provide a camping experience for children and adults with challenging illnesses or special needs. The mission of the camp is "the universal camping experience." Camp for All tries to provide all children, no matter how severe their disability, the true camping experience: cabins, campfires, archery, horseback riding, canoeing, swimming, and, of course, wheelchair sports. Kurt Podeszwa, the optimistic director, says that he would recommend to every camp that they offer wheelchair sports. "The chairs are expensive," he says, "a couple of thousand apiece, but they are a great leveler." Many of his children, of course, come to camp with considerable experience in their chairs and easily outperform children who have never operated one.

Fifty-six different groups pack the annual schedule of Camp for All, almost every weekend during the academic year and weeklong camps during the summer. Each camp has its own name, for example: Camp PHEver, Camp Smiles, Camp Extreme, Camp Discover Dermadillo, and Camp Hope. These playful names represent the camping hopes of children with, respectively: phenylketonuria, cerebral palsy, spinal cord injuries, several dermatological disorders, and HIV/AIDS. The ones I have named represent only a fraction of the total. Each group also brings its own medical personnel, its own cabin counselors, and, of course, its campers with their special requirements. They are met by a staff of seventy, thirty full-time staff and forty summer staff, who mold the camp setting to meet the special needs, both physical and psychological, of the campers. At times, the kitchen is turning out seven different types of meals for a single group of campers with varying dietary and other special needs.

In this chapter visit to this highly unusual camp, we're going to see and hear a version of the sleepaway camp story that is dramatically different in many ways from the iconic camps we have visited up to now and those we'll visit in the rest of the book. Most of you will never need a camp like this and may never have a reason—or an opportunity—to visit one. But I want to take you inside this place, inside the conversations among children and between children and staff, and inside the elaborate efforts made to accommodate the children's needs, so you can get a sense of the children's experience there and learn from them, as I did. They teach us not only about special-needs children, but about all children and the role that sleepaway camp can play in their development.

Here, and at any camp where a child with special needs embarks on a sleepaway experience, the act of letting go can be especially challenging, often more so for parents than for children. A child's illness intensifies parents' natural protective instinct. If the illness is serious, chronic, or life threatening, it can intensify their protectiveness even more because it removes the normal expectations that one's child is growing and developing, preparing for an independent adult life. But as surprising as it may be to adults, a child's need to feel his or her own growth and development, the yearning for competence and mastery, and the need to feel that they matter in the world, comes from inside. It is universal. It is no less for a child with serious disabilities or one whose life expectancy falls far short of adulthood. Everyone wants to feel that they're growing and developing until they die. Kids who are seriously ill don't stop growing and developing, and wait to die. They need to feel they are continuing to develop: That's the inner imperative.

———

I FLEW DOWN TO TEXAS to visit Camp for All when it was hosting Camp Hope, a one-week camp serving children with HIV/
AIDS and founded by the AIDS Foundation of Houston in 1998.
Children with the virus come to Camp Hope from all over Texas,
Louisiana, and Florida. Because of the stigma, fear, and preju-
dice that still surround HIV/AIDS, many families of children
who suffer from the virus are not open about their illness to
their communities, schoolmates, or even their extended families,
which means that the camp is "nondisclosing." Not all of the
children at Camp Hope, especially the younger campers, are
fully aware that they have the virus, or understand the implica-
tions. In some instances, their caregivers haven't yet told them
about the disease. Younger campers are assigned to nondisclosing cabins, where cabin activities and group discussions
don't include HIV as a program topic.

The teens, all of whom are aware of their HIV status, are in
disclosing cabins, where they receive support by talking with
other kids who suffer from the illness. I signed a tightly worded
medical confidentiality agreement when I walked onto the camp
grounds and have disguised the names of everyone in this chapter other than the director's, a pediatrician, and a couple of staff
who allowed their names to be used.

Almost all of the children who attend Camp Hope contracted
HIV through perinatal transmission, that is, when they were in
the womb, or in the process of being born, or through breast
milk from moms who were infected with the virus. About half of
the campers have lost their mothers to the disease and are being
raised by fathers, grandparents, aunts and uncles, foster and
adoptive parents. Camp Hope staff does not use the term *parents,* they prefer *caregivers.* Marc Cohen, the director of Camp
Hope, also suggested that I use *caregivers* instead of *parents* and
explained why. Several years ago, one well-meaning counselor at
Camp Hope asked a child, "What do your parents do?" The

child answered, "My mommy's in Heaven and my daddy's in jail." The staff member was shaken by the reply and didn't know what to say next.

Before flying down to Texas, I asked a social worker at Texas Children's Hospital whether she could find some caregivers willing to be interviewed for this book. Two volunteered: Dan and Jane Crawford, a warm and welcoming couple in their late thirties. Both are clergy, deeply involved in the missions of their churches. They are also the parents of three children: two adopted daughters, Deborah and Melissa, and a son, Randall, eighteen months old, who is their birth child. They adopted Deborah when she was two years old knowing that she was HIV positive.

I first met the Crawfords at the camp pick-up center in the Meyer Building at the Texas Children's Hospital in Houston on a hot July afternoon. Entering the building I stood behind families and children who were signing in at the camp registration table and then walking over to the medication tables. "Dr. Heidi," a pediatrician from Texas Children's Hospital, who oversees the medical care of about a third of the Camp Hope campers, greeted her families warmly. She took the medications they offered her in rectangular, plastic pill containers, some with fourteen or twenty-eight compartments. She snapped open the lids and counted the pills. Once she was satisfied that a camper had all the medications that he or she would need for the week at camp, she placed them in a large plastic bag and moved them into two large cardboard boxes, which were overflowing with medications. Dr. Heidi would then reassure families that although she wouldn't be at camp for the first few days, her colleague from U.T. Hospital would be there and she would join the children later in the week. Dan and Jane Crawford told me that the fact that Deborah's doctor—Dr. Heidi—would be present at a camp was the crucial variable in their decision to send her to Camp Hope the first time.

I got my first glimpse of the Crawfords' daughter Deborah, a cute and outgoing nine-year-old African American girl, in a classroom at the Meyer Center that had been pressed into use as a waiting room. Families who had registered their children for camp were sitting around a square of long, rectangular tables, waiting for the call to head for the bus. Most of the children and adults were African American or Hispanic; there was a sprinkling of white caregivers like Dan and Jane. Deborah had immediately located three friends, girls with whom she had attended Camp Hope the previous years. They were sitting on the floor, playing and chatting. She only occasionally sat up and gave her father an inquisitive look or interjected a quiet question while he talked to the stranger from Boston. She was mildly curious about her parents' conversation, but it was clear that Deborah was really focused on camp. She first attended Camp Hope when she was seven years old, and, according to her parents, she loved it. She was never homesick, not for a second. This was to be her third summer and she was eager to be with her friends again.

Dan and Jane met in their early twenties when both of them were working at a children's home in Tennessee. They respected the efforts of the institution and the house parents to provide a homelike environment for the children, but they wished for the children that they had forever parents. So they agreed, almost without discussion, that they were going to adopt a child long before they considered having a biological child. They went to the United Way office, where they had reviewed a book that contained short descriptions of the children available for adoption. On their way home, Dan and Jane questioned each other. "Did you see a child who called out to you?" It turns out that they had both been drawn to the description of Deborah, so the matter was quickly settled.

Deborah came to them with more baggage than just HIV. As an infant, she was diagnosed with failure to thrive, and the child protective services in the state of Texas had taken her away from her mother, along with her two older siblings. There was no one to adopt all three of the children. The father of her older sister took the two oldest children, even though one was not his biological child, but he did not think he could meet Deborah's medical needs. Deborah was made available for adoption by herself. Watching her play with her friends, returning periodically to touch base with her parents, and check in on their conversation with me, I could see immediately that she loved her parents and was deeply attached to them. She had obviously overcome many of the failure-to-thrive problems from which she had suffered as an infant except, of course, the HIV virus.

Growing up with HIV-positive status presents serious challenges for both children and caregivers. There is, obviously, the constant threat of an early death. Children become aware of the possibility when they learn that their biological mothers died too young, or when they figure out that they take a lot more pills every day than their friends take. At some point, sooner or later, they are going to have to learn the truth about the disease. When AIDS was first identified, it was a certain killer. Twenty years ago, HIV-positive children did not live long; they soon developed AIDS and died. With the new medications developed in recent years to treat the disease, HIV is no longer the overwhelming threat to life that it once was, but it still requires constant medical care and it remains extremely scary. The older children at camp are all well aware that their HIV could switch over to AIDS at any time. However, because of the stigma associated with the illness and people's irrational fears about casual transmission, they cannot talk to their friends about their fears. Taking the medicines may be a guarded affair at home not witnessed by outsiders. These are not children who have sleepovers or go away with friends. These children are not often far away from their caregivers, and their caregivers worry about them constantly.

That is what makes Camp Hope, and other specialized camps like it, so significant in the lives of seriously ill children. Marc Cohen, who was sporting an Australian bush hat and beard dyed lime green on the first day of camp (it was pink the next day), told me that the camp works so well for children because when the children realize that everyone there is in the same situation that they are, "the walls come down." The camp develops a feeling of family and community where, according to Marc, the children "don't have to hide." Or, as one teenage girl said, "We have our own world here."

For younger children who aren't consciously aware that they have a disease in common with the other children, the comfort of this world of their own is like that of any camp. For Deborah and her friends who live in the nondisclosed cabin, Camp Hope is just camp. When they arrive at their cabins—given names like Planet Venus and Wildwood—they find them decorated with balloons and colorful red, white, and blue streamers. Once settled in, they get to ride horses and go on a ropes course, they paddle canoes and play softball. Camp Hope fulfills the function that camp does for all children by offering them a place to be on their own with their friends and counselors.

Deborah's parents both hoped the camp experience would work classic camp magic for their daughter. "I don't know that we've ever looked at the camp as a camp for kids with medical issues," Dan said. "This is just summer camp for her. . . . We don't say, 'You're going to a special camp.' "

Jane's dream for her daughter was that camp "would teach her independence. That is so important for anybody growing up." She wanted Deborah to "see what she could do without us."

The older children at Camp Hope, of course, know exactly what they have in common with all the other children: their HIV-positive status. That makes this an important week of the year for them, the only place they can drop their guards and be honest about their struggles. I was invited to sit in on two volun-tary teen talks led by volunteer counselors, all of whom are HIV positive. The first one was held in the camp chapel in the late afternoon on Monday, the first full day of camp. The setup could not have been simpler: a circle of folding chairs, a cooler full of soft drinks, some bags of Goldfish crackers.

The volunteer session had a sobering title, "Stigma and Dis-closure." An engaging young health educator for a pharmaceuti-cal firm that manufactures some of the medicines responsible for saving these children's lives, started the discussion. "Let's go around," he said to the eight attractive young people, aged thir-teen to fifteen, who were sitting a bit uncomfortably in a circle. "Let's say our names, our favorite food, and what scares us most about being HIV positive." He, like many of the volunteer coun-selors at Camp Hope, is HIV positive himself, so he literally embodies the future—much as camp counselors do so at any camp—for these children: on medicine and health. Reminiscent of the personal stories that counselors typically share around opening night campfires to put campers at ease, his self-disclosure set the tone for the group.

The teenagers didn't hesitate. In spite of the fact that not all of them knew one another, they were very honest. One girl said, "I'm Jen, I love pizza and what scares me the most about having HIV is that I will pass away before they find a cure." Another girl said, "My name is Shannon, I like lasagna and I'm afraid that if I disclose my status to my friends they would shun me." Once a high standard of honesty is set in a teen group, everyone rises to meet it. But running a discussion group isn't ever easy because teens are extraordinarily self-conscious, there is always a bit of sexual tension between boys and girls (especially after the group leader had asked the group to review how the HIV virus is transmitted: blood, mother's milk, semen, which the boys called "skeet," and vaginal fluid), and teens always experience older people as being potentially clueless about their emotional lives.

We sat together for an hour, eight teenagers, three assistant counselors, and three adults. It was certainly the frankest discussion I have ever had with teens about the hard facts of their lives and the possibility of their own deaths. The leader talked with them about the nature of stigma and discussed frankly when disclosure is optional, and when disclosure is an absolute responsibility, as it is with sexual partners. The group then discussed the right time to tell a potential sexual partner and how to deal with the inevitable and sometimes repeated rejections from kids who do not want to risk kissing or hooking up with an HIV-positive teen.

Discussions about sexuality and dating are such common fare at most teen camps because that aspect of adolescent development dominates the conversations in their everyday lives at school and in their social circles at home. But questions and ideas they might be hesitant to share among familiar friends are less risky in the camp setting. Not so long ago, a conversation among healthy teens about HIV and AIDS had a distant can't-happen-to-me quality to it. As talk about HIV, AIDS, sexually transmitted diseases, pregnancy, and safe sex has become part of most school health education programs, the conversations have become more pragmatic. But for this group of infected teens there is no safe haven for conversation in everyday life, and here the conversation is not only pragmatic, it is remarkably and painfully personal.

Most of the younger boys held back, as did one of the oldest boys. It is hard for thirteen-year-old boys to talk in front of mature fifteen-year-old girls. One of the older boys stated somewhat angrily that he would never disclose his status to anyone; that absolutely no one could be trusted with that medical information, but here he was at Camp Hope, taking the risk that everyone was taking. An older girl told the group that she had disclosed her HIV status by speaking on a television show and giving some newspaper interviews; it was clear that the relief she got by speaking out was enormous. However, she still had friends and extended family out of her hometown to whom she had not disclosed her status and she remained fearful about their reactions.

What moved the discussion forward was the participation of three assistant counselors, ranging in age from seventeen to twenty-three, all of whom were disclosed to the world. One boy said that he had revealed his status to his entire high school. He had spoken at an assembly in which he educated them about the nature and transmission of HIV and AIDS.

Finally, Annette, a charismatic young woman from Florida and a first-time assistant counselor at the camp, talked about her own struggle to come to terms with her HIV status and how she had spent years in angry denial of her condition. Over time, however, she had accepted what could not be denied or changed, and eventually felt drawn to help younger children, and pursued the required training to be a camp counselor at Camp Hope. She had attended the camp once in her younger angry years and had left early, determined to distance herself from anything having to do with her illness, and quite certain she would never return. Now, she says, she's glad to be back as an assistant counselor.

"I see a little bit of me in all the girls," she says. "I have a girl with the spunky attitude, another who likes soccer."

Regardless of the nature of a child's medical issues, camps like Camp Hope work for teens at two levels: as a medical and educational experience, and as a simple camping experience. It gives them peers who face similar struggles, and the opportunity to be open about their medical and psychological struggles. That experience has an enormous impact on their medical care and their psychological lives. Ann Puga, MD, a pediatrician from the Children's Diagnostic and Treatment Center in Fort Lauderdale who was accompanying the thirty-one campers from Florida, has observed this effect on children both at camp and in her continued work with youth in the community.

"You can tell them that other kids have it, but when they see it they come home and say, 'I can't believe there are other kids like me.' They stay in touch; they have a system of social support." Dr. Puga encourages her pediatric HIV patients to come to the camp because she finds that in the fullness of the camp experience—not only the HIV support programs but the chance to tackle the more ordinary challenges of sleepaway camp—her patients come to believe they have a future. Certainly community-based programs offer invaluable help in providing the time, place, and counseling services to support teens. But for whatever reason, the camp experience is almost always transformative, she says. Children struggling with hopelessness, who feel that life with HIV is pointless and futile, typically return from summer camp with a new sense of possibility and purpose.

We might assume that the sickest children would be an exception, but Dr. Puga says that some of her sickest patients have valued the camp experience the most. In the early days of Camp Hope many more campers arrived with full-blown AIDS and were essentially dying. One girl who was very weak was determined to do the high-ropes course. It took her twenty minutes to do each element, Dr. Puga recalls: "You could feel every ounce of energy that it took her to do it." The girl talked about that memory with joy for the last year and a half of her life. Another one of Dr. Puga's patients, so sick that he was hospitalized indefinitely in the intensive care unit, talked only about getting out and getting back to camp. She remembers that at a certain point the boy realized that he was not going to get back to camp; he wasn't even getting out of the ICU. From his hospital bed he asked her for a favor: "Tell all the kids at camp that I'll be with them in spirit."

For the adults and medical personnel these most poignant stories make a compelling case for camps like Camp Hope, those designed to take on the special medical responsibilities and other accommodations needed to create a sleepaway camp for special-needs children. For the campers themselves, the experience is mostly and happily just about camp. At Camp Hope a group of campers volunteered to talk to me during their rest time after lunch. I asked them how camp had changed their lives. This is what my group of thirteen- to fifteen-year-old boys and girls said:

> When I left my dad's home, for a week I felt free. I'm away from his rules.

> You don't have your mom saying, "This is my daughter," so it makes you more confident and you have to introduce yourself.

> The rules here are really simple and they don't really contain you. It is easier for you to be yourself here.

> When you are in camp, you have something in common. You don't have to do stupid things that your friends are trying to do.

> Everybody here encourages us. They say, "Get up and dance with us."

> Camp can change everyone. When you come to camp you're open. You never get judged here. You get accepted, everything you do gets accepted.

Even if it is not Camp Hope, everyone needs a little paradise to go to.

Here, even the [HIV] "negative" counselors hug you.

With the exception of one camper's unusual remark, that, "even the 'negative' counselors hug you," what is extraordinary about these statements, of course, is that they are not so extraordinary. Camp Hope campers hit the same themes that teen campers everywhere talk about: They are on their own, away from their parents and they don't feel judged; they are making friends and feeling more confident.

When Kurt Podeszwa talks about the "universal camping experience" at Camp for All, he is certainly talking about archery, canoeing, and the ropes course, but he is also talking about a psychological experience for a child. He wants every camper to find out what she or he can do on her or his own. The camp is set up in a way that makes success possible for the widest variety of children.

"We don't want campers to think that we are going out of our way to make a special exception for them. People have asked me, 'How do you adapt that activity?' and I have to think about it because I don't think of adapting our activities for other people." Of course the camp does adapt activities, but what Kurt means is that the adaptations aren't made to eliminate the challenge, but to make an appropriate challenge accessible to every child. In that sense, every child gets a shot at normality.

At a practical level, making activities doable for every camper means that when Camp for All staff teach archery, they teach several different methods, including relying on dowels installed in a railing to brace the bow horizontally, so all the camper has to do is pull back the bowstring to release an arrow. For children who lack the trunk support to hold the bow up vertically, the horizontal method is key, but other campers try it, too, as an interesting variation on typical archery.

When Kurt got to Camp for All, he got rid of the mid ropes course that required a high adult-to-camper ratio up on the course and was not usable for all campers. With the help of a grant from the National Recreation Foundation, Camp for All has built a high-ropes course, with adaptations including a four-to-one pulley system so that children with spinal cord injuries can leave their wheelchairs and scale the heights. He told me he has climbed up an incline wall alongside a child with two amputated limbs.

At one weekend family camp the mother of a girl with mito-chondrial disease, a genetic disorder, was so anxious and over-protective that they couldn't let her daughter do anything athletic at all. The staff, unable to convince this mother to let her child try some things, made the decision to distract her, got permission from the father, and let the girl scale the climbing wall while they videotaped her accomplishment. Later that night they showed the parents a videotape of the girl's climb. The mother was astonished and she wept, seeing that in her efforts to protect her daughter, she had become overprotective of her. In the days that followed she loosened her hold and allowed the girl to try more things. Loosening the parental grip is, of course, the chal-lenge for every parent who sends a child to camp. It is just much more difficult for the parent of a special-needs child.

Once parents decide they can let their child go away, the next challenge is finding a camp that meets the child's needs. That arouses two impulses in all parents: to protect their child to the maximum extent or to put their child in a program that is as normal as possible. For parents of children with serious special needs or chronic illnesses the choice to send them to a program tailored to meet their needs is obvious. You have to send a child with a disability (Kurt Podeszwa prefers the term *differently* abled) to a camp where the staff is trained to make things work for kids with that particular disability. When Camp for All is hosting Camp Dermadillo, a camp for children with serious dermatological diseases, there are children who cannot tolerate any sunshine on their skin whatsoever, so they cannot be out during the day. All daytime activities are conducted indoors; some children need to be wrapped in sheets if they have to move from building to building. The only time they can do the high-ropes course is at night. Kurt Podeszwa had lights installed so that was possible. Not a lot of camps run their high-ropes course at night.

Perhaps your child has special needs or circumstances, but not so severe as those requiring the level of medical support and vigilance of a camp like Camp Hope. If you cannot go along to protect your special-needs child at a more conventional camp, you naturally wonder whether he is going to be able to handle the challenge. And if you pick the wrong setting for your child, you may worry: Will he be either underchallenged or overwhelmed and devastated by the experience? These are not theoretical questions for me. Every year when I consult at camps, counselors bring me a few cases of children who are struggling or seem mismatched for the camp, children who might have been better served in a special-needs camp than they are in a typical camp. Occasionally, I have to tell a camp counselor or director, "This isn't working." The child needs to go home because he or she requires a more specialized setting. That is rarely a surprise to the camp directors. They know, and they allow me to explain the reasons for my conclusion to the counselors who are working heroically to make the program work for a child who, for example, is on the autism spectrum and is overwhelmed by the pace and social demands of the camp. They don't want to feel they've given up or come up short on effort for any child, and they need to hear the truth: that the child's specialized needs are beyond anything they can satisfy.

It is possible for some children with special needs to have successful experiences at regular camps. The key is realistic expectations and honest communication between parents and the camp during the selection process. If both parties agree that the camp would be a good fit for the child, then all that may remain to be resolved is a parent's underlying concerns about the camp's preparedness should their child need special attention.

Fran Miller, a nurse in Lexington, Kentucky, wanted to send her son Andrew to the same camp that his two older brothers had attended: Camp Sea Gull, an oceanside camp on the North Carolina coast. Her oldest son, Ethan, had gone to the camp for a month when he was a seventh grader and never looked back. He loved it. Her middle son, Paul, had a mixed first season, but when he returned for a second summer, his first letter home summed up his experience: "I love camp."

Andrew watched his older brothers go to camp and began asking to go away when he was five, but he presented a different challenge. He suffered from a triple whammy of troubles: severe eczema, asthma, and dramatic allergies to foods and other irritants, including sheep's milk, walnuts, pine nuts, and coconuts, as well as shellfish and latex balloons. A cat licking his face could cause a localized allergic reaction. The severe eczema was a real trial day to day. Fran had spent much of Andrew's childhood bathing him, wrapping him in wet sheets, and applying ointments to keep his skin moist. Andrew had spent much of his childhood not sleeping at night, scratching his skin until he bled and developed infections.

For Fran and her physician husband, Jim, Andrew's medical issues were a constant source of concern. He had spent eight days in a hospital in Denver getting treatment for his eczema when he was five, and twice almost died from anaphylactic shock. The first time, when he was six, Fran was alone with him in an airport restaurant. He ate spaghetti with clams and a bit of

Romano cheese. He had a systemic—whole body—reaction and his breathing grew labored, so his mom called for help. When the EMTs arrived, Andrew was in very bad shape, needing more than just an EpiPen; they took one look at him and decided they couldn't treat him there. "Can we scoop and run him?" they asked. Though she rode to the hospital in the ambulance with him, it was Fran's first experience of having her son taken away from her for medical reasons.

Not surprisingly, the story of almost losing her six-year-old was still vivid for Fran when she told it to me twelve years later and, naturally, it haunted her when she considered sending him to camp. After all, they had had difficulty just hiring babysitters, since the long list of warnings and instructions intimidated them. Because Andrew's elementary school was only two miles from the house, Fran had been his mom-nurse on standby throughout his early childhood, ready to race to get him. Camp Sea Gull, however, was a thirteen-hour drive from home. How could she let him go to camp? She could not imagine him being able to go to camp without her. She hatched a plan to become a camp nurse and returned to get her recertification as a pediatric nurse. But the problem was that she was aware that at some point she was going to have to change the way she dealt with Andrew's medical difficulties. "I was exhausted from trying to keep his skin whole," she told me. "It is a very solo journey. There is a lot of grief."

The first summer that Andrew, age ten, tried camp, Fran and her husband loaded him, his brothers, and all their gear into a car and headed for the coast of North Carolina. She had signed Andrew up for a five-day starter session for first-time campers. His brothers were going to the one-month session that followed immediately afterward. They dropped Andrew off at camp, got back into the car, and drove a few miles down the coast where they stayed in a hotel. Fran made a good-faith effort to enjoy herself even as, internally, she waited for the emergency phone call from camp that never came.

Andrew was fine. If he was anxious about managing himself at five-day camp, he didn't let his mother know. It was only later when she saw his essay from fourth grade—the teacher assigned the topic "something that has scared you"—that she had insight into what he had been feeling. This is what Andrew wrote:

> I remember when it was my time to go to a spend the night camp. I was really scared because I thought that I would have an allergic reaction while I was there. I have had many allergic reactions before, but this would be different because I would not have my parents with me. One day I was on the decks I almost got stung by a jellyfish, so I became really scared again. I thought, what are my solutions? They were: don't eat anything I don't recognize and don't touch things I don't normally touch. In the end everything turned out just fine and I didn't have a reaction. **The End**

That first year at Camp Sea Gull, Andrew made friends with all the nurses and got them to bend the rules for him. He wangled a couple of nights in the air-conditioned infirmary. Though he made it through his five-day stay, when he asked to return for a longer stay, his earlier success wasn't quite enough to reassure Fran. After all, she had been staying just down the road. Though he wanted to go back, she could not yet wrap her mind around a month of camp for Andrew. Her husband advised her to talk with a camp nurse for reassurance; after all, the camp of seven hundred children had an infirmary of forty beds, and air conditioning!

Then Fran had a chance conversation with the mother of a diabetic boy who had gone off to camp with a brochure prepared by his mother—and had survived. The idea that Fran could write up all she knew about Andrew's illness and turn it over to the camp personnel was somewhat reassuring, but still not enough to give her the courage she needed. She knew that she had to see things in a different way. She had to give herself permission to share his care with others, to *not* be Andrew's one-and-only-around-the-clock nurse and protector.

Finally, she consulted a psychotherapist and told him of her thoughts about applying for a job as the camp nurse. He told her flatly, "He's going to camp and you are not."

She realized that she had to change her thinking from *if* to *when*. Andrew was going to have a crisis without her at some point in his childhood. It was just a matter of when, so she asked herself: *He will have anaphylaxis. What are you going to do?* In this light, the brochure idea became the answer to the question. She set about writing down everything she knew about Andrew's medical issues to create a two-color, five-by-seven-inch brochure entitled, "Andrew's Session Camp Plan." It included nine phone and pager numbers for his mom, dad, aunt and uncle, pediatrician, and the family's health insurance. It also offered easy-to-understand explanations of his severe eczema, asthma, and food allergies and a guide that a counselor could use to differentiate a local allergic reaction from full anaphylaxis. She offered specific coaching tips, suggesting, for instance, that counselors focus on his breathing and ask him, "Does your chest feel like it does when you are having asthma?" and check his thighs, normally clear of eczema, for hives. She encouraged them to listen to Andrew, who had quite a bit of experience evaluating the severity of his own exposure and allergic reactions.

When they dropped him off for his one-month stay, Fran gave the brochure to the camp director, the chef, the counselors, and the nurses. Andrew never had an anaphylactic crisis. Two months after his second summer at camp, when he was eleven, his parents went to Europe for their wedding anniversary, leaving him at home for the week with a babysitter, a registered nurse the family knew and trusted. That option had been available in years past, but it was Andrew's successful experience at camp and his mother's successful experience of letting go that made it, finally, an option they all felt comfortable with.

Throughout his high school years, Andrew has become more independent and better able to manage his medical issues. As a tenth grader, he went on a trip to London. The first photograph on his cell phone was of a hospital down the street from the hotel where he stayed. He showed it to his mother when he returned. What was the message? Without talking to Andrew, I imagine that it was a photo for both their benefit that proclaimed, *I'm okay, Mom. I can find a hospital anywhere. You don't need to worry about me.*

Fran now makes herself available to other families in Kentucky who are sending children with severe food allergies off to a new school or a camp. She reassures nervous parents, explaining the psychological challenges of sending a child with medical needs away from home; she helps them write camp plans for their child. When it goes well, and almost all of the time it does, a child returns home more confident, more grown-up.

Deborah's father described precisely that change in his daughter when she returned from her first summer at Camp Hope. "I had the feeling when she came back that she wasn't Daddy's little girl anymore," Dan said. "She used to always hold my hand, but it wasn't such a big deal for her anymore. She came back a little more . . . independent."

That away-from-home experience is so important for children that we should go to great lengths to make it possible for even very sick children to experience the independent feelings and confidence that come with it. A central tenet of camping is challenge by choice, but if you are sitting in a wheelchair, you cannot choose to go up on a high-ropes course unless someone has made it possible. Kurt Podeszwa goes to great lengths to make that possible.

Finally, as with any parent's willingness to let go, when the parents of very sick kids let them go to camp, they are giving them hope for their own futures in a very concrete way. To a child—any child—the message is clear. *If my mom and dad are always glued to my side, I can never grow up like other children,* the child thinks. *But if they let me go off to camp, I can grow up to be something.*

six

OMG, I LOVE YOU!

THE FOUR WOMEN—Johanna, Kelly, Amanda, and Cortney—arrived for dinner in their green Camp Downer sweatshirts. "See?" they said, pointing to the logos, and then they laughed, only the first of many laughs they shared that night as they described the history of the collective friendship that had started many years earlier. I had asked—actually, challenged—them to come for a meal and explain to me why camp friendships can develop into such powerful, lifelong bonds. Time and time again, former campers have told me that their camp friendships are closer than other ties in their lives. These declarations are always backed up by the camp name, as if that provides a sufficient explanation. "Chimney Corner friends are the best friends," they proclaim, or, "Songa friends are the best friends." I have appreciated the intensity of these sentiments—camp folks are passionate people—but I wanted to know *why*. What is it about camp that fosters friendships that become so meaningful and lasting for so many? I needed a way to get inside a camp friendship.

Johanna Liskowsky-Doak opened the door for me. We were working together at a weekend family camp when I told her I was writing a book about sleepaway experiences. She instantly and enthusiastically declared: "My Camp Downer friends are my closest friends."

I jumped at the chance to interview her about her friendships and she said yes, but about ninety minutes into our interview, when she was discussing some late-adolescent risky behaviors that she and her buddies had engaged in, she stopped suddenly.

"I can't talk to you anymore," she said.

"Why not?" I asked.

"My friends have to be here if I am going to talk about these things."

Okay, I said, did she think her friends would be willing to do a group interview?

"Yes," she replied, "but you might have to get us a little drunk."

And that's how I came to be hosting a dinner for four beautiful thirty-four-year-old women, all married mothers, all hardworking professionals, and all incredibly funny.

Our conversation had been under way for only five or ten minutes when the four women sitting in my family room insisted that they had to bring the missing member, their friend Emily, into our discussions via cell phone from Alaska. The group painted a portrait of her with quick verbal brushstrokes, revealing their deep respect for her.

"She's a certifiable badass," Kelly said.

"She did everything bad way before us," Johanna chimed in. "She was telling me how she was making out with some guy in a field somewhere and I was, like, oh my God."

"She is the most proper badass you'll ever meet," Kelly reiterated.

I wondered who could command the respect of these four women who were pretty accomplished themselves. Cortney (yes, that's how her parents spelled it) is a lawyer, Johanna a science teacher, Amanda a paralegal, and Kelly a social worker. It turned out that the "badass" woman joining us from Alaska was a recently retired Air Force captain, an Iraq War veteran, one of the first women to attend Virginia Military Institute, the wife of an F-16 pilot, and the mother of two. The respect for her among her friends was total, and she returned their love through the phone, staying on the line for three and a half hours.

Toward the end of the evening I asked whether they loved one another better than anyone in the world other than their husbands, children, and parents. They all shouted, "Oh, yeah!" Amanda, feigning forgetfulness, asked, "I have a husband?" implying that being in the presence of these friends made her lose track of everyone else in her life. I asked them how a friendship that close got started. Which two of them became friends first? They couldn't remember.

"We always talk about that," Kelly said in a tone suggesting that as many times as they discussed it, they never came up with the definitive answer.

"We knew *of* each other," Amanda said, pointing to Johanna.

"What I remember is seeing you at school," Johanna recalled, but they were fuzzy about that since they hadn't attended the same school. They lived in the same school district in Franklin County, Vermont, and their parents knew one another, but they'd gone to different schools. And they didn't immediately become friends when Johanna came to Camp Downer at age seven.

"My first memory is with van Armen," Amanda concluded, using Emily's nickname.

Emily joined in the discussion from Alaska. "The first person I remember was Johanna," she reported. "She was seven. I couldn't talk to Amanda because Amanda was the director's daughter and a superstar. And then Kelly was in my cabin, and then Amanda saved my butt."

I had no way to know at that moment, but Emily had just skipped freely ahead in time, from the age of seven to the age of sixteen, to that crucial year when they were all counselors in training (CITs) and she hadn't gotten her application in on time, but Amanda, the director's daughter, made it possible for her to come anyway. Amanda volunteered to give up her bed in the CIT cabin in order to make room for Emily.

Cortney, pointing to Amanda, had her own memory of beginnings: "I met you because you and I wouldn't eat." She described the camp food as disgusting, and continued: "We weren't friends. We would only eat PB and J. We sat next to each other and whoever the counselor was, would tell us we had to eat. I think I met Kelly that same summer. What summer was that?" she asked, looking for help remembering their shared past.

Kelly shared her first memory of Cortney. "We were walking up the road and I noticed that Cortney had her period and I walked up and told her."

"It was so embarrassing," Cortney said. It was her first period and even though she had come prepared—her mother had packed the necessary supplies—she was too embarrassed to use them. "My mom had packed Maxi Pads, these *huge* things. How could I wear those when I was in my shorts?"

They had all heard The Talk at school only recently, she said. "It was around that time at school that we were taken into groups, the girls to talk about their periods and the boys about wet dreams, and then we came back together and kind of looked at each other."

Both Kelly and Cortney vividly remembered the episode of

the bloodstained shorts. They also remembered that after such an awkward beginning to their relationship they hadn't been able to talk for a while.

But the budding friendships had continued, and now, nearly twenty-five years later, the women were reconstructing their collective memory in a flurry of random details about girls, guys, cabins, and crushes.

I mentioned to them that with the conversation moving fluidly back and forth in time, from age seven to age thirteen and then to sixteen, and with all of the inside jokes, it was like listening to a private language.

"Oh, yes," Kelly agreed. "But there is a whole other level of private language, like 'middle stall.' You don't usually have relationships with anybody else where you can say one word and everyone knows what you mean." I did not follow up on the meaning of "middle stall," but it didn't matter; the stories got funnier and raunchier.

Suddenly, they were talking about the bachelorette trip and the legendary fart machine. As the members of the group had finished graduate school and approached their thirtieth birthdays, Cortney and Kelly were both engaged to be married. The group saw it as a turning point in their lives; soon they would all be starting families. It was time for a road trip, time to visit Emily and her family, who were stationed with the Air Force in Italy. Johanna and Kelly, who described themselves as being the followers in the group, surprised themselves by organizing the trip. As Johanna put it: "We're going to Italy, bitches! Let's buy tickets."

On the plane they drank, talked, and slept. It was a long flight and at one point they were startled awake by a flight attendant on the public address system asking if there was medical personnel on the plane. Johanna and Kelly grew wide-eyed with the same thought, *Oh shit! Where's Amanda?* Amanda had experienced numerous epileptic seizures in front of her friends (usually Johanna) as far back as camp days, and eventually she had undergone brain surgery to ameliorate it. All of the women had been keenly aware of her medical vulnerabilities. When they didn't find her in her assigned seat, they were panicked that she had walked down the aisle and had somehow become a medical emergency. They frantically searched the plane and found her in the back, stretched out sound asleep on some empty seats. They were incredibly relieved; they "laughed and laughed . . . It was the best."

When they arrived in Italy, the two bachelorettes were required by their friends to pass an initiation, the last imposed by the group. Kelly explained, "Cortney was getting married in August and I was going to get married the next summer so they organized this We're-going-to-totally-embarrass-you-in-front-of-the-country-of-Italy, and that included a fart machine. It's like a remote control device." The group required the bachelorettes to wear the tiny speaker of this machine on them in a bar as they were supposed to hit on men they didn't know. As Cortney and Kelly engaged men in conversation, Amanda, Johanna, and Emily stood some distance away and pushed the fart button at random moments, unsettling even the most ardent new admirers. By the end of this much-told story, my dinner companions were roaring with laughter.

It was difficult not to envy the profound safety and earthy intimacy of this tight group. When the Camp Downer Gang of Five party was over that night, the young woman who had been helping to serve the dinner and had overheard much of the conversation said to me, "I wish I had camp friends as close as that." But my original question remained. I wondered if I was just witnessing a great friendship among five women, another version of the Ya-Ya Sisterhood, or whether their deep and lasting bonds had been uniquely shaped by a mix of factors common to overnight camp.

Johanna made the case that the depth of their friendship was camp specific. She said she feels closer to these friends than the girls with whom she attended high school and college. Several of the women said the same thing; they decorated their college dorm rooms with photos of their camp friends and experienced classmates' efforts to befriend them almost as an intrusion into their sisterhood. "Our summers together on staff are when we became sisters," Johanna told me. Camp Downer, she continued, is "kind of like a cult" where, "the counselors love Camp Downer and the campers love the counselors and it is one good time. The counselors are goofy and playing pranks and singing songs and being totally ridiculous. All the ritual activities just really create a cultlike community."

There is also the freedom that comes with Camp Downer. "You get to be the person you want to be," Johanna explained. "You get to choose the activities." Even though Johanna's older sister, Emma, attended Camp Downer, the experience for Johanna was that she had no family influence or family protection at camp. She was on her own. She remembered thinking, *It is time for you to become independent and learn more about who you are as a person. . . . It could almost be like you sink or swim. . . . You have to be able to fend for yourself.*

The women confirmed this, telling me that what makes a camp friend different is that, "*you* get to choose and then you get to really focus on forming a relationship." A camp friend, apparently, occupies a different place in the psyche than a school friend because the teacher didn't seat you together, you aren't being graded, you aren't in assigned seats, and you don't see each other's parents at the end of the day. Your mothers are not arranging play dates or even conversing with each other; your dads aren't coaches together for the town soccer league. There is only you and your new camp friend and best of all, *your parents can't have an opinion about your new friend because they don't even know her!*

IT MIGHT HURT PARENTS to think of themselves as a barrier to their children's friendships, because most parents really want their children to have close bonds with peers, but of course parents can be an impediment. Because you are a parent, you can't hide your feelings from your children; when children look into your face, they know immediately what you think of their friends. So your daughter can tell if you are warming to her new friend, and she also senses immediately if you are not drawn to her, or if you have concluded that she is a bad influence. Because the mother-daughter bond is so powerful, once she knows how you feel, she has trouble sorting out her own feelings about her friend. In other words, she cannot make an autonomous judgment. At camp, children are free to feel whatever they want to feel about their friends. But it is only the first step on the way to a deeper relationship.

As I listened to the Camp Downer Gang of Five, a number of stages seemed to define the evolution of profoundly close camp friendships. Making an independent choice of a friend is the crucial first step. Having enough time to cultivate the friendship is next. Maintaining the bonds in the off-season deepens the commitment. Perhaps the most important factor is the shared love of camp, the process of creating fun skits and participating in rituals. For those campers who aspire to become counselors, the experience of working side by side as CITs, being evaluated and waiting nervously to be picked for leadership positions becomes a bond. Also, sharing the responsibility for children creates a bond like no other (just ask parents). Finally, the physical intimacy of living together and coming of age together creates lifelong memories.

Camps cannot be the only place that people form such close relationships. I asked Emily to compare her relationships with her military friends to her camp friends. She told me that her military bonds are "amazingly close" and that she is very grateful for them, but it was "these ladies," Amanda, Cortney, Kelly, and Johanna, whom she can "really trust, really rely on. It's hard to pinpoint why I have this bond with these girls but . . . it's just because we do, and that's the way it is and that's the way it works. I love them for who they are and they love me for who I am and it's just, it's like stronger than any bond that you could build in any career or any military."

Perhaps this chapter on friendship could stop there, with Emily's declaration, "that's the way it is," but as a psychologist, of course I needed more evidence. I was determined to get up to Vermont, to visit Camp Downer and see if I could witness the process of friendships growing in the moment between campers and campers, counselors and counselors.

Before we join Camp Downer in progress, a quick aside: Everyone associated with Camp Downer is keenly aware that the name comes across as an ironic joke, something like Camp Bummer. The reason for the name is simple. The camp is located in Charles Downer State Forest in Vermont. Mr. Downer was an early Vermont environmentalist who bequeathed eight hundred acres to the state of Vermont for educational purposes. A counselor told me that sometimes people who have heard her talk about her love for the camp say, "If you love it so much why don't you call it Camp Upper?"

One thing that makes Camp Downer so special to its alumni is that it is a bare-bones camp. "The cheapest camp in Vermont," one counselor boasted to me. The "least expensive camp" is how Amanda puts it, but even she admits that when she got married at camp (her father, Mitch, is the director and he officiated the marriage there), many of the wedding guests who had heard her rave about the place for years were put off by how simple, even shabby, it was. Camp Downer was built by the Civilian Conservation Corps during the Great Depression and it has one of the last, if not the last, CCC-constructed dining halls still standing in the United States. It isn't that the board of directors at Camp Downer hasn't thought about a new dining hall; they have just never had the money to build one. Or, more accurately, they put whatever surplus money they have into scholarships. Originally a 4-H camp, Downer was founded to serve the children of Vermont farm families, to get them away from the hard physical work of farming so they could swim and play. The director and the board continue to strive to keep the cost down; there is a constituency for its mission.

The camp has thrived since the recession of 2008. Children whose parents might have signed them up for fancier camps in better economic times, are grateful to be at Camp Downer. The two-week session fills up within five days of when the brochure is mailed out. The governor of Vermont sent his children to Downer, as did the ice cream gurus Ben and Jerry. I stood with Mitch in the gravel driveway that doubles as a dodgeball court during activities period. We gazed at the beautiful hillside and the big trees under which the campers gather for brief assemblies. The hillside is surrounded by the dining hall, the rec hall, the infirmary, a bathroom, and residential cabins. He told me that when the kids and the counselors leave and he is closing up the place in early fall, he often looks at the place with a gimlet eye and has to admit that it "isn't much." But kids don't fall in love with Downer for the amenities. As Johanna pointed out, they fall in love with one another.

When you watch children walk around camp, you see them walk in pairs and trios and quartets intensely focused on one another. Girls hold hands or link arms, boys sometimes race each other, sometimes they amble in slow motion. When they sit down for assemblies, they sit tightly together, sometimes hugging. I saw children take a friend's face in their hands and just stare into it: forehead to forehead, nose to nose. A counselor in training at Camp Downer told me, "When we're here, time doesn't exist." That free time allows friendships to blossom. Mitch, who combined a career as camp director with that of school counselor, theater director, and elementary school principal for thirty-six years, told me that he thinks children have more time to make friends in one week of Camp Downer than they do in an entire year of school. I challenged that claim; after all, the school year lasts for thirty weeks. He stood his ground and I was forced to do the math.

Let's posit that you have thirty-five minutes per day in school when a teacher isn't talking or you aren't working and you can just hang out with your friends. Multiply that times five days per week for thirty weeks a year and you get about eighty-eight hours of "friend time" in a school year. At a one-week camp, because you are living together 24/7 (and assuming that you sleep ten hours per night), potentially you have ninety-eight waking hours when you could be with your friend. In a two-week session you have 196 hours of friend time. And we shouldn't underestimate the power of sleeping next to your friend. The women told me that when Amanda offered to give Emily her bunk so that she could be a CIT even though her application was late, three of them ended up sharing two bunks for the summer. Children find that sleeping in the same cabin creates a powerful connection between them. Frank, a seven-year camper, happily described a two-week session at Camp Downer as a "two-week sleepover."

This comparison of the friend-time equation doesn't include the after school–socializing time factor, of course. But perhaps that only underscores Mitch's point. If at home, sleepovers, and nonschool socializing time together and away from parents nurture close friendships, then Frank's comment about camp as a two-week sleepover explains why camp friendships can grow so deep so quickly.

Frank was one of four sixteen-year-old CITs at Camp

Downer, two boys and two girls, whom I interviewed. My questions, of course, were about why they came to camp, and about their friendships. Betsy, like the original 4-H campers, said that the alternative to camp for her was harvesting hay on her family's land. She and the others were there in hopes of being chosen as counselors at the end of their CIT2 summer. Being a counselor, they told me, is the only way to get back to Camp Downer after you are sixteen and the thought of not being picked was close to unbearable. Larry, one of the four CITs, told me that the possibility of not returning reminded him of the pop song lyric: "I nearly cried to think of you without me." I could feel the tension and the intensity of their desire to be picked.

For the Gang of Five, the CIT2 summer was also the "golden session" and for them it all came down to Amanda's selfless act. Emily's application hadn't arrived on time. She was out of luck. Amanda gave up her bed so that Emily could come for the session and be in a position to apply to become a counselor and later a director. "If Amanda hadn't given up her bed," Emily said, "I would never have ended up being friends with them now." In the end they were all picked as counselors. Only when the selection process was over could they relax and metaphorically fall into one another's arms. Cortney dates the collective friendship as starting when they were counselors. "I don't think our friendship was solidified until we came on as staff."

It was fascinating to sit with the current CITs and look at them through the lens of memory supplied by the Gang of Five. Over the course of the summer of 2011 there had been three classes of counselors in training, composed of six sixteen-year-olds. They live in the cabins with the children and assist the counselors. Many of the younger children simply consider them staff. Out of a total of eighteen, however, only six of them would be picked. I could feel how close these four were, how proud they all were of just having taught children for the first time.

"You have to be selfless," Betsy proclaimed, "and it's not

hard." They all wanted to make the campers happy and prove themselves in the process. Susan, the second CIT girl, said that while she had had leadership programs at school, until she was put into a leadership position she had no idea. They were proud of being evaluated every day by the program directors. They were also clearly rooting for one another to be picked as counselors, but each one also wanted to be chosen. I asked them if their best friends were with them at camp. Susan said that her best friend was not, but many of her good friends were there, and with camp friends "there is no drama." Frank said that his best friends weren't there either, but that they had attended prior sessions (presumably as CITs). Perhaps he was hoping to be reunited with them next year as staff. Perhaps he would be on staff with the three CITs who were part of my interview. Nothing could really be settled until they knew which ones among them would be picked to continue into late adolescence and young adulthood at Camp Downer.

The future was in other people's hands, so they returned to discussing their love of camp. They described it as a place of peace, where you are secluded, where there are no electronics and no Facebook, but you always have company. Betsy liked that you don't have to do anything alone at Downer. The girls talked about how relaxing it was not to have to put on makeup or worry about the way you dress: "You can be a little smelly and a little frizzy."

The girls were pretty complimentary to the boys, saying that the "boys at home are such jerks in comparison." Betsy loved the fact that the boys at camp "sing along to slow songs." I asked if they used the word *love* to talk about one another. "That's not too strong," Frank said. "That's what we feel for each other." Larry said that the reason he comes to camp is for the people, but he had a hard time articulating it for me, saying he wished he could take me back in time, that it was "something you had to live." Susan declared charmingly, "It is so unexplainable I cannot explain it to you."

If sixteen-year-olds struggle to articulate their feelings for camp, women in their thirties do not. Cortney put it into words. Her father had died after her first summer at camp and she did not come back the following summer because her life was chaotic as a result. The following year she begged her mother to let her return, and rejoined the group of friends that began to consolidate and build toward the highlight of their staff years.

"You'd get to the camp road and you'd be driving down it and it was the feeling, Oh my God, it's the best part of my summer," Cortney said. "When you go to camp, it's always the same. You can count on that . . . it's a feeling of stability and absolute happiness."

Once Camp Downer picked these five women to be counselors, after years of knowing them and two years of explicit evaluations, the camp trusted them with the lives of children, *when they were only seventeen years old*. To me this is the most striking aspect of camp counseling. Late teens whose parents find it difficult to trust them ("Who's going to be at the party?" "Is there going to be drinking?" "Are the parents going to be in the house?") are hired by camps to serve as counselors and are trusted to an extraordinary degree. They take children canoeing, supervise them swimming, and take them up mountains and into caves. The leadership on a caving trip may be provided by a twenty-seven-year-old instructor with vast experience, but most of the work is done by eighteen- and nineteen-year-olds.

Unlike some other camps, Downer does not require campers to go away for a year when they are seventeen, inviting them back as staff only after they have turned eighteen. As a result, Camp Downer has a younger-than-average counseling staff, almost all homegrown. And they have to precociously make decisions that are typically made by older counselors. It means that seventeen-year-olds are doing the same work as twenty-two-year-olds. It also means that seventeen-year-olds are socializing with twenty-two-year-olds. This leads to powerful role modeling, extraordinary maturity, and some precocious growing-up experiences.

The maturity, of course, comes from taking care of children at all hours of the day and night. At Camp Downer there are children from poor families who arrive with their belongings in garbage bags. There are, of course, the usual number of bed wetters and homesick campers who cannot fall asleep, or who wake up their cabin counselors in the middle of the night, who have to be helped to change their beds, or who have to be comforted and consoled. Eighteen-year-olds have to deal with children who are afraid of swimming, fearful of heights, and terrified of spiders. They have to judge the seriousness of plaintive complaints that "I'm sick," when they are out on trips. They have to figure out how to handle tricky situations creatively.

"Remember, Emily, when the girls were fighting and we pretended to fight to distract them?" Amanda says. Cortney replies: "Remember when that girl vomited off the top bunk and I came to get you?" Then Kelly: "And that was part of being a Vermonter. Problem solving . . . it was intuition."

Most people, I imagine, think there is a steady supply of young women, experienced babysitters, who can do these things for children; typically, we do not picture young men doing this for boys. But at camp, teen boys look after little boys in this way, and teen girls care for little girls. They all have to clean up vomit, and they all have to be good at it. Camp directors live in fear that they have chosen the wrong people, and that their counselors might misjudge a situation. That is what keeps them up at night.

The other thing that keeps camp directors up at night is the extracurricular lives of their counselors. Pete Hare, the director of Camp Keewaydin on Lake Dunmore, where I have been the consultant for ten years, told me that much of his energy goes to "managing the libidinal lives of late adolescents and young adults." Nearly every summer at camp he has to fire a counselor or two for drinking, smoking weed, or crossing some other lines. If Pete doesn't have to fire someone, Ellen Flight, the director of Songadeewin, the girls' camp across the lake, has to. What is interesting to me is that the following summer, Pete hires back many of the people that he fired. They reapply and make the case to him that they have grown up and are more mature—and they almost always are.

The answers to the questions that I posed to the Gang of Five might give a camp director pause if he or she were an inexperienced camp director. But veteran directors understand that they are running a camp for two age levels of children, older and younger, and they have different rules for them because they are at different developmental periods in their lives. Part of the way the counselors show their maturity is by living double lives: taking super-responsible care of children when they are on duty, and pursuing their social and sexual interests when they are off duty, or, as it is called at Camp Downer: "off-off." On a weekend when there are no kids around, or when you get far away from camp with your buddies, things happen. As Amanda put it, "It is amazing what you can cram into twenty-four hours."

When I again asked the Gang of Five why they were such good friends—a question I asked fifteen different ways that evening—one of them told me: "We've all been naked in front of each other. . . . There is no other place in life that you are together that much so the level of familiarity is different than any other part of your life."

THIS DISCUSSION OF CASUAL NUDITY led to memories of "streaking," and who had been involved in these naked runs, which led to a conversation of "the summer of firsts" when they had all lost their virginity, and finally to a discussion of how many of them had, in fact, slept with a particular male counselor who shall remain nameless, or rather, who shall go under an alias. The conversation went more or less like this, accompanied by laughs and much good will.

"I think there is a very interesting sense of never feeling competitive with any of you."

"[That's because] we've all made out with the same guys."

"We all had sex with Robert."

"I never did!"

"That is bull!"

"Why would I lie to you? No, no, no, never. We just hooked up over time."

"I swear you told me you did."

"We both made out with Brian. I never made out with Don."

"I made out with Gary who is gay now."

"You came the morning after I had sex for the first time. . . ."

Amanda summed up the discussion: "BOYS DROOL, FRIENDS RULE."

WHEN I VISITED THE CAMP, I asked Mitch about his role in monitoring the activities of counselors in their "off-off" times. He explained that the counselors have a day and a half on weekends between sessions and a longer break at midsession, and that some stay at camp to be with one another, while others travel to one another's homes. During midseason, there is a tradition of counselors pooling their money and renting a condo over at Killington. Mitch told me, "I think they go there to pray." When I pushed for a bit more information about the five women I had interviewed, he reminded me that he was Amanda's father. "I think you know more than I do."

I promised the Gang of Five that I would never write anything to hurt Camp Downer. They wanted to be honest with me about the lives they led in their late teens, but they wanted to make sure that I wouldn't portray their camp as Liberty Hall. I hope I haven't because I do not believe it is so different from any other summer camp. When you put a group of seventeen- to twenty-five-year-olds together for a summer, things are going to happen: Some counselors are going to drink, some will drive too fast and get picked up by the police. Young people are going to fall in love, they will have sex (or at least some will), and they are going to take risks. That's what young adults do. Their hormones are running wild and their prefrontal lobes aren't yet completely developed. After describing some risky driving behaviors, Johanna said to me, "You wonder about it now and wonder why we thought it was a good idea." We've all been there. What makes a successful counselor is someone who can switch from responsible caretaking of children to more private late adolescent behaviors.

Most of the time, counselors succeed in doing so, but not always. Twelve-, thirteen-, and fourteen-year-old girls are intensely interested in the romantic lives of their counselors. They spend a lot of time talking about the imagined private lives of their counselors, or trying to interest them romantically. In a charming collection of essays about summer camps called *Sleepaway*, Mark Oppenheimer writes about his experiences at leftist Quaker camps that encouraged nudity, an idea which, as a modest eight-year-old boy who played Little League baseball, he found appalling. Nevertheless, one night he and three friends were aware that there was some kind of counselor get-together. They waited until the rest of the kids in his cabin had fallen asleep, then they followed the sounds of "twang and laughter" floating through the woods. Soon they came across articles of clothing, halter tops, and clogs littering the ground, and within moments were witness to the sight of his counselors, activity directors, chefs, and lifeguards dancing in their birthday suits. "As young as we were," he wrote, "we knew that this was a momentous moment, to be savored . . . a hundred nude, square-dancing Quakers." This kind of story, however, is not the one that directors want their eight-year-olds to be telling their parents when they get home from camp.

I share these details about campers' and counselors' adventures and responsibilities not to idealize camp adventures or relationships, or to suggest that a lifelong friendship is the only desirable outcome, but to show how this particular context for friendship serves a child's developmental needs from early ages through adolescence.

When you come to the end of your childhood, when you start to think of yourself as an independent actor, you need someone with whom to share that experience. That's why a friend is so essential in middle school; only your friend understands who you truly are. Your mom and dad don't really get the new you, they still treat you like a baby, they don't understand how really cool and responsible you are. When you enter puberty, you can see that your relationship with your family is going to change, and change radically. You need a friend with whom you can share notes about your bodies, your sexuality, and your future. Your mom might think that your crush on a rock star is stupid. Your friend understands; she is in love with a different rock star. Your dad thinks you dress like a tramp, and is upset, but your friend thinks you look great. Most especially, you need a friend as a whetstone against which (or whom) you can constantly sharpen your new self.

Erik Erikson, the renowned developmental psychologist and psychoanalyst, said that all conversation in adolescence is about identity. Friends need to talk about *Who I am and who you are and how we are really different from what our parents can see.* That's why friendship becomes so intense in adolescence. And then, finally, you may need a friend to engage in some high-risk behaviors with you and remain the lifelong witness to your courage and independence. That is what we can see so clearly in the Camp Downer Gang of Five and other camp-based friendships.

I TOURED THE GROUNDS of Camp Downer with Jamie Thabault, a recent graduate from Wesleyan University who had come back after an absence of a couple of years to take the position of assistant program director, a job that some members of the gang had also held in the past. As someone who had competed in soccer, ice hockey, and field hockey at a high level, both in high school and college, Jamie had an interesting perspective.

"Sports camps are fun," she told me, "but not as much fun" as camp. Despite the fact that she was a varsity player at Wesleyan, she always chose to return to Camp Downer even though it caused her to miss the University of Vermont field hockey camp. "The best days of my life," she avowed, were, "the day I got the letter saying I would be a staff aide, when Mitch called me to say that I had a counselor job, and the day we won the state tournament."

The rank order of her top three achievements provided yet another testament to the kind of psychological hold that any such camp has over its community, what Johanna had originally described as "cultlike." The activities we observed—canoeing, volleyball, swimming lessons, dance, and arts and crafts—were all standard camp fare. The Trash Can Band, kids making music using garbage can tops, buckets, and other found items, was unusual and clearly fun. It stood in stark contrast to a very wealthy camp I had visited the previous week that was able to stage a concert with thirty different electrified bands. One staff aide, who had herself attended one of the more expensive camps in New England before coming to Downer told me that there are camps with better facilities than Downer, but no place with more love.

I had planned my trip to Downer for a Thursday so I could be present for the final campfire of a one-week session. That afternoon, Meg, a first-year counselor, told me that she was going to be "bawling her eyes out tonight." "Why?" I asked. "You can be yourself at camp," she told me. "And you can make such genuine friendships." She was grieving the departure of campers. The pathway down to the campfire site is known as The Trail of Tears.

For years, Camp Downer, like many camps around the United States, had Native American themes. The children were split into tribes that had names like "Iroquois" and "Sioux." Mitch had starred in the campfire play as an Indian chief for twenty-five years. In 2002, the national office of 4-H asked all of their camps to remove the Native American symbolism from camp life. The tribal names disappeared and were replaced by animal clans: the bear clan, the owl clan, the catamount clan, et cetera, all animals native to Vermont. Mitch rewrote the script for the campfire, basing it on the worship of Nature, with counselors playing characters representing earth, water, and wind. The role of fire is, of course, played by fire itself.

WE WALKED DOWN to the pond before the campers and took our place on the plain wood bench that formed a big enough circle to accommodate 160 children and 40 adults with front-row seats. In the middle was the fire pit, filled with a conical tower of long pine boards with the bark still on. Peeking through the logs, one could see kindling and tinder. Four women characters were roaming the circle: one in a green-and-brown dress (the earth, naturally), one in blue (water), another in a tattered gray (the wind), and a fourth woman dressed as a farm wife in overalls and a checkered shirt. The children filed into the circle in a single line, focused and serious. Once everyone was in place, the woman in the overalls shouted, "Let there be fire!" and instantly flames shot up from inside the cones of pine boards. The woman next to me leaned over and answered the question I was about to ask—How'd they do that? "That's a secret," she said.

We were taught to say "Aw-Wa-Ni-U," and move our arms in a prescribed motion at any moment of transition in the ceremony. Although the language of origin was unclear, the context suggested it might be Native American. We learned that it means, "All Good Things Through Nature." Then the counselors played Deer-Stop, a silent, blindfolded variation on hide-and-seek; then they invited other campers out to make six pairs for leg wrestling. The girls beat the boys and two girls ended up leg wrestling for the championship. When there was a clear winner we all intoned "Aw-Wa-Ni-U." It was more comforting for the loser than, "Yeah!" or "Hoorah!"

A young man with a bandana walked into the circle and began a skit featuring a clueless farm mother (the counselor in the overalls and checkered shirt) and her wayward, disrespectful son. He had been away for three years and because his mother didn't use Facebook or email, she hadn't heard from him. She was reproachful. Somewhat pathetically, she had kept asking the mailman whether she had a letter. The answer was always no. The boy asked about his childhood pet cow, Bessie. The mother tried to avoid the question, but the truth came out. She had sent Bessie to Sharon Beef, the slaughterhouse in Sharon, Vermont, right down the road from the camp, and she had been turned into hamburgers. The son was outraged, "My only childhood friend!" The counselor's improvisation managed to work in references both to mistakenly drinking pee and eating deer poop—surefire winners with young children—and this slow-moving skit commanded the attention of every camper in the circle. Why? Because it spoke directly to the issue that every camper faced the next day: changes in his or her relationship with parents as a result of being away at camp. In case we missed the point, we were all invited to join in singing Cat Stevens's youthful anthem, "Father and Son," with the father pleading for his son to take his advice and stay, and the son answering: "I know that I have to go away / I know I have to go."

At the end of the campfire, we all took one another's hands and sang "Rowan's Song," a homegrown tribute to summer, community, and the present moment.

> So take my hand like this, palm to palm
> Tell me that this is where I belong. . . .
> Sometimes I wish that everything else would fade away
> And I could live my life like it was summer every day.

Then, in the dark, the counselors distributed small candles and we all watched as two counselors paddled toward us with a lighted torch. The torch was brought on to shore and the candles of honored campers were lit from its flame; they then distributed the light from hand to hand and, just in case you weren't feeling tearful, we sang the Downer Camp song.

> Please remember me
> In the depths of winter, singing
> Please don't go away
> Why can't we stay?

The five women I interviewed for this chapter, my Gang of Five, had sung this song as little girls and as young women. They had held one another's hands and cried together. As they grew older, as counselors, they held the hands of small children who had cried when they left their parents but who, by the end of a week or two at camp, were now crying because they had to leave their friends from camp.

Returning to the dinner scene that opened this chapter, toward the end of our (four-hour!) repast, Johanna went to her car and brought back the predictions that they had all made for each other fifteen years ago, when they were nineteen—before graduate school, before husbands, before children. They had predicted the order in which they would get married, who would be first to have children, who would still be smoking (nobody, and they were right!). They had speculated randomly about the kind of bodies their future husbands would have and where they would live. They were right about Emily getting married first. She had always done everything first. They were more or less wrong about a lot of other stuff.

The one thing they never doubted was that their friendships would last. When Johanna sent them all copies of the predictions she wrote, "OMG, I love you!" on the bottom of the sheet. Emily, the "badass," the graduate of VMI and the Air Force captain, said, "That's one of my all-time favorites. . . . I think I like it because I saw it written on everything I sent to you, it's always, 'OMG, I love you!'"

Seven

PASSAGES

At age eighteen, some months after completing a forty-nine-day, six-hundred-mile canoe trip to Hudson Bay in northern Canada, Keith attempted to articulate his feelings about the experience. "Nowhere else can you experience such a clean satisfaction," he insisted, "and I'll miss it, and I'll crave for it." He believes that it made him, "better, stronger, smarter, more . . . you know, morally secure, more religious, more emotional." That was quite a list, but I was not surprised to hear it.

In August 2010, I interviewed two groups of campers, twelve boys (Section A, of which Keith was a member) and twelve girls (Section 1), within hours of their return to camp from their respective Hudson Bay trips. Before sitting down on the ground with them to talk, I watched them paddle in to Camp Keewaydin on Lake Temagami, a beautiful lake three hundred miles north of Toronto. Their strong arms and bodies were clothed in worn flannel shirts and torn blue jeans; their canoes were full of the moose racks and caribou antlers they had purchased from members of the Cree First Nation. They had paddled a long way; they had been cold and hungry, exhausted and bored; they had seen wolves, eagles, and moose, Beluga whales and polar bears; they had suffered and they had returned. We cheered as they lifted their canoes onto land.

I have almost never seen adolescents as happy, as confident, or as emotionally open as the members of these two groups. They were completely in love with one another, hugging and laughing, and they were totally satisfied with all that they had accomplished. Any parent would have been proud to be the mom or dad of one of those young adventurers, and, indeed, most of the arriving canoe trippers had a smiling parent on the dock waiting to greet them. However, I noticed that many of the parents were somewhat tentative and respectful in the way they approached their youngsters. It was as if they did not quite recognize their children, or know what role they were now supposed to play. One father said to his son, "I don't know how to describe it, but you look like a different person." In June they had sent boys and girls away for their final year of camp, and in late August they were embracing young men and women who had realized their dream.

Not every camper is going to complete a trip like a Section 1 or Section A canoe trip. Very few people in the world ever complete a trip like that. I have included it in this book because it is a particularly compelling example of a rite of passage provided by a camp. Every teen who chooses to leave home, whether it is to go to camp or a semester abroad, or just to do a road trip with a friend at the age of nineteen, has a dream of what will happen and how he or she will grow from it. Kids may not always share that dream with their parent, but it is there. When they are young, that is, ages eight to twelve, campers dream of having fun, making new friends, and winning the respect of their counselors. When they are a bit older, ages thirteen to fifteen, they are looking to develop some skills in a setting where they can assert their independence. But if they continue to return to camp at sixteen, seventeen, or eighteen, they are mainly looking for one thing: a path to adulthood and some companions on that journey.

The goal of childhood is to grow up. Children always want to be bigger and more competent; they say so repeatedly throughout childhood, asking to stay up later or be trusted to do this or that grown-up thing. However, becoming a mature person is not easy; it involves sacrifice and the loss of the protections of childhood. Children want the respect of adults—and deserve the respect of adults—for giving up privileges of early childhood. You see that in thirteen-year-olds who are independent and strong one minute, and whiney and sitting in your lap the next minute.

By late adolescence, however, almost all adolescents want full independence from adults and yearn to do something *big* on their own. (If you doubt it, try recalling your teenage daydreams.) They want to have an adventure, to find their own Golden Fleece, to slay the Minotaur, something that involves some risk, perhaps danger. Then they want to return home to receive the recognition for their conquests and their new maturity. One of the greatest failings of our society is that we do not have a ceremony to mark the passage from childhood to adulthood. Traditional societies have rituals in which a cohort of late adolescents are taken away from their village, where they symbolically—or literally—shed their childhood clothing, are covered with ashes or paint, then are challenged to complete difficult tasks. After they have completed the tasks, they return to the community where they are celebrated as adults. In American society, we do not have a powerful ritual for this transition. The ceremonies we do have are anemic: high school graduation, the departure for college, college graduation. I have known many young people for whom school was a demoralizing ideal that did not bring them anywhere close to a sense of accomplishment. Short of the military, we have virtually no shared cultural milestones where adolescents can find a real test of adulthood. For the young people who go to canoe camps, the Bay Trip is that rite of passage.

JUDGING FROM HIS FIRST SUMMER, Keith was not a boy looking for a heroic quest. As he tells it, at fourteen he was a portly child, not "'fat' fat," but heavy and nonathletic. He hadn't asked to go to camp, but other kids his age were heading off in the summer and he did not see a ready alternative. A friend of his mother's urged them to look at the camp video for a canoeing camp in Ontario. His parents had no particular investment in canoeing. Neither of them had gone to such a camp. Keith agreed to go in the spirit of curiosity, once his parents assured him that they would take him home at midseason if he hated it. And hate it he did. Keith must have used the word fifteen times in our conversation, describing his first year at camp.

He still remembers it vividly. He sensed that his counselor had his number and that made him uncomfortable. He was not terrible at canoeing, but he really didn't like it and he had no desire to get good at it. He went on a five-day trip ("hated it") and a ten-day trip ("hated that"). He could barely wait for midseason and his parents' arrival. He had a frown on his face from the moment he saw them. Finally he confronted them: "Okay, I hate it. I want to go home." His mom and dad must have anticipated his request, because they were united in their response. They told him, "Keith, you have to stay. You have to. You have to stick it out." He protested and reminded them of their deal. They pointed out to him that he had already lost a lot of weight in the first fifteen days and argued that even if he didn't enjoy it, he should think about it as a physical exercise sort of experience. Canoe camp as fat camp. How humiliating.

Keith was convinced that it was the worst decision his parents had ever made about him, and he was furious. In retrospect he now believes that it was "the smartest parental decision they'd ever made." However, there was no way that he could see that immediately. He faced the second half of the summer with the attitude that all the camp people were stupid, and his parents were stupid, too.

"I hated everyone, I hated myself, and I hated being out there," he said. He played out his frustrations on everyone until one day something shifted inside him. He was sitting in the woods in the sunshine, listening to the birds singing, when he had a reflective moment, wondering what he actually hated about it all. In that moment, he realized that what he really disliked was (in his fourteen-year-old vocabulary) "like, I can't control, like, being out here or something like that."

Once he saw that the issue was control, he realized that he had worked hard all day and had been sweating, and he felt good. "I felt like . . . I felt whole and clean." He began to feel that this might be an "awesome" experience. At the final campfire of the season, when he heard the stories from the Section A trippers, he began to think that he might someday complete the Section A trip, from Northern Ontario (or Quebec, depending on the route, which changes from year to year) to Hudson Bay, arguably one of the most strenuous canoe trips in North America—the Holy Grail of Canadian canoeing—and perhaps the longest wilderness trip completed by seventeen-year-olds anywhere.

"I cried a bunch of times" that first summer, Keith said, and he "cried a bunch" the second summer and "cried a few times" the third summer, but he kept coming back with the goal of Section A in mind. He wondered aloud whether you had to be a sadist or a masochist to return to Camp Keewaydin year after year, and laughingly concluded that you had to be a masochist. Keith wasn't alone in his experience of hardship. It was fascinating to hear how many of the young men and women who went on to paddle the Section A trip to Hudson Bay had a tough first summer on Lake Temagami. Most of the Bay trippers I interviewed did not employ the words *whole and clean,* like Keith had.

"Dirty," "cold," "wet," and "hungry," were the descriptors most often used. All one boy remembered about his first year was sleeping in a wet sleeping bag after failing to put his tent up properly and experiencing a flood that soaked everything he owned. A girl recalled that on the first day canoeing she got a horrible sunburn, the worst she had ever had in her life. Many recalled putting on wet boots and socks every morning, day after day. Even Bruce Ingersoll, now the director of Keewaydin Temagami, had a tough first year as a camper there trying to negotiate tenting arrangements with kids who had been at the camp longer than he had. Another camper, Mac, on the eve of his departure for the Bay after four summers on Lake Temagami, captured the feelings of many when he said: "Actually, I hated it that first year. I wanted to go home. I hated paddling, I hated portaging."

In spite of the hardships they endured, something hooked these young men and women. In the interest of full disclosure, I must acknowledge that I had a personal reason for wanting to know why they were drawn back to Lake Temagami for a second summer. I was a camper there in 1961 when I was fourteen years old and I chose not to return after a pretty positive first year. I have some personal regrets about that decision; fifty years later I realize it was a once-in-a-lifetime opportunity and I passed it up, despite my love for the outdoors. However, my curiosity isn't just about the rigors of Camp Keewaydin or, for that matter, about Camp Wabun or Camp Northwaters, the other two camps on Lake Temagami that offer a Hudson Bay trip to the oldest campers.

My curiosity is about why young people voluntarily choose to undertake such scary and grueling endurance trips, whether they involve hiking, canoeing, or kayaking, ocean sailing, horseback riding, or mountain climbing. Why do they give up the comforts of home, their cell phones and computers, the support of friends, closeness with parents, the possibilities of summer romance, sex, and fun times in order to experience what one camper described as "pain . . . and more pain"? Are they masochists, as Keith suggested? No, absolutely not. Like all adolescents, they seek the milestone adventure that will mark their passage to adulthood. What makes them different is the degree of adventure they need to satisfy that yearning.

The boys and girls—perhaps I should call them young men and women—who choose to paddle to Hudson Bay are looking for three things: first, they want to know they are capable of making a difference in the lives of others; second, they are seeking a passage to adulthood; and third, they want a wilderness challenge to last them a lifetime. After interviewing more than thirty people who made the trip to Hudson Bay, I believe that most of them find those three things, and many get an added bonus: They develop extraordinary psychological resilience. Later in this chapter, we will follow these young people on their journey to Hudson Bay, their passage to adulthood, but before we do, we need to take a short side trip into the psychological problems of contemporary youth, their feelings of uselessness and anxiety, and the role that the outdoors can play in offering them a passage to adulthood.

A wilderness endurance trip is one of the few places where a contemporary American adolescent can feel that he or she *really matters,* where she or he can really make a crucial difference to the lives and safety of others. In one sense, all children are aware that they are vitally important to their parents. Their moms and dads tell them that they love them and they couldn't live without them. Their parents do everything to protect their children's health and safety, thereby communicating to them how precious their lives are. Being cherished gives every child the message that he or she is loved, and that is wonderful, but there is a problem. A child's sense of worth may come from the actions and feelings of others, and not flow from much that he or she does. As a result, children experience a passive sense of being *valued* rather than being *valuable,* and that leaves them feeling incomplete. A high school senior once said to me, "My parents' love for me is kind of extreme. It makes me feel really guilty." Grateful children may face the problem of how to give back to their parents or, more generally, how to give back to society. Young people in modern suburbs who want to feel that they really make a difference have precious few opportunities to show that they can.

American children generally do not spend much time looking after younger siblings; they are rarely responsible for the life-and-death care of animals *(I forgot. Oh well, Mom will feed the dog).* They do not protect property or contribute to the wealth of the family. Well-behaved kids earn their parents' gratitude and studious children earn high grades, but every thoughtful child has to wonder whether his or her efforts really matter. Getting an A on a history paper does not change the world. Whether or not you do your homework does not affect anyone else. As a psychologist, I have served as therapist to many studious, hard-working teens who, deep down, felt pretty useless and often very anxious. Though I did not meet him until he was an adult, Matt Kolan was one of those high-performing, highly anxious adolescents.

You may recall from the Introduction that three young men in their early thirties managed to cajole me, against my better judgment, into jumping into Lake Champlain in late October. One of those three men was Matt Kolan, a lecturer in environmental science at the University of Vermont who also teaches an undergraduate course on rites of passage. Matt was the son of a high school guidance counselor. His dad had dreamed of being a doctor but was not, for financial reasons, able to go to college. Out of love, he subtly handed down his medical school dream to his son.

"By the time I was eight I could name all of the Ivy League schools in order of ranking," Matt says. "I grew up in a world that valued a certain type of learning and a certain type of success." He went on to be a gifted basketball player, valedictorian of his high school class, and a premed student in college. An academic superstar, he graduated early from William and Mary. Indeed, he did everything right academically until he failed to show up for the MCAT (Medical School Admissions Test) exam three times, a clear indication that he was deeply conflicted about being a doctor. One summer late in college he volunteered to work in a health clinic in Nicaragua. Seeing the poverty and poor health of the people threw him into despair.

"I couldn't see how my wildly privileged life was really going to impact the world," he says, and around that time he began to experience serious anxiety attacks and had to be hospitalized for a racing heart.

Late adolescence is never an easy time, and many young people go through periods of turmoil and uncertainty in their late teens and early twenties. This phenomenon used to be called an identity crisis. Whether you choose to see it as a transformational moment or a mental illness is a matter of perennial debate. What research tells us is that increasing numbers of college students in this country are reporting that they are depressed and anxious; more and more are on psychiatric medication; many are arriving from high school with existing psychiatric illnesses. Matt, the valedictorian and Golden Boy, was one of them. After his early graduation from college, he returned home, which was, he says, "exactly the wrong place." Sitting at home was not a cure for his anxiety disorder. He applied and was accepted for a job at an environmental education center in Delaware even though he was, by his own admission, "completely unqualified" and would not have known a bear track if it stared him in the face.

While he stayed on the job for only three months, it profoundly affected his life, because he met a "tribe" of people who were passionately connected to nature. The outdoors became part of his healing process. Looking back, he notes that as a result of doing simple things like jumping into waterfalls at night and catching frogs, he was suddenly living "elements of childhood experience that used to be true for 99 percent of humans." Such adventures "awakened in me the kind of vitality that comes with life spent outside," he says. Matt threw himself into the wilderness, hiking the Long Trail across Vermont on his own, carrying all of his own gear and food.

Matt applied for a graduate program as a field naturalist at the University of Vermont and soon morphed into an outdoor educator and eventually entered a doctoral program in environmental science. Even though he has been offered tenure track positions leading toward a professorship, he will not take them because he still wants to spend time outdoors training young men and guiding them toward adulthood. He believes that our boys are very much in need of a rite of passage to help them get to manhood. (I'll address the issue of a rite of passage for young women later in this chapter.) For him, there are four stages of life: the childhood into which you are born, youth, a rite of passage into adulthood, and finally a transition from adulthood to elder-hood. He has committed himself to seeing young men through that critical transition from the teen years to the adult years, which he sees not as one simple ceremony, but as a long process involving the death of childhood (for him it was realizing that he did not want to go to medical school and his subsequent anxiety attacks), a formidable challenge, and a passage to adulthood mentored by adults.

For him, the crucial dimension of that rite of passage is moving from the selfishness of adolescence to a stage of being of service to the wider world. I agree. I have many times employed the word *useless* to describe the feelings that many boys—especially angry boys—have about their experience of school, and their place in the world. Almost everyone I know who works with boy development, whether they serve inner-city youth at risk for joining street gangs or upper-middle-class boys facing endless years of graduate school, believes that boys yearn for some kind of clear ritual that takes them from the uselessness of late adolescence to the focus and mission of manhood.

Bret Stephenson, the author of *From Boys to Men,* writes that an endless, open-ended adolescence puts boys at risk, both because they are natural risk-takers, especially when they are in groups, and because they lack the mentors to help them harness their energy. In the United States we tend to rely on organized competitive sports to provide the mentors. Indeed, some boys find their mentors among their coaches and teachers, but too many boys do not find a role model there. It is too easy to go through a school day without really making personal contact with a teacher. Without guidance, they get stuck in a state of idleness, or in an oppositional and defiant behavior. Stephenson calls it "head-butting," and observes that

> Rites of passage and initiations were created not only to foster a healthy transition from boyhood to manhood, but also to put a limit on the time required for the whole process to unfold and to give it a definite end point. Promoting youth to adulthood quickly enabled our forebears to avoid years of head-butting with teens.

When Mark arrived at Camp Keewaydin on Lake Temagami at age twelve, he was quite ready to butt heads with almost anyone. He had already been a camper at two other traditional camps. He described himself as a basically unhappy boy, not because of his family but because he didn't have many friends at school. A restless person, never quite satisfied, he was always hungry, on a physiological and a psychological basis.

"I was this kind of, you know, obnoxious, fat, messy, lazy kid who started fights with everybody . . . started fights with the staff," he says.

Things did not go well. On his first trip he argued with his counselor while they were sitting on a rock by the lake. He shocked the twenty-year-old by pushing him off a rock into the water. The counselor was fully dressed in his only woolen clothes. He retaliated by tossing all of Mark's stuff into the water.

When Mark told me the story, I realized that seven years earlier, in my role as psychological consultant to the camp, the staff had presented his case to me. I cannot remember what I said to the counselors when they described this angry boy, but it was probably something along the lines of, "Don't worry. He probably won't come back for a second year." Consultants can be wrong. Mark returned, and when I interviewed him eight months after his Section A trip, his seventh year at Keewaydin, he explained that although by any definition he had a bad first summer, "there was something so kind of magical about it that I wanted to come back even though it was bad." I asked him why he used the phrase, "kind of magical." Like most canoe trippers, he fell in love with the structure and simplicity of the life and the equipment. He was also getting thinner and growing stronger, and he wasn't thinking about his next snack or what he was going to watch on television. He began to feel proud of his ability to "streamline."

> You know, so your sleeping bag goes in your roll and your rain jacket goes in your backpack and your cup clips on your

boat . . . right underneath the gunnel. So then you quickly un-
clip it, drink some water, and keep paddling really fast. . . . So I
really can't describe how happy that made me, you know, *to
slowly have faith in a system.*

Having faith in a system created by adults, especially flawed authority figures, is one of the great challenges of adolescence. By
the time girls and boys reach their teen years they are natural
critics. They are thoroughly acquainted with the system of
school and the system of home and are often quite cynical about
them. They often express independence by rejecting the guidance of adults. A witty person once described the job of a high
school teacher as that of a fireman employed to "put out fires
that are already out." I often remember that phrase when I get
up to speak in a school assembly and look into the sullen "show-
me" faces of tenth-graders. They are not much interested in the
wisdom of their elders. Many have learned to work the system
by doing just enough work to get by; they are grabbing what
they can, breaking the rules, binge drinking, taking drugs, or
engaging in promiscuous sexual behavior. A minority—we call
them dropouts—have simply given up on what adults in school
have to offer. Once kids are headed down the road of self-
destructive behavior, it can take a lot to get their attention.

WHAT MOST YOUNG PEOPLE have not seen is the wilderness,
and what they have not encountered are the real-life problems of
living out in the woods, on the sea, or in the desert. That's why
so many therapeutic boarding schools and programs like Eckerd
Youth Alternatives and Outward Bound provide outdoor experiences not only for paying customers looking for an outdoor
challenge but for adjudicated youth: angry, oppositional teens
who have completely lost faith in the system and gotten into
trouble with the law. Outdoor programs offer them a totally

new perspective on life. Mother Nature is impersonal, and the problems of sun, wind, rain, and cold are real. If you take a group of adjudicated youth—what used to be called juvenile delinquents—in canoes out into the Everglades for two weeks, as Outward Bound does, you don't have to provide them with rules and boundaries. The water, the poisonous snakes, and the alligators provide all the reality that any angry teen could want. Suddenly, they need to learn a system in order to stay alive, and they have to turn to their counselors in order to learn those skills.

That's what happens to all campers at Keewaydin or in any other program where you have to master skills in order to be safe. I remember vividly being a student at Hurricane Island Outward Bound School when I was eighteen. On the first day, we were told that the survival time in the cold Maine waters of Penobscot Bay was less than thirty minutes. A fact like that focuses your attention. You do everything in your power to stay out of that water, for example, rowing with all your might to keep the boat pointing into the wind so that it does not get hit broadside by the waves, take on water, and capsize. Naturally, the instructors require the students to participate in a morning swim in the ocean, which reminded us—it always knocked the breath out of me—exactly how cold the ocean was. While your own survival is crucial, you don't just learn skills to save your own skin. Often the techniques you learn mean you are literally supporting others.

One example is belaying, part of a system of climbing that all rock climbers on a cliff or campers on a high-ropes course must use to break a serious fall. Everyone who climbs must take a turn belaying another climber. It is one of the clearest, most vivid lessons a child can receive in helping other children, because as she is watching her fellow campers climb higher and higher on a climbing wall or ropes course, she is always thinking, *When I am up there, I hope the person who is belaying me is* really *paying attention,* and when it is her turn to belay someone else, she is keenly aware that she is the only person who can stop their fall and save their life. For most children, being responsible for someone else's life is a totally new experience.

WHEN YOU ARE CANOE TRIPPING, there is no single act as dramatic as belaying, but there are a lot of moments when you are essential to the well-being of another person and he or she is essential to you. While it is possible to paddle a canoe full of gear by yourself—fur trappers in the north woods did it 150 years ago—it is extremely difficult and requires great strength and skill, especially in a high wind. Most canoeing is done by two people paddling in rhythm, one in the bow and the other in the stern. When you have to cover six hundred miles in forty-nine days, you have to paddle all day almost every day, and there will be days when you paddle thirty miles. Sharing a canoe with someone else is an intimate connection. It is very easy to tell whether your partner and you are paddling at about the same level of effort and effectiveness. If your partner is not pulling his or her weight, it makes you angry, or it can make you feel like a leader. If he or she is stronger, a more skilled paddler than you, that can make you feel inadequate.

A member of the Camp Songadeewin 2010 bay trip for girls, Dora recalled that her first year at Songadeewin, she was in a canoe with a nine-year-old girl who really wanted to paddle but who almost immediately began crying and dropped her paddle into the water, "because she thought if she dropped her paddle then she wouldn't have to, like, paddle anymore." Luckily, there was a third girl in the canoe; Dora, who was older, was riding "mojo" in the middle, so she was able to take over for the nine-year-old, but then the girl had to sit there all day realizing that she was dead weight being carried by other girls. Canoeing gives you a choice. You can paddle, you can become discouraged and find a way to keep on going, or you can sit in the canoe feeling like a burden to others. (It is worth saying that your mother cannot save you at a moment like this. She cannot coax you, judge you, advocate for you, or say, "Take a break, honey, I'll paddle for you." She is literally a thousand miles away.)

The canoe is heavily loaded with all of your personal gear: tent, clothes, shoes, camera, and journal. If it tips over, there is a risk that everything will get wet, so you and your canoeing partner have to be careful as you approach the rocks. If you are in a high wind or a thunderstorm producing whitecaps, you struggle to keep it balanced; if you are in whitewater, you must both strain as hard as you can to keep the boat on course, away from the rocks, and if the boat hits a rock, you must bail out fully dressed into cold water before the rock punches a hole in the bottom of the wood-canvas canoe, crippling it.

The wood-canvas canoe is a remarkably trustworthy vessel, able to carry two paddlers and hundreds of pounds of equipment through smooth and rough waters. It glides beautifully, and unlike an aluminum or fiberglass canoe, it won't get blown around in a high wind on a lake. After you have paddled a wood-canvas canoe for a few days, you may never feel completely satisfied by another type of canoe. The price for that smooth ride and stability, however, is weight. A wood-canvas canoe weighs approximately 106 pounds at the beginning of a summer; after two months absorbing water, it can weigh over 120 pounds. When you go for an extended canoe trip, it is not always possible to get where you want using lakes and rivers, so there are times when you are going to have to carry the canoe, called portaging, for a hundred yards or for a couple of miles between bodies of water. The only efficient way to carry it is on your head and shoulders. Old-fashioned canoe tripping revolves around five pieces of equipment: the wood-canvas canoe, the paddle, the wannigan, the tumpline, and the ax. This equipment is so recognizable to devotees of canoeing that I once met a woman in Toronto who introduced herself as a "tumpline-and-wannigan person." Having wrestled with those duties myself some years earlier, I knew exactly what she meant.

The tumpline is a twenty-foot-long leather strap with a head-band in the middle developed by the First Nations people of Canada; originally made from moose hide, it is now made of cowhide. By tying and knotting the thinner ends around the thwarts of the boat you create a loop in the middle, so when you flip the canoe over your head onto the shoulders, you put the tumpline just above your forehead and it puts much of the weight of the canoe onto your head and neck so that the canoe isn't just sitting on your shoulders. (Women all over the Third World carry heavy bundles of wood on their backs using a head strap just like a tumpline.) It is usually the responsibility of the larger boy or girl, the "sternman," to carry the canoe. Mean-while, his or her partner, the bowman, has to wrap and knot the tumpline around the wannigan, a rectangular plywood box filled with dry food, canned goods, pots, and silverware, and hoist it onto his or her back. Both the canoe and the wannigan are heavy and awkward. It takes a lot of practice to flip a canoe up without hurting yourself or the canoe; it takes an equal amount of skill to swing a wannigan up on your back without rubbing off all the skin along your spine. The phrase "fucking wannigan" is often heard on a portage.

It takes at least several years of training to be able to paddle all day and to portage with relative ease. Discouraged first-year campers sometimes sit down in the middle of a trail, refusing to portage, refusing to carry their loads. That works about as well as the throwing your paddle into the water. When someone sits down on the trail, defiantly saying they won't carry their load, either the child's section mates have to add the additional weight to their loads, or everyone has to wait for the straggler at the end of the portage while being eaten alive by mosquitoes. If you are on a canoe trip and you want to make any progress as a group, everyone has to paddle and everyone has to portage. Brian Back, the historian of Keewaydin, writes, "Once the portaging has been mastered, though, love affairs can develop." The campers who go on the Hudson Bay trip need to practice because they are often carrying canoes and wannigans on trails that haven't been used in decades, or they are portaging where there are no trails at all and a path needs to be cleared. Everybody takes a turn with the ax and the task of trailblazing.

Carrying loads this heavy gives campers the chance to take care of one another in meaningful ways. If you are carrying a canoe and have bumped into a low-hanging tree branch (it is hard to see with a canoe covering your head), or if you are struggling with weight or balance, someone can step in front of you to relieve you temporarily by "tenting" the canoe, resting one end on the ground, and relieving you of its weight for several minutes. The gratitude you feel toward your section mate at that moment is enormous, and because you are looking directly into his or her face, having someone help you in that way feels intensely personal. With constant portaging, constant challenges arise, and there are never-ending opportunities to help one another by taking the weight off someone else's shoulders.

Not every camper who comes to Keewaydin is temperamentally ready to complete the longest trips. The woods, lakes, and mosquitoes of Ontario are not everyone's cup of tea. At the end of every summer, each camper must assess his or her commitment and make the decision to return (or not) the following year to tackle the next level (Outpost, Section B) leading to the Bay trip. Everyone has doubts; a few campers have to take time off from camp in order to really know whether this experience is vital to them.

Dora said that she had become addicted to canoe tripping and never doubted that she would do her Section 1 trip, but during her next-to-last summer there, she had a crisis of confidence. In the middle of a hard portage she started thinking about not coming back. *I love it,* she thought, *but I just don't know if my body can do it.*

Another camper, David, nicknamed "Bones," was five-feet-nine-inches tall and weighed ninety-five pounds when he first came to Lake Temagami. "I was as tall as my counselors," he said, "but half the weight." After two years, at sixteen, he took a summer off from camp. All of his neighborhood friends told him how much he had been missing by being away during the summers; they were starting to smoke pot and have sex. During his tenth-grade school year he threw a big party at his parents' house and a lot of things were stolen. He had already made the decision not to return to camp that year, but his parents told him that had he not done so, one of his punishments for the party would have been losing Keewaydin. He knocked around the house that summer, feeling lost and dreaming of being up on Lake Temagami, but the next summer he returned for his Section B trip, and then again for Section A.

After three to five summers of skill building and psychological preparation (not to mention the financial support of parents who pay high fees for this expensive undertaking), the young people who have made the commitment to go to the Bay, climb into their canoes and paddle away from the camps on Lake Temagami, heading for what they believe will be the adventure of a lifetime. Ben Brown, a member of the 2010 Section A, wrote optimistically (if somewhat understated) in his journal: "This summer promises to hold many good memories."

Because the actual distance from Temagami to Hudson Bay is well over a thousand miles, beyond the reach of any summer canoe trip, the first two days of the trip are spent in a van, driving to the end of a string of mining and logging roads in northern Canada. Once they put their boats into the water, the campers enter a vast wilderness. They will not see any signs of civilization for three weeks. They will have to be resupplied by a pontoon plane midway through their journey. The staff carry satellite phones in case of emergency; however, no rescue in the wilderness would be easy. Everyone is aware that on previous trips campers have sustained injuries and their mates have had to paddle for hours to get them help.

The destination for Section A in 2010 was Peawanuck, a small First Nations Cree community at the confluence of the Winisk and Shamattwa rivers, a few miles upriver from Hudson Bay. The village is close to Polar Bear Provincial Park. If they are lucky, the Section A boys and the Section 1 girls will get to see beluga whales and polar bears at the end of their trip. The Section A group launched their canoes into a river shrunken by abnormally high heat and a lack of rain. The tributary was shallow and their paddles hit the mud. Ben's early journal entries reflect his focus on the weather and his discouragement. His later entries reflect a preoccupation with food, respect for his section mates, thoughts about two different girls of interest, and some unmistakable philosophical growth.

DAY 2: Another day on the shit river.

DAY 4: Today was a long day of paddling through "the shit" or swampy little lakes and "rivers" with a foot of water.

DAY 7: We spent the better part of the entire day knee-deep in frigid water. The other time was spent portaging or battling the wind in some way or another. By the end of the day we had 15K of hard earned river behind us.

DAY 9: Gary, Mike and I tried our luck fishing in the rapids. We caught 15 brookies between the three of us, keeping nine for dinner. It was the highlight of the trip for me so far. These Brook trout are truly wild, with a distinct burnt orange streak running along their bellies, beautiful spotting and distinct white tipped fins on the mature fish. I was so excited . . . Tasty.

DAY 23: We had three portages over 1000 yards among others. Arielle carried the canoe and struggled, but I continue to admire his tenacity . . . Brandon asked me how I was doing today during lunch. To which I replied, "I'm not complaining just living." This is certainly the best way I have discovered to live life—continuing to find the enjoyment in everything I do.

DAY 33: Starting out this morning we stopped to listen to the howling of wolves . . . It was a scorcher as the intense northern sun shone down on us mercilessly . . . Caught a few fish today, just between rapids. I had my first shitty day, burning myself with sun. Slicing my finger and snuffing a rod. It's a wakeup call for me to get my act together, stay assertive, and enjoy my last eight days as a camper without stupid regrets.

DAY 38: So close to the bay! We woke up this morning and it was still dark. We passed 70K today. The morning was a long, strenuous paddle. My mind was spinning with thoughts about home. Then came food thoughts, which were quickly dashed after I started thinking about Allison *[thoughts about two girls redacted to protect Ben]* . . . This rant is but a portion of what seven hours in a boat will do to you. Not to be forgotten: Everett and Warren killed two geese and we put them in the jumbolia I [sic], a delicious Section A tradition continues.

Ben's journal reports that their five-day stay at the Cree community was, perhaps, the most meaningful time of their journey. While they waited for a once-a-week plane to pick them up, they played softball with the men of the village and bought moose and caribou racks to bring home. They got to know a Cree leader who shared stories of his childhood; he told them about shooting his first moose. Several of the Section A campers talked to me about this man, who eventually invited them to a sweat lodge ceremony, which was so powerful and so meaningful to them that they had decided as a group to keep it confidential. I have respected that in this chapter. They are entitled to their memories and the mystery of what they did when they were away.

IN KEEWAYDIN'S HISTORY, the Bay trip was originally celebrated as a feat of muscularity and manhood. It was also viewed through a competitive lens: *We're faster, we're tougher than anyone.* That's the way I remembered hearing about it when I was fourteen. It remains an unparalleled endurance test, to be sure, but since the canoe trips opened to girl campers in 1977, the shared experience of the extreme wilderness challenge has become a rite of passage for young women and men alike. The fact that young women now do the exact same trip—paddling routes as long as the boys do and carrying the same heavy canoes on three-mile portages—has produced a measure of humility in the young men. It also helps that the leaders of the three camps are modeling a different kind of masculinity: one that doesn't need to exclude women in order to find hard, challenging accomplishments a source of masculine pride. It was Bruce Ingersoll, the director of Keewaydin, who introduced me to the two other Temagami camps.

Camp Wabun was the first to start trips for young women. Dick Lewis, the longtime director, told me that a Wabun alum and the father of a daughter more or less forced him to do it in 1977. Dick says that in addition to this being the right decision because it finally provided girls with equal access to the wilderness challenge, their involvement was the best thing possible for countering the swaggering attitude of his boys. The fact that boys and girls paddle the same trips produces a deep mutual respect, and the girls' trips have "heightened and transformed us," he says, providing benefits for both.

The Bay trips appear to be equally satisfying to boys and girls, though the significance of the trip may touch on some different history for the two sexes. Dick notes that for the boys, the trip links them to all the men who have gone before them, from the trappers of one hundred years ago to those recent alums who the boys admired when they were eleven and twelve. Boys like to feel that they are mastering natural skills and joining a male wilderness tradition. Girls clearly revel in the mastery of natural skills as well, and may be inspired by strong outdoorswomen of the past, but just as likely they may feel they are breaking new ground for the girls who follow them.

At those final campfires, Dick says, boys tend to tell stories of risk taking and humorous stories of monumental screwups, while girls tell more poetic stories of personal discovery. At Northwaters, the most psychologically minded of the three Temagami camps, the trips are coed. In the tradition of Joseph Campbell, they are seen as mythic journeys of self-discovery, with this generation creating new traditions of shared passage.

What interested me when I interviewed the boys and girls from Keewaydin's Section A and Section 1 was that the girls said the trip had helped them think in new ways about their bodies. Instead of constantly worrying about beauty, they are concerned about strength and health. One of them pointed out that instead of using your body "to please other people," you valued it for its strength and what it could do for the group. A girl who had been date-raped in seventh grade found that the Bay trip helped to heal her; helped her reclaim her body for herself. Rites of passage for women have traditionally focused on biological or cultural markers: first menstruation, first intercourse, betrothal, marriage, pregnancy. For modern young women there seem to be three things that they need to develop a strong sense of self-worth and confidence as they move into adult life: 1. to take possession of their own bodies, celebrating their own strength and beauty; 2. to demonstrate to themselves that they can do anything men can do; and 3. to connect with other women by relying on one another and knowing that they are responsible for one another's lives. For the Keewaydin women there is also the possibility to connect with a tradition that has been available only to men for a long time.

Dora, whose father and sister were Keewaydin veterans, said that family tradition was important to her: "The way that my dad spoke about it, and the way that my sister spoke about it. Like it was never a question in my mind, you know? I was, like, I want to experience that. And my entire life, I had pretty much been told, 'That's when you will became a woman. That is when you will become an adult. Like that, if you can do that, you can do anything.'"

The young women flexed their arms to show me their muscles; as I looked with genuine admiration (okay, envy) at their biceps, one young woman quipped: "Sun's out, guns out." When I mentioned that they didn't seem to hug one another as much as girls at other camps did, they pointed out, "We smell pretty bad."

In the end, for both boys and girls on a challenging trip like that, everything boils down to character, the willingness to carry your load, take initiative, and help the other person.

Virtually everyone who paddles to Hudson Bay writes about it on their college application. No surprise. Dick Lewis believes that the one place in America where Wabun is best known is in college admissions offices around the country. On college essays, Bay trippers often describe what they learned about themselves on the worst, most grueling days of the trip. I have read quite a number of these essays and they always emphasize the closeness of the group, the physical challenge, accepting help, and being of help to others. A young woman named Tricia wrote:

> The daily labor and work pursued at this camp . . . has taught me more about myself and how to learn to find the good in others and [to] understand how respect is earned or granted. . . . I frequently find myself finishing a task like portaging, carrying equipment overland toward water, and meandering back along the trail to gather another load, even if it was not my personal responsibility.

Ben wrote:

> Together we were cold, together we were hungry and together we coped with adversity. There was nobody to do the work for us; day in and day out we worked constantly for the little things. A meal required someone to chop wood, another to split, and yet another to build a fire and cook. Nothing comes for free out in the woods. . . .

I have talked to college admissions officers about their reaction to these camp essays, and, frankly, they light up when they see them. When they hear about this kind of tenacity and ability to get along with other people, they know they are accepting a young adult who has some resilience, someone who isn't going to fall apart during freshman year. At a minimum, they know they are accepting a student who has the capacity to get him or herself out of bed in the morning and do some serious work. Campers on Lake Temagami believe that it is the essay about the Bay trip that will be most impressive to colleges; that is because it ranks highest in *their* camp mythology.

I learned that it isn't just the children who go to Keewaydin who write about their camp experience on their college application essays. Almost all seventeen- and eighteen-year-olds who have gone to the same camp for multiple summers write about some aspect of it, because it has been camp that has provided the setting, the challenges, the mentors, and the rituals to accompany their rite of passage. Camp may be only four weeks a summer, but it gives those teenagers a bright pathway to adulthood.

Cassie, at sixteen the youngest girl on the Section 1 trip that year, wrote to me to explain that, "The section is the only thing that matters . . . and camp itself is a ritual. I value it more than anything in this entire world. I wouldn't trade anything for my experiences." Another girl, Ilana, said, "Once it was over, I didn't remember the pain, I didn't remember being hungry, I didn't remember being bitten by bugs all the time. . . . What I remembered was, like, the sense of camaraderie that I had with my section mates and the amazing feat that I had just overcome, and that was just really awesome."

eight

"I WISH YOU LUCK
IN BEING YOURSELVES"

S HY, SHUTDOWN, WITHDRAWN, *apathetic, angry,* and *unmoti-vated.* Those were the adjectives that David McDonald used to describe himself as a fourteen-year-old. A challenge for anyone who attempted to motivate him, McDonald writes in retrospect, "I was a kid who was lousy at school and sports. Got picked on by local bullies and had a difficult relationship with my parents." It is hard to imagine that McDonald would have enjoyed many of the camps I have described in the preceding chapters of this book. I do not know how his parents managed to get him to Buck's Rock, the camp that he credits for changing his life, but he did go there for two summers and, "For the first time in my life I found something that I was actually pretty good at, glassblowing. It changed the way I felt about myself forever."

I took McDonald's words from a brief essay that he wrote in memory of Ernst Bulova, the founder of Buck's Rock. An Austrian educator with Montessori training, Bulova fled the Nazis in the thirties, founded a school in England, then moved to the United States in 1940. He looked at traditional American summer camps and was not impressed by their regimented programs. He was especially critical of their "Arts and Crafts" programs. He declared that they were "neither art nor craft." Some of his relatives sold him a parcel of land in New Milford, Connecticut, where he started a "work camp" that was designed along many of the principles of hands-on learning of Maria Montessori. Bulova's Buck's Rock Work Camp began to attract the children of left-wing New York parents. Like many progressive educators, Bulova recognized that, "Children like to learn, but they do not like to be taught."

That observation is true for all children, to a greater or lesser extent. Some children have a high tolerance for the tempo and reward systems of traditional schooling; others react against these structures with every cell in their bodies. There is no parent or teacher who has not had the experience of starting to teach a child who immediately appears weary, rolling his or her eyes with the unspoken cry, *No more, not again . . . I don't want to be taught something!* That is especially true of young people for whom traditional educational institutions do not work well, and there are lots of them: children with learning disabilities; intuitive, nonlinear thinkers; the dreamy and the imaginative; children who are not good at sports or do not care about who is wearing what; "geeks and freaks," or kids who don't fit in. Even if we do not always recognize who they are, *they* know who they are. Just as some children are psychologically allergic to school—everything about it is deeply uncomfortable and remains that way—large numbers of kids are positively allergic to traditional camps because they require everyone to do an activity with their cabin or to sing some inane lyrics with the community. Throughout this book I have praised camps for their community building; for that reason it seems essential to me to also write about a camp for people who don't like camp. Lee Kraft, a former camper, writes that when she is asked about Buck's Rock, she is hesitant to even use the word *camp*.

> I find it extremely difficult to describe the place where I truly found myself and had some of the best experiences of my life as "merely" a camp. A camp is a place where kids have swimming lessons. At night they sit around a campfire roasting marshmallows and singing songs . . . [H]ow could the word "camp" ever begin to scratch the surface of the shows, the people, the ideas and the life I discovered?

I am sympathetic to Lee's passionate defense of her noncamp, though the irony that a community exists to which many travel every summer to live in cabins, eat in a communal dining hall, sit outside in nature, make friends, tell stories, listen to each other sing, and watch one another's performances but declines to call itself a camp is not lost on me. As Shakespeare pointed out, "A rose by any other name would smell as sweet," but let's just think of this collection of brightly colored, funny-shaped buildings spread out on a hillside in Connecticut, all of them filled with young artists, as an Arts Colony for children. There are others. And Lee is right in one sense: They *are* different psychologically from the classic woods-and-waters camps. Four things set them apart. The first is that at an arts camp the focus of children and adults alike is on creativity. The second is the depth and range of choices offered to children every day. The third is the amount of freedom granted to children in service of their identity formation. The fourth is that more than any other camps, arts camps tend to attract children who experience themselves as different, as outsiders. It is a challenge to create a community of the more-or-less alienated, children for whom being an outsider is an essential part of their identity; the result is often something like an arts colony.

A few years ago, on the last day of the summer at Buck's Rock, I strolled away from the crowds of parents and children visiting all the exhibits, down the hill, past the clown workshop and the radio stations, across to the airy batik studio, past the jewelry-making shed, the leather-working and ceramic studios, and finally to the glassblowing shop. What fascinated me, what drew me close, was, of course, the fire. Each of the three ovens heats to 2,200 degrees Fahrenheit, and their doors stand open so that their contents are accessible to the glassblowers. The mouths of the oven are like archways; they allow you to look directly into the white waves of heat with their shimmering orange edges. It is absolutely mesmerizing to stare at them. During the summer session there are always observers—most of us are drawn to fire—but on this final day there were only two older girls working together.

Guessing from their ages, which appeared to be about seventeen, I imagined that they were probably junior counselors. They worked hard, sweating, moving in a practiced ballet. One girl held a steel pole that held the glass in the oven, twirling it along the flat edge at the bottom of the oven's mouth. When the molten glass was hot enough, she lifted it out, swung the pole around, and placed it on a set of railings where she rolled the pole slowly with one hand while she molded the glass with a tool she held in her other hand. Meanwhile, her companion, who had been patiently waiting, crouched down and blew into the open end of the pole, forcing air up and into the center of the slowly growing glass creation that her friend was skillfully shaping.

Though I was standing only three or four yards away, these young women either did not notice me or they were not remotely interested in me. They were totally focused on finishing up their beautiful glasswork, absorbed in the act of creativity. As they worked, they talked, their voices filled with disdain for the last-day-of-summer activities.

"Parents' Day!" one of them said. "What a waste of time."

Even though I was a parent, I took no offense. I understood. Anything that took time away from creativity was a waste of time. The chance to work with these ovens, to make glass, to do it on their own (there was no grown-up in sight) was precious to them. Where else could two high school girls get the chance to create these kinds of pieces? How many high schools have these kinds of facilities? Not many. How many places trust adolescents this way? Not many. This was a rare opportunity for them and they were taking advantage of it right up until the last possible minute.

This drive to create is the most prime characteristic of children who choose arts programs. Children are not all equally talented, but they all have a drive to express themselves creatively. In order to better understand the arts colony experience, I interviewed Toby Dewey, who was for almost thirty years the director of the Charles River Creative Arts Program and is now the founding director of the Summer Arts Program at the Cambridge School in Weston, Massachusetts. (Like Lee Kraft, he also declines to use the term *camp*. He dismisses camp as "canoes and war games.")

"There is something about a creative environment that is very unusual," Toby said. "Very few people get to experience it." When they are part of an arts colony, children inspire one another. Everyone gets up in the morning to make something, carve something, or write something. Everyone in the community looks forward to the publication of the daily paper. The children may express feelings and viewpoints in it that push the boundaries a bit; their sentiments might well be censored by administrators at school, but not in an arts program.

The climax of the day at an arts program is the noontime assembly where children see one another's work: musicians play, animators project their work up on screens, and clothing designers see their creations modeled on the runway. There is some singing, but not camp songs. The emphasis is not on the collective, but on performances by individuals and small groups. A boy plays the guitar and sings a solo, a Beatles song such as, "Blackbird Singing in the Dead of Night." Four children get up to improvise, trying to make the same faces that the animators have created on the screen.

Improvisation is a constant, both by the children and the counselors. Every child who gets up in front of that audience is taking an individual creative risk. The job of the community is to celebrate that risk taking.

I walked into a musical theater class just as the director told a group of about twenty young people, ages ten to sixteen (with three or four counselors in the mix), to create a musical number based on a the idea of a stage kiss. There was no preparation time. She announced it and sat down to play some Broadway-style music. The group of children and adults huddled briefly, talking as fast as they could, coming up with a script and some lyrics on the spot. Almost instantly, it seemed. As the director began to play the piano, the crowd on the floor began to sing the chorus to "Stage Kiss," the lyrics to which were only minutes old. A boy of about fifteen leaped out and began to sing lyrics of his own creation. Kneeling on one knee with his arms thrown out, the classic position of suitor, he began to sing to a girl, professing his love. Suddenly, he stood up and approached her. Someone—a camper or counselor—handed him a plastic ID card. He placed it between their lips and they kissed, with the card in between. As soon as the girl and boy rejoined the chorus line, another boy stepped forward and began to profess his love for . . . another boy. Ultimately, they also kissed, using the card between their lips as well. After several of these quick improvisational scenes, the group finished up with the rousing chorus of "Stage Kiss," a song that had not existed ten minutes earlier.

The fluidity, the creativity, the speed of it all was breathtaking; the group was exultant. If the period had not been ending, they would have improvised an entirely new song. The spontaneity, mutual respect, and support in this group enabled everyone to take risks.

Psychologists have been studying creativity for a long time, trying to identify the personality traits that make a person creative, predict in advance which artists will produce great art, and analyze the family and contextual factors that drive the artist. After a century of efforts to nail it down, creativity remains a mystery, shining and ineffable. The best we can do is to create an environment of support, provide artists with skilled teachers, and then give them the time, space, and freedom for their creativity to emerge. Artists must choose their medium; you cannot force people who want to paint to dance, you cannot force pianists to play the oboe or do printmaking. It does not work like that. That is as true for children as it is for adults, which means that an arts colony for children lays out the widest possible range of choices every day. Toby Dewey said that his program offers 130 different kinds of classes over the course of a summer. The list of choices is extraordinarily long: dance, theater, set design, lighting design, instrumental and vocal music, leather and batik shops, jewelry making, painting, printmaking, photo shop, publishing, and on and on.

Each of these arts requires a teacher who is both a skilled artist in his or her own right and a gifted teacher of children as well. Here is where arts colonies really part company with mainstream camps. At most camps, counselors can fill multiple roles and they work with groups of children who are all learning the same thing or playing the same game. In an arts colony, everyone is working in his or her own area of expertise. That requires a very large group of specialists.

Indeed, at Buck's Rock, there are really two different staffs:

art specialists and guidance counselors. The art specialists teach their craft, the guidance counselors staff the dorms and cabins, fulfilling the role that cabin counselors do in other camps. And what do the guidance counselors do during the days, when their students are all making art? They talk to children who have chosen not to make art just then, who are more focused on their feelings and themselves. A child can choose not to go to a workshop and instead spend the day talking to a guidance counselor, because basically there is only one rule at Buck's Rock: You have to go to meals. (Actually there is a second rule: You are not supposed to have sex.) The meals rule means that kids cannot stay in bed all day; they cannot withdraw from the community. However, what is striking is that this art colony lacks any rule requiring you to make art.

It is a moot point for most of the campers—making art, making music, experimenting with creativity is what they've come here to do. But the freedom to choose is paramount, and for some campers it is their medium for experimentation. One boy told me that he had spent most of his first summer there playing sports with his friends. He downplayed his art productivity. Playing sports all day at an arts camp is a countercultural choice. Looking back, he wished he had taken more advantage of the facilities and staff, but he was clearly proud of being able to pick and choose and even reject the opportunities around him. The American psychiatrist Thomas Szasz once wrote that "A child becomes an adult when he realizes that he has a right not only to be right but also to be wrong."

More than any other camp I visited, Buck's Rock gives children the chance to make mistakes—learn what they like and don't like—by offering them so many choices, along with the choice to reject all the choices. That can be crucial for children who are in the process of creating an identity. Szasz also pointed out that adults often use the phrase, *finding yourself,* or *find-*

ing your identity. But, he says, "The self is not something one finds, it is something one creates." Everyone in an arts colony understands that the creation of art and the creation of the self are intertwined. You make art when you are ready to express yourself; the way you express yourself becomes your identity. You may recall the "angry . . . withdrawn, unmotivated" fourteen-year-old David McDonald at the start of this chapter. Mastering glassblowing changed the way he felt about himself forever.

What is so fascinating in this arts colony for children is that they are all (or most of them) learning skills and making art, but many are very self-consciously engaged in the process of self-creation. Many of the former campers who wrote essays in memory of Ernst Bulova described a setting in which they were able to grapple with the eternal questions, master a skill, create some art, fall in love (there are a lot of marriages between campers who met in New Milford), and, without fail, experience their true selves for the first time. They believed that the choice and freedom of camp was deliberately created so that they could engage in that process, which takes time and adult trust. One quoted Ernst Bulova as saying, "I wish you luck in being yourselves."

MOST OF THE CHILDREN I talked to had gotten to this arts colony after going to some other more traditional kind of camp and having what could be described as a not-me experience. Harry Stack Sullivan, the great American psychiatrist, said that all experiences fall into either the me or the not-me category. It is the first distinction babies can make; if something is scary and uncomfortable they cry and draw back instinctively. If they like it, they smile and move toward it. Throughout life, adults make the same distinction. Everyone has had the experience of walking into a room and encountering a situation or a group of peo-•

ple who definitely give you that not-me feeling. It may be subtle, but it is unmistakable and it rarely goes away. The only question is how long you take to acknowledge your discomfort and choose something else. I talked with a high school junior named Steven who was spending every bit of his time at the glass shop. At first he joked, "I'm a little bit pyro. I like playing with fire." Then he grew more serious and told me that he had switched camps. "I went to a regular camp in the Adirondacks," he said. "I didn't like it, but I don't remember why. It was in the woods; they had a lake. I loved going out on trips." So he kind of liked it, but it also did not work for him. He said he disliked the regimentation; he didn't like the schedule and the competition. He was happy here, doing as much glassblowing as the schedule would allow and trying other things. "You can go to any shop you want to anytime you want." That, he liked.

IF THIS ARTS COLONY for children sounds like a paradise for fickle teens, it is not; not any more than adolescence is a paradise. It is nothing of the sort, because choice can be confusing and growing up is never easy. It takes some teens a few years to get their act together. Some parents find it uncomfortable to offer children this much choice and freedom at the ages of twelve, thirteen, and fourteen, but the present directors, Laura and Mickey Morris, speak for many summer camp directors who believe that it is important to listen to children and give them the chance to choose what they want.

"Parents so often provide the answers," Laura said. "Children need to make decisions on their own, they need to make mistakes. We believe in second and third chances." To illustrate the point, she said she had told a child that very day that she was glad that they had given him a third chance after two previous stays with complications, because he had turned out to be such a "mensch-y kid"—by which she meant a good sort. Then she laughed, and said, "We have a high tolerance for the quirkiness."

Codirector Mickey described a boy who had a "lot of social issues," and had been briefly in a boys' home. He was not very well behaved when he got to camp. What he did do was spend all of his time playing Ping-Pong. He didn't participate in shops. At the end of the summer Mickey and Laura reluctantly concluded that the boy had squandered his time and were surprised when he enrolled again. The boy returned the next summer and he was standing in the registration line with his father when Mickey asked him, perhaps a bit defensively, "Are we going to see something more than Ping-Pong?" In this case, it was the father who had seen the positive results from that first summer in his son. "Because you let him do that, he got good at Ping-Pong and now he's ready," he told Mickey. The boy painted huge Goth paintings his second summer; his third year he tried some performing arts, which naturally required him to cooperate with other children—and he was ready to do so.

ANN KLOTZ, WHO WITH HER HUSBAND, Seth Orbach, runs an ensemble theater company for children in Eagles Mere, Pennsylvania, explains that creativity-based programs benefit children whether they perceive themselves as "creatives"—artists or performers—or not. In their program, she says, the focus is not on pre-professional training for rising young stage stars. "We're about using theater for transformational purposes." Seth adds, "Many kids who are wicked smart come to do theater because they can't in their school, or they are learning disabled and can't take the time. Our whole shtick is ensemble theater." Their little company lives all together in one building. They cook together, wash dishes together, do laundry, and clean the bathrooms together. Ann tucks them in and gives them all a kiss good night. "They get mad if you don't." She listens to girls unburden themselves at bedtime, describing their friendship or family troubles. They create a sanctuary where a number of gay boys feel safe coming out to their peers for the first time. The group does plays in repertory that are well attended by the summer folk in the town. Like many others in the creative camp category, they do not refer to their program as a camp. It is instead the Ensemble Theatre Community School.

I've chosen to visit the programs I have—and I consider them all camps of a sort—because for me, camp is a psychological experience. If a child goes away from his or her parents, encounters new people and new challenges, learns the moral rules of a new community, absorbs the traditions, makes some choices and faces some challenges—on a horse, in a canoe, in a dance studio, blowing glass, or doing a musical—and discovers something about him or herself, that's camp. Camp is any place where you find a great new friend or discover a skill, and in that process you learn something new about yourself that you could never have learned if you had stayed at home with your mom and dad. And because they weren't there, your achievement belongs to you, your new independent self.

AFTER MY INTERVIEW with Mickey and Laura, I wandered out on the front porch of the dining hall and found a thirteen-year-old girl sitting and reading at 10:30 in the morning, right in the middle of one of the periods when most of the other children were working in one of the shops. Her back was against a pillar, her blond hair flowing over her shoulders, her long legs out in front of her, a book propped in her lap. While I was pondering whether or not to interrupt her reading, a handsome, dark-haired boy named Steven came and sat next to her and began to chat (and flirt a bit). I joined the two of them and we, in turn, were joined by a friend of Steven's named Ari.

I asked the girl, named Marissa, whether the counselors were okay with her not being in a workshop. She said yes, as long as she was being productive.

"You self-assess," she assured me. "I'll know in my own mind if I'm being productive here or need to do more."

Steven jumped in authoritatively: "They just don't want you hanging around the bunks."

Marissa was a first-year camper at Buck's Rock and was surprised at how different it was from other camps she'd seen or attended. "I've never seen any place like this," she said. She previously had attended a horseback riding camp and it was fun, "but not anything like this . . . This is so relaxed. No one tells you what to do." She contrasted it with home. "My parents don't give me the chance to prove to them that they can trust me and that I can manage myself." Even though she is a good student, her parents are frightened, she said. "I'm growing up too quickly," she added. "They want it to last longer." When she talks about her future, she sees them shy away from it. "They'll say, 'You've got a long time.' "

Steven agreed that camp was a great psychological break from his highly competitive honors track program at a New York public school. He said that his mother wanted him to go to camp because his school is so demanding and rigid, and doesn't allow much time for art. Like Marissa's parents, his parents struggle with his adolescence. "My mom's always telling me, 'Stop growing up.' "

We talked about the counselors to whom they are close. Marissa suggested that there is a "very guidance counselor-type relationship between kids. Mostly I'll talk to my friends," though she had felt homesick a couple of days previously and had gone to her counselor crying and had been comforted. Had she let her parents know that she was homesick? "I didn't really want to tell them because my mom said she'd be happy as long as I was happy."

As we were sitting there, two girls walked by wearing shorts and suspenders, with tight white T-shirts tucked in, and their hair in Pippi Longstocking–style pigtails. They were both wearing sunglasses. "It's change-your-style day," Marissa explained.

I asked them why they had chosen a coed camp rather than a single-sex camp.

"I can't stand anything all boys," Steven said. "Boys can be dicks and girls can be bitches. Boys insult people." Boys will call each other gay, Steve explained, then admitted that sometimes he slipped and used the word as an insult even though he did not approve of it.

Marissa chimed in: "Girls can get—both girls and boys—can get *yechhh,* and if you're fed up with one, I hang out with the other. It's nice to have the option."

"What I like about this camp," Ari added, "is that you can go sit under a tree."

What about romances at camp? I asked. Steven said he doesn't talk to anyone about that. He also mentioned the counselors who patrol the grounds at night. They are called the Safety Crew, "but that's not what we call them," he said. "We call them the Screw Crew." Steve explained, "[they try] to keep you out of the dark spots, so they can really see what you are doing, like Truth or Dare. You could get into trouble for that." I asked them, if they ran a camp, would they try to keep tabs on kids like that? Marissa shrugged yes. Steven said, "Yeah, if I ran a camp I'd do that. It does keep people safe."

As we talked more, Steven told me how worried he was about his twin sister, Cassandra, who had come to Buck's Rock for the first time this year, but had gotten so homesick that her father had just come to pick her up to take her to his house. (Their parents are divorced.) He hoped she would come back to camp, perhaps that night for his rock concert, but he clearly felt at a loss to help her, and he was confused about the stage fright from which she suffered. She has a beautiful voice, he said, but no confidence about getting up on stage to let other people hear it. He, by contrast, is a performer, a member of the cast of the summer's final production, Cole Porter's *Kiss Me, Kate*. I had accidentally stumbled into a group of kids devoted to the performing arts.

I spent the rest of the day with Marissa, Steven, and their cast friends. I watched them rehearse the musical numbers in an upstairs room in one of the dorms where it was incredibly hot. They worked hard, going over and over the numbers as the temperature rose. Marissa, the languid reader on the dining hall porch, had been transformed into Bianca, the flirtatious and unfaithful actress who sings, "Tom, Dick or Harry," and Steven became the blustering Harrison Howell, the army general who intends to marry Lilli Vanessi, the star of the show.

I also met Seth, a twelve-year-old playing one of the gangsters who sing "Brush Up Your Shakespeare," the show-stopping comedy number at the end of the show. Seth was a round boy with a comic personality and a wonderful voice, and a great stage presence. Throughout the rehearsal Seth was playing with a yo-yo, doing tricks with it, sometimes walking the dog with it so that it banged on the floor. It drove me a bit crazy, but it did not apparently disrupt anyone else. Later I asked the music director, Helen, a teacher from Sweden who comes over to Buck's Rock every summer, whether it bothered her. She said that she had of course noticed it, but that Seth was "always singing and he is very talented." She told me that she doesn't like to teach in schools where she has to discipline children. She wants to teach children "who want to be there." Back in Sweden, she teaches rock bands of children from ages thirteen to twenty. She tells me that her rockers talk all the time, and "they can't keep their fingers off the synthesizers." She appreciates their talent, too.

That night Steven's sister, Cassandra, did in fact return with their father. Their mother came in from New York and joined them, and the three of them watched Steven perform in a musical variety show. Steven was clearly a rock star. When he and his friend, Ari, took the stage, a number of girls in the front row shrieked and swooned a bit. The boys were totally in their element: cool, relaxed, and clearly having fun.

I got a chance to interview Cassandra later. She told me that she hadn't joined Steven during his first year at camp because she did not want to sleep away from home. She had used him as something of a scout for her, checking out the place and making friends whom she got to know on Facebook. She hated her day camp ("I got tired of being told what to do. I felt like I was in school") and felt secure enough to go to Connecticut that summer. But homesickness gripped her almost immediately. "It was the first or second night . . . It was like I had to be away to realize that I missed people at home that I couldn't see. I missed my older half sister in California, I missed my dad, my dogs. I have three dogs. They always follow me around."

She wasn't able to use her phone for the first week at camp, but after that she got her cell phone back and called home, asking her dad to pick her up for a break from camp. (Not many camps would allow this, and most camp directors would say this is the worst possible way to manage homesickness, but remember that Buck's Rock sticks to the principles of freedom and choice for children.) Her father came and took her home. Her mom reluctantly agreed to it, worried that Cassandra, who is pretty anxious, might keep calling him to get her from camp. That's not what happened. Cassandra went home, got a good night's sleep, knocked around her dad's house thinking about how she missed her camp friends, and then asked him to drive her back. Though she was quite nervous about saying good-bye to her parents and remaining at camp that night, she was determined. And she made it through the rest of the session.

On the last day of camp that August, I returned and talked with Cassandra again, asking her thoughts about the whole homesickness episode. She described the role that her new camp friends had played in her success on the second try. "I kind of just thought I would try to stay. I hoped I wouldn't feel homesick anymore. I think it was 'cause of my friends. When I came back they were really mad at me for leaving. They helped me get into things and helped me stay here."

Steven hadn't tried to help—he said he hadn't felt it was necessary. "Not helping was a help," he declared. "I didn't think she needed it."

Cassandra told me that she still hoped to get over her stage fright. Though she performed with a group of girls as backup singers, she was not yet ready to solo. I asked her how Buck's Rock had changed her.

"I think I'm a lot less shy," she said. "I really love it here. I don't want to leave. I think I've become a lot more independent."

Throughout the day, camper by camper, car by car, parents and children loaded up the cars with all their gear from the summer. Parents attended the final dance concert and visited the wood shop, leather shop, and metal shops to see their children's work and the work of their friends. You could tell from the way they walked and the way the parents deferred to their sons and daughters, that the children were in charge. They were at home; it was the parents who were visiting. As families left, children hugged each other and cried.

GIRL 1 (crying): Now I hate you. You've made me cry.

GIRL 2: I love you!

GIRL 1 (still crying): F—— you. . . . I'll miss you . . . call me.

Not all families stayed for the musical, but many did and lots of former campers and former counselors had returned for the final performance. Steven and Seth greeted their returning friends. They all made admiring comments about each other's cool clothes and life achievements. They were clearly proud of one another's growth.

The audience gathered under the white tent in the outdoor theater. The hard wood benches were packed with families and children when the orchestra started playing the first notes of "Wunderbar," the familiar first notes of the *Kiss Me, Kate* overture. Marissa was totally wanton as Bianca, Steven was bluff and arrogant as the general; they sang well and Seth, along with his partner and minus his yo-yo, was a comic sensation in "Brush Up Your Shakespeare." After the final curtain, all the cast members and the children hugged one another, cried, hugged their counselors, and made pledges to stay in touch. Their parents stood to the side, waiting for their children to come back to them. Over the loudspeaker came Mickey's voice, declaring the 2010 summer season to be at an end.

nine

THE MAGIC OF CAMP

CAMP IS HOGWARTS. While only a tiny fraction of children in the world will ever go to boarding schools, and none will ever go to an academy that fields a Quidditch team, all children imagine themselves going to Hogwarts, because it is the iconic place where kids are on their own. Part of the genius of J. K. Rowling's Harry Potter stories is that she understands that adventures start only after you leave your rule-bound caretakers, namely your parents (or, in the case of Harry, his awful aunt and uncle, because he has lost his parents). Once you are free of your vigilant mom and dad, you can go places where you have adventures with your friends, where there are new rules, risks, exotic adults, and wild creatures. The same literary device of freeing children from their parents is at the center of every classic animated film: Bambi's mother is killed; Nemo is separated from his father; Ariel, the Little Mermaid, escapes from her overbearing dad and her mother was never in the picture; the Lion King runs away from home after his father is killed. If real children cannot actually go to Hogwarts or, as the Lion King did, hang out with meerkats, what they can do is go away to camp.

In my interviews with campers and former campers, one of the phrases that they used over and over was: "This isn't the real world." It was always used as a compliment to suggest that things could happen here that never happen outside of camp. I believe that is because camp memories genuinely belong exclusively to the child. A woman in her fifties recounted that being sent away to camp by her parents for eight weeks at age eleven was a turning point in her life. Her parents, who were autocratic Europeans, had not consulted her about the decision. She had been very frightened by the prospect of camp. Although the decision to go was not hers, by the time she left camp she owned the experience completely. When her father drove to northern Minnesota from Connecticut to pick her up, she got into the car and made him listen to her sing every camp song she had learned. The concert lasted for hours. Looking back, she realizes that she was boasting, "Look at all I learned. I have a separate life."

Camp experiences can be so vivid, so life-changing that they are remembered forever, and later events are unconsciously measured against those peak moments of camp. I was once seated at a dinner table with seven middle-aged people when I began talking about my work as a consultant to residential camps. Immediately, stories of sleepaway camp began to tumble out of everyone there who had attended camp. Mitch Zuckoff, a professor of journalism at Boston University and the *New York Times* bestselling author of *Lost in Shangri-La*, declared with complete conviction, "There is absolutely no award in life as meaningful as a camp award," and then he began to talk about a blue sweater with an M on it that he won at his camp when he was twelve. As he described the sweater and talked about his camp, with its corny, made-up Indian name, its precious rituals, and the waterfront and hiking achievements that had led to the win, his voice was transformed. He sounded as if he were remembering his first love. His wife confessed that he had never thrown away that blue sweater; it was in a drawer at home, and she knew right where it was. "Honey," he said slyly, "we should look at that sweater when we go home tonight." Though he made it sound like a piece of marital seduction, it was nothing of the kind. Everyone at the table recognized that he *really* did want to go home and look at his camp sweater and be reminded of the moment he received it.

Michal Sager, an art teacher from Minnesota, had an emotionally powerful experience at a Jewish girls' camp in Canada (now closed) when she was twelve. She spent a month with a charismatic counselor who was obsessed with the movie *Five Branded Women*, starring Jeanne Moreau. The movie was about Yugoslavian women who were punished for "consorting" with Nazi soldiers. They had had their heads publicly shaved and were expelled from their town. On a two-night overnight trip away from the main camp, the counselor had the girls pretend that they were all alone in the world, banished from their towns and reliant only on one another. This is not, perhaps, what every Jewish parent hopes for in a summer camp experience for a daughter, but the art teacher said it was the single most powerful experience she had in moving her from being a little girl to identifying with the challenges and painful choices of adult women. A painter in adult life, Michal reported that she still has camp-related dreams and is still, in her fifties, painting abstract depictions of water, shoreline, and things emerging from water that she connects directly back to her days of awakening as a young woman, when she was in the thrall of a young counselor and felt the imagined terror of being all alone, reliant only on her female comrades.

Is what I am calling "camp magic" really different from the

universal dreams and terrors of childhood? Don't we all have powerful memories deeply wired into our brains because when we first lived those experiences they were so new and exciting and we were little and innocent? Yes, of course. I do not for a moment contend that sleepaway camps are the *peak* of early life experience for every child who attends them. Some children have just an okay time at camp; others have a lousy time and do not return; still others love their downtime at home. They have what they need for the summer: a town pool or a beach, friends, a bicycle, and the freedom to go where they want.

It is also the case that other life experiences trump camp experiences: falling in love, the first job, traveling abroad, an inspiring teacher. I am not suggesting that camp beats everything else that is good for children. After hearing the Hollywood writer and producer Jeff Melvoin use the word *magical* to describe a production of *Peter Pan* that he directed at North Star Camp in Wisconsin—his directorial debut—I quickly made the assumption that camp theater had been the most important factor in pushing him toward a television career. He corrected me: "Camp for me was more of a holistic experience. It helped shape me as a person. It was my high school drama teacher who shaped me as a theater person." That said, he told me that he always felt more "individuated and confident" when he was at camp, compared to the way he felt at school. He speculated that perhaps it had to do with the large shadow that his successful father cast over him, or the achievements of his talented older brother. Whatever the reason, he always felt strongest when he was at camp. And then he recited some lyrics from his camp song, the one everyone sang together at the closing campfire.

Carry on, keep those fires burning
We will soon be returning
Carry on.

He added that a middle verse, "Don't give up when life is rough on you," had been a source of strength to him throughout his life.

So why is it that a fifty-seven-year-old television producer is still able to sing his camp songs with great feeling, a Minnesota artist is still drawing inspiration from that long-ago make-believe banishment, and a professor keeps his camp sweater in a drawer at home? All of these stories flow from what I call the magic of camp. That magic is neither mysterious nor hidden. It is in plain sight. However, it is not captured by gushing testimonials. From the point of view of a psychologist, there are ten elements in the camp experience that create emotionally powerful experiences for children.

1. Opportunities for imagination, play, and creativity

"Do you want to be a judge for the Miss Ugly contest?" a counselor asked me on the first evening of my visit to Camp Evergreen, a girls' camp in New Hampshire. My heart fell. I hate judging contests of any kind; I am reluctant to declare children to be winners and losers. But I was curious about the Miss Ugly title because it went straight to the central psychological worries of teenage girls: Are they pretty? Are their bodies okay? Will they be considered attractive? This competition was obviously going to stand that classic worry on its head. The girls were going to compete to be the very thing they fear the most.

It turned out that I was the only male present at the contest, attended by 160 girls and twenty counselors. My presence was completely irrelevant; no one cared what I thought. The eyes of the nine- and ten-year-old girls were focused on their CITs, all just a few years older than the girls. The contestants were dressed in their best ugly costumes as Snookie, "hairy hippies," Madonna, Ke$ha and P. Diddy, Lady Gaga and her daughter (for skit purposes anyway), Ken and Barbie, and Oompa Loompas.

They had put a lot of work into their costumes and makeup. Each girl had to introduce herself to the audience through a brief skit and demonstrate a "talent." Most costumes mocked the female celebrities that the media offers as models of womanhood or sexually attractive female behavior. A few girls made a real effort to look ugly, stuffing their tights with articles of clothing that gave them hideous bulges, and makeup that was truly dreadful. The younger girls were fascinated.

At the end of the judging, the results of which no one cared about, an older counselor got up and looked into the earnest, beautiful faces of the younger girls. "I am glad to see that so many of you have the potential to be very ugly," she professed with great satisfaction. "I hope in years to come that you may work on your ugliness and possibly win this contest." They were clearly looking forward to someday having grown-up bodies as those of their admired CITs, as well as their confidence to perform in front of the camp and mock their own fears in public. I was not surprised to hear that the Miss Ugly contest, an act of homegrown imagination, is one of the highlights of the summer. The meta-message was, Relax girls, you are safe here, you don't have to carry all of your "Do I look good?" feelings with you every day. You can enjoy yourselves. (Almost every girl camper I interviewed for this book mentioned that camp was wonderful because you didn't have to worry all the time about the way you look.)

I have attended a lot of campfires, lunch announcements, and camp skits while researching this book. I have laughed a lot and groaned a bit; I have also learned that not too many of these entertainments bear retelling. You kinda have to be there to appreciate "Spit Spitter and his Round-the-World Louie." Many skits were obvious and derivative, many were dumb, a few were painfully half-baked. There were some moments, however, that were brilliant and, most important, all were home-baked. Most were very different from school assemblies, where most material is carefully vetted and "appropriate." At camps you get credit for simple effort, because imagination is a pot that is constantly boiling. At a traditional camp, every gathering is an opportunity for creativity and performance, morning, noon, and night. If you wanted a child to stretch his or her imagination every day, it is worth witnessing how any gathering can become an occasion for math problems (too complex for me), guessing games, creative announcements, jokes, and songs. If you wanted your daughter to find her voice, to take some risks, to try her hand at scriptwriting, to be willing to stand up in public, camp would be the place for her to practice. Most of the younger girls hold back, but all you have to do is see their faces to know that they are learning important lessons in creativity and in projecting themselves out into the world. Camp days are an occasion for constant creativity and invention.

Yong Zhao, the presidential chair and associate dean of Global Education at the University of Oregon, observed in a speech that the talent show—the amateur variety show with its skits, singing groups, and would-be stand-up comedians—is a peculiarly American invention. He says that you would never see such a thing in China, his native country, because there adults decide which talents are valuable and then train children to practice and perform them. A talent night in China showcases the best young pianists and string players, because that is what adults have deemed important.

Yong Zhao has written extensively about creativity and learning in his book, *Catching Up or Leading the Way: American Education in the Age of Globalization,* and contends that governments and authorities in every country work very hard to define "useful skills and knowledge" and teach them through "the curriculum, standards, text and high stakes testing," which is why the majority of American schools have narrowed their curriculums to two tested subjects: math and reading. He points out that instructional time for arts, music, sports, and foreign languages has been shortened or eliminated. All the emphasis is on logic, analysis, and verbal skills. He concludes that "Lady Gaga proves that such a paradigm no longer works." For him, the 412 million YouTube viewers of Lady Gaga reveals "the tremendous expansion of possible ways that the full spectrum of human talents and interest can be useful" to a global audience.

Author Daniel Pink, in *A Whole New Mind,* suggests that "design, story, empathy, play and meaning," are becoming "essential in the Conceptual Age." I don't know whether Pink has ever visited a campfire at an American summer camp, but he is describing exactly what happens there every day: *design, story, empathy, play, and meaning.* Jeff Melvoin's famous (at least to a small generation of North Woods campers) production of *Peter Pan* could not, of course, utilize wires, harnesses, and flying gear. The camp didn't have any of that equipment; the musical was staged in a rec hall with low ceilings. There were, however, open beams about eight feet up, and Jeff had at his disposal some large male counselors, including one nicknamed "the Hulk." They dressed the Hulk in a black T-shirt with the words FAIRY DUST on the front. Every time a character in the play was supposed to fly, Fairy Dust would pick the child up and sit him or her on one of the rafters from which the actor delivered his or her lines. A moment like that is theater magic. No one who saw it ever forgot it. It is also camp magic.

2. Camp is not school (No tests, judgment, or evaluation)

If the single most important thing about camp is that a child's parents are not there, that is still only part of the story. Camp is also *not school.* That simple fact can produce an extraordinary change in the climate of a child's day, and therefore in his or her emotional life. Good things, certainly different things, happen for children when they are relieved of the pressure of judgment, comparison, evaluation, and striving that are an inevitable part of the school day. Let's be honest; it isn't just the school day. Judgment and comparison are often intrinsic in town sports. Adult conversations are dominated by talk of who has been picked for the "select team" (that varsity experience for nine-year-olds). On school teams, at music lessons, and dance lessons, children are bathed in high expectations and constant informal and formal evaluations throughout the academic year. However, because that pressure is part of the air that they breathe in schools, children mostly accept it and do not remark on it as much as they might, even though they are always aware that it is there. The stakes of school are high; both good and bad performances have consequences. Children feel that every day.

I talked to the mother of an academically gifted boy who was enjoying a high level of success at his demanding school. He was the kind of ninth grader whom all teachers recognize as a future Ivy League or Caltech kind of guy. If it is possible to identify high-fashion models and future athletic brilliance at fourteen years of age—and it is—it is also possible to spot brilliant professor types by the beginning of high school. This boy was one of them. His mother was extraordinarily proud of him, but she also spent a lot of time thinking about his academic future. One day she was sitting in her study poring over brochures for summer internships that she believed would be impressive on future college applications. Her son appeared at the door, immediately understood what his mother was thinking, and explained ironically, "Mom, I'm not going to be gifted in the summer."

We no longer have the original agricultural rationale for a long summer vacation (in previous centuries, children were needed to help their families harvest crops). But there remains a strong argument that young people need a break from the pressures of school. As the federal government and the states consider increasing the number of school days or going to all-year school calendar (the United States typically has 180 school days per year compared with 220 in Japan and 251 in China), proponents of year-round school cite research about "summer learning loss." However, "summer learning loss" tends to affect children from low-income homes who, sadly and sometimes tragically, do not enjoy many stimulating summer activities. Research does not show learning loss in middle-class or upper-middle-class children. There are those of us who believe that the summer break can be beneficial for *all* children and that camps can provide both an opportunity to de-stress and a chance to explore different types of learning for all children. Lance Ozier, author and educator, sees summer camp as "vibrant settings for skill building and socio-emotional growth through the arts, media, music, sport, and a range of other activities." He agrees with Richard Louv, author of *The Last Child in the Woods,* that camp addresses the "nature deficit disorder," but he takes camp one step further and views camps as potential classrooms where children can build upon their proficiency, skills, and competencies. I certainly saw a lot of learning going on in summer camps, not least the fact that so many children were trying to keep up conversationally with their college-age counselors.

Pete Hare, a camp director and the son of a legendary long-serving camp director, worked as a successful history and Spanish teacher at two schools for close to fifteen years, then chose to return to the camp life full-time when career options required that he choose between pursuing school leadership or camp leadership. I asked him why he chose camp. He explained both his choice and the difference between school and camp in simple terms:

"First of all, camp is a far happier place than school. When kids and staff arrive at camp at the beginning of summer, the positive vibe and the smiles on their faces are incredible. The energy is crackling." By contrast, he continued, "When faculty arrive at school . . . I don't deny that there is some excitement, but there is a lot of drag-ass as well." That's understandable; they are teachers. They are facing a long and serious school year. Time is an important variable in the distinction between schools and camps; camps last a maximum of two months, so it is easier for everyone to stay "up" for that short stretch of time.

The essential difference between the two, however, has to do with the high stakes of school and the lower stakes at camp. You could argue that camp is full of contests, competition, and evaluation. That is true. One team wins the color war; the races are timed; there are awards for best camper. Perhaps it is not really so different from school. However, my experience visiting camps suggests that many of the competitions are, in fact, play or pseudo competitions that throw our intense need to win into a laughable light. Camp contests teach you to be able to make a heroic effort, laugh about it, and move on. Camp contests, done right, are group play.

When I visited Chimney Corners Camp for Girls in western Massachusetts, I arrived on the last day of the color wars. A counselor new to Chimney had introduced a novel culminating event: the frozen T-shirt contest. When I heard the name, I blanched inwardly, because it evoked the wet T-shirt contests held among college students vacationing on the beaches of Florida. This was nothing of the sort. Four T-shirts had been thoroughly wetted down, balled up, and placed in the freezer. They emerged looking like white papier-mâché balls, except that they were rock hard. There were four color teams and each had *chosen* a champion to represent her team. The first girl who could crack open the icy T-shirt and don it over her team shirt would win.

It was a ridiculous exercise into which these four champions threw themselves with a kind of insane devotion, slamming the T-shirt onto the floor of the outside basketball court to break up the ice and free the fabric. It was an extremely demanding task, and by the time they had been at it for ten minutes, the four girls were panting and sweating profusely. The girl representing the Blue Team was trim, muscular, and a total maniac. If I had to face a pack of wolves in the wild, this is the woman I would want beside me. Over and over, she would pick up the frozen T-shirt and hurl it to the ground, then tear it apart with her fingers and teeth, accompanied by the cheers and chants (recently composed) of the Blue Team while the Yellow, Green, and Red cheered for their champions.

The organizers had left the shirts in the freezer for far too long. It was clear that our heroines would be exhausted before they succeeded, so the rules were rewritten on the spot and teams were allowed to fetch warm water from a sink in the kitchen. Girls ran for buckets and plastic pitchers; bucket brigades were formed to melt the ice. The T-shirts, torn and battered, were donned. One team won the color war. Everyone cheered the winner, then the teams retired to create a cheer/skit for every other team, which they then performed for one another (out go the athletes, in come the lyricists and playwrights). Everybody hugged and laughed and headed off for the next activity. No state championships, no college scholarships offered to these ferocious queens of the frozen T-shirt contest.

Whether they specialize in soccer, tennis, or football, camps that teach particular athletic skills that connect to the skill sets valued by schools and coaches will, naturally, create a more competitive and stressful environment because everyone present, adults and children alike, are looking forward to real-world judgments and rewards for the summer's work: *Will I make the varsity? Will a college coach see me at camp?* That kind of pressure comes with the territory of high-stakes sports, and for young people dedicated to their sport or looking for a college scholarship it can seem like the only rational choice.

My daughter, Joanna, played three varsity sports all four

years of high school and at a pretty high level. (Some of her teammates went on to play in the Olympics.) I watched some of her practices and a majority of her games, and she always looked comfortable on the field. But there was something joyful about her when I would pick her up after a summer at Spirit Sports Camp for Girls. The director of Spirit, Margie Anderson, who was herself a former all-American lacrosse and soccer player, would not allow her girls to specialize in one sport. They had to choose three different sports per day, each for an hour and a half, plus an hour and a half of swimming, plus evening activities.

Margie encouraged girls to play sports at camp that they did not play at school. And yes, there was a color war at the end of the season, with teams competing in silly competitions like rotating rapidly around a baseball bat held to the ground or the ultimate camp game, Capture the Flag. Miranda, my daughter's friend who also went to Spirit Sports Camp, reports: "It was play . . . it was fun. I was never as happy as I was playing sports six hours a day, but it was never competitive." She saw her Spirit Sports Camp experience as an antidote to the judgmental voice that she associated with school. All of her report cards read, "Miranda is bright but she is too social. She doesn't focus." That assessment was a cloud over her head. At Spirit she never felt judged. "We were respectful and we listened to the coaches, but we also chatted and fooled around. They never told us we were 'bad.'"

Camp is an escape from judgment. I sat in on the Torchlight ceremony at Camp Champions in Texas while the results of the cabin inspections for each division were announced. The results were greeted with excitement, with cheers and little dances on the part of the winners, but no one there was fooled about the stakes of this contest. Being recognized for a clean cabin is a sweet pleasure; a messy cabin, however, is hardly a life-and-death matter. Even the choice of the boy and girl torch lighter, a real honor for the campers who are chosen, is largely forgotten by the next day. It does not go on your permanent record. The feeling that what happens at camp is sweet and fleeting is such a relief compared to the feeling of school, where everything is remembered and it all goes on your permanent record, something for your parents to worry about and for some unknown, future college admissions officer to frown over.

3. Character development: "I feel part of something bigger"

One of the most striking things about the camps that I visited was how readily campers talk about the impact their camp is having on their moral development. I have visited over seven hundred schools in my career; I have been given many tours by students. With the rare exception of church schools, where students sometimes talk to me about chapel services, students never stop to read me the posted rules or to discuss the values posted on the walls. Those signs are there, of course, everywhere. I walk through schools where bulletin boards are filled with anti-bullying posters and praise for good citizenship, where Bill Bennett's (endless) list of virtues decorate the hallways. Students never mention them to me. Perhaps these sentiments have become invisible over the many months of the school year; more likely there is too much going on in the building and the children conclude that these statements are present and pleasant, but not a priority.

As I was touring YMCA Camp Becket for boys with Randall and William, two staff aides, both sixteen years old, William avowed, "One of the reasons I keep coming back here is that I feel a part of something bigger." They walked me to the dining hall where we stood together and looked up at the eight values carved into wood over the dining hall doors:

Do your best

Help the other fellow

Each for all—all for each

Peace through understanding

I can and I will

Play the game

Manners make the man

Better faithful than famous

These instructions are clear, simple, and memorable. Randall and William knew them by memory; they had listed them for me before I viewed the carved statements high up in the dining hall (I admit that I tested them). These rules are discussed every week at chapel and in cabin chats led by counselors after lights out. They become part of the fiber of campers, just like the Girl Scout Law, which nearly every woman who was ever a Girl Scout can recite from memory.

I will do my best to be honest and fair, friendly and helpful, considerate and caring, courageous and strong and responsible for what I say and do, and to respect myself and others, respect authority, use resources wisely, make the world a better place and be a sister to every Girl Scout.

The boys at Becket informed me that seven of their posted values had always been a part of the ethos of Becket, almost since its first season in 1903, though I was told that number four, "Peace through understanding," was added in the sixties over much opposition from the Becket boys of prior decades who felt the sentiment was too abstract, perhaps too antiwar, and potentially divisive. The fact that these two staff aides in 2010 saw themselves as caretakers of the cherished values they shared with all the boys who had gone before them said a lot. These are the codes that bond Becket campers together for life.

New York Times columnist David Brooks writes that sociologist Craig Smith and his colleagues at Notre Dame have found that young adults in America exist in an atmosphere of "extreme moral individualism." Many are lost when it comes to meeting the moral demands of communal life, Brooks writes, because they "have not been given the tools to cultivate their moral intuitions, to think more broadly about their moral obligations, to check behaviors that may be degrading." One young adult reported to the researchers, "I don't really deal with right and wrong that often."

My experience at the camps I visited is that many campers had a keen sense of right and wrong, and were not shy about saying it. There are many definitions of what good character is. Not everyone agrees on all that should be included, but almost all definitions include honesty, compassion, courage, and some capacity for sacrifice on behalf of other people. At sleepover camp, because children are together 24/7, because they are sharing cabins and boats and must cook together on hiking trips, they know immediately which children help and which do not. In school you can ignore a child who does nothing to help; on a four-day horseback trail trip, you cannot. I am not saying that campers are perfect. They can be gossipy and cruel, they can exclude and tease; they can avoid work and make excuses. That said, in my experience, the level of consideration at camps is extremely high and campers are proud of operating at a higher moral level than they do in the real world. "This is a bubble," they tell me. "It's not like the outside world." They told me that they don't behave as well in the real world as they do at camp. What is noteworthy is that this effect is felt very quickly when children leave their home schools and travel to some setting away from home.

Vicki Pastor, a teacher from Jefferson Township in Maine, says that her seventh graders have been coming to the Kieve Leadership School in Nobleboro, Maine, for fifteen years, and every year she can see that the sleepaway experience has an immediate impact on the way her children think about teasing and bullying. "The whole class is changed," she says, after a sleepover experience of only four days. Kieve, like many private camps, is in a gorgeous setting. Throughout the fall and spring, the camp opens its doors—and provides generous subsidies—for groups that might not otherwise be able to access a camp like this: Iraq and Afghanistan vets and their families, 9/11 first responders and their families, and most notably middle-school children from all over the state of Maine.

Vicki says that it is sometimes difficult for her children to have perspective on the way they treat one another at home. Almost all of the children I met from the Jefferson and Chelsea districts had been in school together "forever," and most had never, as one boy put it, "slept away from parents." What he meant was that he had slept over at friends' houses down the street, but never out of town. From the moment they arrive at Kieve Leadership School, the children focus on values. I asked Vicki why it happened so quickly. She reported that the Kieve Leadership staff always ask her seventh graders questions and help the children develop a new language. They are confronted with the question, "Are you part of the solution or are you part of the problem?" The staff are also trained to debrief the children after activities such as the ropes course or the climbing wall, which involve belaying, turn taking, and tolerance for one another's fears.

The most important thing about the straightforward list of values at camps, like the Boy Scout and Girl Scout codes, is that all the tenets are understandable and every camper can see how they are applied—or not applied—every day. If you need help tying up your boat and another boy just turns his back on you and walks away with two of your cabin mates, you know he has not lived up to "Each for all and all for each." "Help the other fellow," might sound old-fashioned, but a woman counselor told me how important it was to her because she uses it every day to measure the performance of other people. So do campers. At one camp, when I was watching a final-day triathlon competition of running, swimming, and boating, I witnessed a boy who was far in the lead emerge from the water, then glance around and see that a swimmer behind him was really exhausted and struggling. The leader gave up his position to charge back into the water and help the struggling boy get to shore. There were adults present. The boy in the lead knew that someone else was available to help. He turned back because he considered it his personal responsibility to help his comrade. That is good character in action.

4. Sacred dimensions: "If we only take time to stop and look around"

When I imagined writing a book about summer camps and other away-from-home experiences, I decided not to write about church camps because I did not think I was qualified to do so. As a psychologist who calls himself an agnostic (for lack of a better term), I doubted whether I could write thoughtfully about the religious experience of campers. I am, of course, aware that there are thousands of faith-based camps in the United States—evangelical, Jewish, Quaker, Catholic, Methodist, and many others. The Christian Camp and Conference Association alone, for example, represents 874 mainstream evangelical camps, the vast majority of which are sleepover camps, and that membership may constitute less than half of the evangelical camps that exist in the United States.

Historically, part of the motivation for getting children to sleepover camps was to get them away from city streets and into the country, to keep children from idleness and the "occasion of sin." Some religious groups relied on camps to strengthen the bonds between children and their religious and cultural traditions, and create a community where, say, Jewish boys and girls could meet, perchance to eventually marry within the faith. (Camp romances work for Lutherans and Catholics as well.) There is no question that the fun of camping, combined with a faith tradition, can create an intense and life-changing religious experience for children. If *the* book on camps and organized religion has not yet been written, there is work there for another author.

So while I have not written about religious camps, I do want to touch on the issue of sacred feelings, because in my travels to camps I could not help noticing that even secular camps create a space in which children experience powerful spiritual feelings. You cannot miss it. When children gather around a fire at night, or near a sparkling lake in the morning sunlight, and hear the adults that they care so much about speak of how a particular camp means a great deal to them, it hits children deep in their psyches.

When I visited YMCA Chimney Corners, I learned that there would be a chapel service on Sunday evening. It would be nondenominational, I was told, because Chimney, even though it is a YMCA camp, attracts Jewish campers and children from nonreligious families, and, indeed, I never heard the name of Christ or God mentioned during the ceremony. Upon arriving at the location in the woods where benches were set into a hillside, it looked as if the "chapel" was an occasion for dress-up more than anything; the girls had all put on the best clothes they had at camp. The serious and respectful faces of the girls, however, alerted me that this was far more than a costume show or a campfire with skits.

Four older girls ran the chapel, inviting campers who had prepared talks to speak to the gathering. Girls from every age level took turns walking to the front, some quite nervous, to address the gathering, to talk about themselves, their backgrounds, and their life experiences. They talked about losses of parents to cancer and other hardship, illness and travels; they mentioned significant things that their fathers and mothers had said to them, they read poems. We sang inspirational songs like "I Believe I Can Fly." As always in camps, the songs are about youth and independence, strength and possibility: "I believe I can fly / I believe I can touch the sky."

More than anything, however, the girls talked about what Chimney Corners means to them, read poems, and praised their friends and their counselors. Because it was totally dark, I could not write down what I was hearing, but some weeks later Shannon Donovan-Monti, the director of Chimney Corners, sent me a stack of Candlelight chapel talks that girls had given over the years. One girl, quoting Agatha Christie, wrote that "Just to be alive is a grand thing," and went on to say:

> If we only take time to stop and look around us we can easily admire the beautiful aspects of life: the sunrises, the sunsets, the stars lighting up the sky at night. Even the dark clouds of a thunderstorm can appear beautiful as the bright lightning dances through them. . . . But I must admit that the grandest aspect of being alive is the fact that we get to share our time here with everyone around us.

In 1999, at a Candlelight ceremony "In Remembrance," a girl named Sharon read a poem by an unknown author.

When I die, give what is left of me away to children
. . . I want to leave you something better than words or
   sounds
Look for me in the people I've known or loved . . .
You love me most by letting hands touch hands
By letting bodies touch bodies
And letting go of children that need to be free . . .
So, when all that's left of me is love
Give me away

Then she talked about a counselor, Francesca, who had died (she didn't mention the circumstances), a woman not much older than herself, whom she remembered for having taught her how to walk arm in arm for a prolonged period of time, and how that was actually better than walking alone. "Right now," she finished, "I'm just looking for more people to hold arms with."

In 2006, one girl wrote an ironic introduction to her Candlelight talk apologizing for not having a "life-changing" story about an underprivileged child looking her in the eye or rebuilding a "decimated school." She wrote that, for her, Chimney is a

> bunch of hilarious moments and hugs. Chimney is spirit, it is music, it is dressing up, alter egos, seclusion, losing yourself in the whirlwind of not caring. It is loud, boisterous, politically correct, secretive, private and open-minded . . . endless opportunity, relaxation, confidence, spontaneous and beautiful.

Though I never tire of hearing this kind of testimony, I do understand that much is gushingly adolescent. However, it is also very powerful. The cumulative effect of girls listening to other girls open up at a campfire or Candlelight, four weeks every summer for four or five or seven summers, is profound. When I asked the staff at Chimney Corners how many of them were being raised in a religious home, 80 percent of them raised their hands. When

I asked them for how many of them their sacred feelings about Chimney were stronger than their attachment to their family's religion or their home church, *80 percent* of them raised their hands. "It's not even close," one young woman declared.

THE IMPACT OF CAMPFIRES on the spiritual feelings of campers cannot be underestimated. These women were telling me that a nonreligious camp tapped more deeply into their spiritual feelings than did the church that they attended with their families. As a psychologist I cannot say for certain why this is so, but I believe this happens because of the trust established at camp, the role modeling of emotional openness by veteran counselors, and the setting in nature, "the sunrises and the sunset . . . the stars in the night and sharing it with friends."

My friend Chris is seventy-one years old. When I told him that I was going to visit Camp Becket and Chimney Corners for the book he said, "Oh, I'm a Becket boy." When I asked him about the impact of the lakeside Sunday morning chapel on him, he told the following story. When President Kennedy was assassinated in November of 1963, Chris was twenty-three and a newly married man. He and his wife had been planning to go to a football game that Saturday, which had been canceled after the death of the president. Filled with grief and faced with an empty weekend, Chris suddenly realized that more than anything he wanted to see the huge pine tree by the lakeside chapel at Becket. Even though he had grown up in a religious family, that pine tree at his camp was his spiritual touchstone. That's where he needed to go when his president was shot and his world was shaken.

5. Independence, self-esteem, and identity

Perhaps the single most important finding in the camp research literature is that children who attend camp come home feeling independent and confident. They have higher self-esteem than they did when they departed for camp because true self-esteem comes not from praise but from real experiences of skill building and making a contribution to a community. All camps, whether they are sleepover or day camps, whether the focus is on the water, on mountains, on horseback riding, or hiking, are designed to provide experiences of success for children. Because children are rarely forced to engage in activities but are allowed to choose what they want to do, their successes belong completely to them.

When I sat and watched the Chelsea sixth-graders at Kieve Leadership School, I could see the pride and excitement on their faces as they came down from completing an element on the ropes course. Their confidence was unmistakable. For a skeptical person, the obvious question is: Does this effect last? The answer is yes. Research suggests that 92 percent of campers say that they feel better about themselves as a result of camp. Campers and their parents report growth in confidence, independence, and maturity as a result of camp experiences, and these gains are maintained six months later. These effects occur in day camps, one-week camps, and four-week camps; I observed them in the three-and-a-half-day school trip that the Chelsea students made.

One boy, whose mother was nervous about letting him spend his nights at Camp Kieve—he had never slept away from home before—came to pick him up that first evening so he could return to his bed. Though he had been away for only twelve hours, he was determined to gain a bit of the independence that his classmates were enjoying. From the moment she arrived, he tried to persuade her to let him stay overnight. When he returned to camp the second morning, he had extra clothes and his toiletries for an overnight stay. His mother cried when she talked to me, but understood that he was taking a step at twelve that she herself had not taken until she was six years older, when for the first time she slept away from home. She was a bit anxious for her son, and more so for herself, but she was also proud of him and his newfound independence.

Many campers are changed in ways that their parents can see immediately because when they return, they are willing to help around the house. Camp directors have drawers full of letters from parents thanking them for sending back a child who is suddenly willing to do chores. She now picks up her clothes or helps with dishes, the parent writes, suggesting that there has been some kind of magical transformation at camp. It is not magic; it is simply a change in identity. When your mother asks you to pick something up, it makes you feel like a small child. A twelve-year-old thinks to himself, *She's been asking me to do this kind of stuff since I was little. It is annoying and it makes me feel like a baby.* But when he is away from home and he is being asked to clean up a cabin by a nineteen-year-old counselor, he feels entirely differently about it.

First of all, the voice is different; it is not his mother's. Second, he usually wants to win the respect of his cabin counselor. Third, he is being asked to make a contribution to the group; perhaps they will get the cleanest cabin award and can share in that prize. At the very least, if he helps out, his peers will recognize that he is pulling his weight and will not feel critical of him. I had a number of campers tell me that setting the table or cleaning up feels different to them than doing the exact same task at home.

The one comment about camp that I heard from children more than any other is that "You can be yourself here." That is a pure identity statement. Why can a child be him- or herself at camp but not at home? That is a dismaying idea for parents who imagine that their children feel most safe and most loved at home. That may be true, but feeling safe and loved is not the same thing as experiencing your true self. The choices at home are the old choices, something your mom and dad have always wanted. You do it to please them, or to oppose them, but the choices do not feel fresh. Every child struggles to experience him- or herself as an independent actor at home for the obvious reason that home is the geographic center of your dependence— that's where you were little—and no child can view his own identity clearly when Mom or Dad is nearby because all children view themselves, at least partly, through their parents' eyes. When a boy's father is watching him build a plastic model, or play a video game, the boy is assessing himself in two ways. One, according to his own criteria, *How am I doing? Is this fun for me?*; and two, by the criteria that he imagines his father uses, *Does he think I'm doing a good job? Does my dad think this game is stupid?*

The great American educator John Dewey wrote that "The self is not something ready-made, but something in continuous formation through choice of action." Children are what they do; they are what they choose. Even the best schools cannot allow children that much choice. Camps, on the other hand, offer many choices: most serious, some serious, scary, and silly. What they are doing, in fact, is offering chances for identity formation. A child thinks, *If I choose the Nature Walk, I am a nature person,* and other kids see him or her that way. *If I always choose kayaking, then I am a kayaker.* I have experienced this business of choice in my own family. I sent my daughter to a general activities camp one summer and paid an extra fee for her horseback riding. It turned out that she did not like the horseback-riding instructor, so much so that she avoided the stable and spent her time sailing with a counselor whom she really liked. When she came home, I was annoyed that she had "wasted" the extra fee I had paid for horseback riding. She, on the other hand, was absolutely delighted with her sailing skills. She made an identity choice based on what she liked and didn't like, actually based on the people that she did or did not like. I had to get over it.

I sent my son Will to the canoe tripping camp in Vermont where I served as the psychological consultant. When he was there, he spent a lot of time in the woodshop and a minimum of time on the water. Doing the "wet exit" in a kayak—upside down, underwater—freaked him out. At the end of the second summer he said to me, "Dad, this is your kind of camp, not mine. I don't want to go back there." I made it clear that I wanted him to go to some sleepover camp but let him know that he could choose the kind of camp he wanted. He said, "Find me an arts camp." So we did. It is worth noting that my daughter still remains the only trained sailor in a landlubber family, and my son now attends the Maine College of Art and works as the counselor at a summer day camp teaching woodworking. Neither his mother nor I have any woodworking skills whatsoever. That is his identity, not anything he got from us. He got it from camp.

6. Friendships and social skills

Scott Brody, the director of Camps Kenwood and Evergreen, argues that the primary business of camp is to give children a chance to escape from the social and identity traps of elementary and middle school. He believes that camp offers the opportunity for a "do-over," especially in the social realm. When children come to camp, "It's like the inner dialogue that is in the head of every middle school child stops. And they stop seeing themselves through the eyes of parents and other kids." What happens then? "They see themselves as who they want to be," and that opens the gates for children to develop closer, more meaningful friendships than they had in school.

In Chapter Five, I tried to solve the mystery of why camp friends who are with each other only a matter of weeks in the summer often experience being closer than school friends who spend nine months together. We witnessed the growth of such a friendship between five women at Camp Downer. What I did not focus on was the role that the adults play in creating a space that allows friendship to grow. Scott uses the analogy of a subject in school. If math teachers teach math, then camp counselors teach social skills. "Nurturing relationships in groups is the key." Because of the academic demands of school, teachers cannot always pay attention to the isolated child. At sleepover camp, however, a kid's social life is the purview of the counselors twenty-four hours a day, and in a day camp, nine hours a day. If a child is isolated, everyone sees it and tries to help the child. "We are observing, coaching, calibrating, because that's the most important part of camp." The best counselors are also modeling social skills all the time and the children are watching.

Camp research supports Scott's conclusion that camp has an impact on the social lives of children. Children make great friends at camp; almost 70 percent of them maintain those friendships after camp has ended. Their parents report increases in social comfort six months after camp and an increased capacity to be a leader among peers. "I would say that camp helped me to be more outgoing," reported one ten-year-old girl. What I see in most campers is a growth in tolerance and children's capacity to resolve conflicts. If you are going to live in a cabin with your peers for a month, you had better be able to get over a fight, tolerate differences, and include everyone in the activities. At school you can turn your back and walk away from another child. That is harder if you are in a cabin playing games with the same children every day, especially if the counselor whom you respect fosters a high level of cooperation in the cabin.

Certainly some people have stories of terrible times socially at a camp. That can happen. It is just that the unhappy stories are swamped by the stories I hear of great camp friendships. Ellen Flight, the director of Camp Songadeewin, concludes that all the activities at camp help children "make connections," and that her staff models friendship. You don't have to look far to see it. When I peeked into the rec hall on movie night at Songa, I saw all of the girls lying on the floor, side by side, wrapped in sleeping bags and blankets, holding their stuffed animals. Camp is one huge sleepover.

7. *Making a relationship with nature*

Many people who founded camps in the late 1800s did so because they were worried that urbanized youth lacked the strength, fitness, and practical skills of the early pioneers. If that was a concern 130 years ago, it is—or should be—a far greater worry today. Our children, both from the cities and the suburbs, spend an extraordinary amount of time indoors in front of screens. Too many are growing obese and many no longer feel comfortable outdoors because they spend so little time there.

There have been dramatic decreases both in the amount of time that children spend in free play and in the amount of time they spend outside of their homes. According to Richard Louv, the author of the brilliant book *Last Child in the Woods,* adults born between 1946 and 1964 may be the last American generation to think of the out-of-doors as a place for recreation. According to researchers at the University of Maryland, between 1997 and 2003 there was a 50 percent decline in the proportion of children ages nine to twelve who spent time engaged in outside activities such as hiking, walking, fishing, beach play, and gardening. Of the mothers from the previous generation, 70 percent remember playing outdoors when they were children; only 26 percent of them report that their own children play outdoors daily. We have replaced free play with town sports, and the woods and the backyard with the Wii in the rec room.

When small children first arrive at camp, they are often

frightened by spiders and mosquitoes, by rain and thunderstorms, by snakes and all the imagined creatures that could be at the bottom of a lake. That is understandable, because they haven't spent hours standing knee-deep in a stream or lake near their house. No one likes leeches and ticks, but it is a useful life experience to have had to take a leech off your leg and realize that you do not die from it.

Children normally go through stages of feeling somewhat uneasy outdoors to gradually getting more comfortable. They whine about the discomforts. Some complain about sitting on the ground, about getting dirt or pine needles on themselves. Many panic about going on a hiking trip and sleeping in a tent (there are always imaginary bears) or going to the bathroom in the woods. Every child who goes to the bathroom in the woods, and develops that all-important ability to identify poison ivy so as not to squat in it, experiences it as a step toward independence and maturity. They feel triumphant because they are no longer slave to their fears, nor are they chained to the comforts of a bathroom and a shower. Perhaps you have a memory of the excitement of taking a bath in a lake or stream. Or the thrill of waking up in a sleeping bag when the temperature dropped overnight and there is actually frost on the ground—and yet you are okay. Gradually, most campers grow comfortable with living outside. They come to understand that mosquitoes are just annoying and can sometimes be completely ignored. They learn that skin makes you waterproof; you are not going to melt in a heavy rainstorm even if you are completely soaked. One of the nicest things to watch at camp is a group of children running outside in a heavy summer rainstorm happily getting wet.

As a result of their camp experiences, many fall in love with the woods and the mountains. Most schools teach environmental science and respect for the natural world. Every science teacher who can arrange it has her children doing projects in the park or nearby woods. I walk into Biology labs that have tanks of tropical fish or terrariums with salamanders. All of this is good, but there is no classroom experience that can compete with wading through a swamp at night and hearing the sounds of thousands of spring peeper frogs, or turning over a rock and finding a "wild" salamander underneath. That is magic. There is simply no substitute for seeing Nature when you are living in it, part of it, surrounded by it. The experience changes your experience of the world. One camper talked about his group's last trip of the summer. "On the second to last day of the trip we found this mountain and climbed to the top of it and I literally thought I could see the whole world. It was six thousand feet. I'm not a religious person, but if there is a heaven, that was the view."

8. *Healthy sexuality and body development: "The Naked Brigade"*

Every year for the past four years I have accompanied the senior class from the Belmont Hill School on a thirty-hour senior retreat at Camp Cody in Freedom, New Hampshire. This break from the school routine is designed to help the seniors focus on themselves as the leaders of the school, their responsibilities as older boys whom younger boys will emulate, and to give their mentors a chance to talk to them about their boyhoods and their impending departures from home—not to college, but to young adulthood. Though the trip is a break from school, a chance for the class to bond, and a chance for the adults to impart some wisdom, the trip inevitably involves some group chaos. Going to camp is disinhibiting.

One year there was a late night "pillow fight" in which the boys employed mattresses instead of pillows, running at each other like medieval knights with mattresses for lances. All the adults (teachers, headmaster, and the psychologist [me]) bunk in the counselors' area of the cabins that are occupied by boys. We go to bed early because we are experienced enough to know that we may be awakened, and we usually are. A few years ago I was startled out of sleep at 2 A.M. by the sound of large male feet accompanied by the exuberant shout, "The Naked Brigade!" Eighty-five nude seniors literally flashed through the front door of our cabin and out the back. All that we, the adults, could do was smile and shrug at this healthy display of boyish bonding and male power.

Going away from your family, leaving civilization behind you, and living in Nature makes many people—and perhaps a majority of children—want to skinny-dip. This is exciting for kids and a challenge for camps. As I mentioned earlier, when children live together, the fact that they are all changing clothes in their cabins, swimming together, and showering in the same showers, stimulates their curiosity about each other's bodies. When older boys and girls attend camp together, far away from their parents, some will inevitably experience crushes, romances, and first sexual experiences. All of this is human biology; you can no more stop it than you can stop the tide. In 1929, Hedley S. Dimock and Charles E. Hendry published their widely read study, "Camping and Character: A Camp Experiment in Character Education." Without describing the behaviors, the two researchers noted that almost 7 percent of the boys in their study occasionally demonstrated unspecified "irregular sex behaviors."

What were these "irregular" behaviors? Masturbation? Probably. Sexual exploration and play? Maybe. And the 7 percent figure raises the question: What were the other 93 percent of children doing? They were almost certainly displaying normal sexual interests, but not in a way that brought them to the attention of counselors and researchers. David Sedaris, the great American humorist, who is gay, wrote an essay in which he described his first sexual experience with a boy at a summer camp. It was a sad experience because the two boys turned on each other after their encounter, but camp was where it could happen. One former counselor told me that he arrived at his cabin and through the screen door spotted a twelve-year-old camper masturbating for an audience of four fascinated eleven-year-olds. The counselor did not crash into the cabin, but later asked the boy about the scene. The twelve-year-old explained that he had boasted to the younger boys that he was able to ejaculate; none of them could yet and they all challenged his claim. He had to make good on his boast.

These completely normal behaviors take place in the context of our fears about sexual abuse. If we send our children away from home, and they are dressing and undressing in front of counselors and other adults and not under our protection, will they be vulnerable to pedophiles? Many parents spend a lot of time teaching their young children about "stranger danger." After all that education it seems counterintuitive to entrust them to strangers. Though, as a psychologist and a parent, I absolutely understand these fears. I have a different concern. I think that children today make a quick jump from being completely protected from any possibility of sexual abuse to watching the rawest pornography on the Internet. The average American child sees pornography for the first time before the age of eleven, long before his or her parents think that is possible, or get up the courage to talk about it. (Boys between the ages of twelve to twenty-five are the largest consumers of pornography in the United States.) This leap from protected innocence to raw, impersonal sexuality is scary and abrupt. Camp provides a healthy middle ground for sexual development, to talk about stuff that you cannot talk of to your parents, to gossip about the romantic lives of counselors, and perhaps to experiment a little bit. One teacher, who had attended a Lutheran summer camp when he was in eighth grade, said that every night after the chapel, the kids would go down to the woods by the lake and make out.

Part of the magic of camp is that children get an education about the bodies of other children, and they get a chance to talk about romance and sex. (Lots of it is misinformation, but weren't we all a bit misinformed at the start?) Girls can be infatuated with their grown-up girl counselors and talk endlessly about them. I know camps that have a "girl crush" day, which desexualizes these strong, normal feelings that younger girls have for older girls they admire. Boys have crushes on young men counselors. They don't talk about what they are feeling in that way, except to say, "He's so cool," but they want to jump on their favorite counselors and hang out with them constantly. This is healthy.

My experience of visiting camps is that camp directors are keenly aware of the dangers of pedophiles and live in fear that a person with a sexual interest in children might slip through their screening procedures. They all recognize that in previous decades camps, like schools and churches, were either unaware or turned a blind eye to the existence of pedophilia. That is not the case now. Accredited camps are naturally held to very high screening standards, and many states make CORI checks (Criminal Offender Record Information) mandatory for camp counselors.

What saddens me about our constant worries over the possibility of child sexual abuse is that some parents become so afraid that they can never trust another adult to look after their child's body, so they keep their child from enjoying the kind of closeness that Rebecca Steinitz's daughter had with her close group of friends from camp. Rebecca told me that her daughter and her three friends were "so close and so open to each other. They see each other naked, they all lie on the porch together, they have an intimacy that you can't find in American society."

Camps walk a fine line between providing protection of children on the one hand and fostering close relationships between campers and campers, and campers and counselors on the other. With that many hormones colliding, sometimes "sex happens" between kids at camp. And there is always the possibility of poor boundaries and actual child sexual abuse. But sex also happens at home and after school, and statistically most child sexual abuse occurs in families, not with strangers. My experience of camps is that for the most part, children's feelings about their bodies and their knowledge of their own sexuality grows and develops in healthy ways when they are at camps. A sexual education at camp is certainly healthier than one from the Internet.

Scott Brody, the owner of Camps Kenwood and Evergreen, says,

> I think camps have more control over the sexual behavior of children than either schools or parents. We set up boundaries for kids . . . and our counselors hear almost everything because fifteen-year-olds, bless them, always talk. I would venture to say that kids are less likely to venture into serious sexual territory at camp. It is very hard to violate a major rule at camp because we send you home.

Scott reports that campers do ask him why they have rules against PDAs (public displays of affection), even handholding, and he talks to them about the necessity for safe boundaries in such a tight community.

9. Relationships between counselors and children

Shayne Horan, the principal of an elementary school in California, pulled out a stack of old letters from his file cabinet, some on store-bought stationery, others on scraps of paper torn out of school notebooks. All were from his former campers at Camp Lohican in Como, Pennsylvania. His campers had written to him just to say hi or to talk about serious things going on in their families; some boys had written once, others had written over a period of years. As he showed them to me—they were twenty years old—he talked about each child, his strengths and vulnerabilities, and sometimes about attending that camper's wedding ceremony twelve years after that child had left camp. You could not ask for a better illustration of the closeness that can develop between campers and counselors than these letters. These relationships can go on for years.

THE WOMEN AT CAMP DOWNER, whom I featured in Chapter Five, all talked about their relationship to Sherry Mitchell, who is married to "Mitch," the camp director. Sherry meant the world to them; she was like a second mother to all of them (except for Amanda, for whom she was the first mother); she followed their progress in life and worried about them. They lovingly complained that, like a mom, she sometimes asked questions they didn't want to answer, but they always returned for more talks. Camp counselors can have a lifelong impact on campers.

IF I WERE FORCED to choose which one of the ten elements of "camp magic" is the *single* most powerful, I would pick the relationship between counselors and campers. In a world where children no longer come from large families, where small kids are not much looked after by their older siblings, the power of the relationship between older children and younger children can be life changing. Campers and counselors are teaching each other important lessons. It would be hard to say who is more changed by the encounter. The counselors share their wisdom and their life lessons (such as they are at nineteen), and the campers teach counselors patience, caring, communication skills, and, above all, empathy. The learning can sometimes be difficult, but empathy and leadership skills are the result.

10. Leadership training

Because camps need a steady supply of counselors, they provide some of the best leadership training for adolescents and young adults that I have seen anywhere. The training starts early and is generally nonstop. When I compare the leadership training in camps to that in schools, there is generally no comparison. Schools do not, in fact, do a lot of systematic leadership training. Teachers tend to let leaders rise up organically, on their teams or in their clubs. Class officers get elected by their peers in schoolwide elections modeled after adult democratic elections. Sometimes these elections are serious affairs, other times they are a joke; some of the leaders are great, many are mediocre (just as in the adult world). In athletics, team captains are often chosen because of their high level of skill—how can they be denied the position?—and sometimes because of great leadership capacity even though they may not be the most athletically talented. But in either case, there are rarely prolonged periods of training for school leaders.

Camps, by contrast, cannot take leadership ability for granted. Counselors often have life-and-death responsibilities for children on horseback, at the waterfront, in whitewater, on high cliffs, or just when kids are horsing around. Camp directors need to find young women and men who are capable of personal sacrifice, who will work long hours, and who will shoulder enormous amounts of responsibility. Camp administrators start scouting for future counselors by spotting community-minded campers as young as twelve and thirteen. They designate them as counselors in training, usually at age fourteen or fifteen (while their parents are still paying for the privilege of sending them to camp), then as a staff aide or some similar title at sixteen (parents still paying), and then as junior counselors or cabin counselors at seventeen or eighteen.

Because of the respect that campers have for their counselors and their attachment to the camp, more children aspire to become counselors than can be accommodated, or have the talent for the job. Usually there is a moving, public ceremony where the best staff aides are announced and celebrated; off to the side are the campers who were not picked, coming to grips with the fact that their camp careers are now over. Camp directors tell me that these selections are among the most painful moments of their jobs. After years of running cabins and/or refining a specialty skill, some counselors ascend to jobs as division directors or assistant program directors, responsible for training, supervising, hiring, and firing counselors. A few choose to become camp professionals and apply for year-round positions at camps.

After seven years as a camp counselor and fifteen years as a teacher and school administrator, Shayne Horan told me that "to this day," being a counselor makes being a teacher look like a piece of cake. The hours are so long and the experiences so powerful that "It helps you be a teacher, a role model, mentor; you have to be a friend. . . . There are times when you have to play the mother or father when they are homesick. And then you have to set boundaries and be tough."

When you are nineteen or twenty, being tough with fourteen- and fifteen-year-olds can be . . . well, tough. The longtime humor columnist for the *Miami Herald,* Dave Barry, worked as a counselor at Camp Sharparoon in Pennsylvania along with my older brother, Peter, and my cousin, Bonnie. Dave mentioned his camp counselor experiences in some of his columns. "One of my key counseling techniques," he wrote, "was terror," and he described how he could get his campers to "briefly stop hitting each other and making bodily sounds" by telling them "scary bedtime stories."

The real story of how Dave became a counselor-leader is

more harrowing. Sharparoon was a church-supported camp for underprivileged children from New York, mainly African American and Puerto Rican. Dave grew up in a mainly white, upper-middle-class community of Armonk, New York, where he would only occasionally see a minority child. When he went to Sharparoon as a camper, there were a lot more black and Puerto Rican kids than white kids, and when he returned as a counselor, the campers from the inner city challenged his leadership. He had eight boys, ages fourteen and fifteen; three of them were bed wetters. "We had kids who had been in trouble with the law. They jumped me when we were out in the woods. I don't know what they intended to do." One fifteen-year-old in particular was after him. "The other kids were not going to help me," he remembered. "They wanted to see who won the fight."

Dave won the fight, by punching much harder than he would have ordinarily. But after the altercation he sat down alone with each boy to talk and establish a bond of trust, or, as he tells it, "Actually I ended up telling them that if they tried that again, I'd kill them." He survived that first summer and they did, too. The next summer, when they were visiting a nearby lake, rowing an ancient, crummy rowboat, some white kids came by in motorboats and shouted, "Nigger, nigger!" at his campers and then tried to swamp their rowboat with the waves they kicked up.

"Our kids had heard worse, but I was really angry," Dave told me. That night he did something he regards as immature. ("I don't approve of it now.") He and his assistant counselor waited until their boys were asleep ("That was extremely irresponsible and childish, leaving our kids.") and then rowed across the lake to the marina. They spotted the two offending boats and he and his assistant counselor each "took a shit in their boats." Dave added, "It was very satisfying."

This is raw leadership and rough justice, nothing that any camp director would recommend. However, it arose from Dave's identification with and empathy for his campers. Dedicated counselors will do whatever they can to protect their campers from harm. In my experience, high school students who have been camp counselors stand out from their peers. They are more mature, more disciplined, and have a capacity to build community, which is lacking in many other late adolescents. Being a camp counselor does not necessarily make you love school or make you a brilliant student, but it gives you a chance to practice your leadership skills and think about your role in a community. Sitting in a classroom may not offer you the same opportunities.

When researchers ask human resources directors and other executives at top American companies which abilities are going to be most essential in the twenty-first-century workplace, they cite three critical skills that workers are going to need: teamwork/collaboration, ethics/social responsibility, and oral communication. Watching counselors work with children in camp settings, I am convinced that they are getting powerful, daily training in exactly those skills. For example, Diane Debrovner, deputy editor of *Parents* magazine, attended Buck's Rock arts camp for three years as a camper, CIT and counselor. Unlike her friend who worked in publications at the camp and then went into publishing, Diane took a more circuitous route. She did theater.

"I never got the big parts in the big productions," she said, referring to the musicals. She was part of a smaller group that performed plays. Yet she feels that her experience in theater prepared her well for her eventual career: "I think camp taught me to be independent. And theater, well, a lot of what I do is communicate. I have to communicate with writers, and that skill was definitely nurtured at Buck's Rock."

Andy Hiller, now an officer in the Marine Corps, was a counselor at Camp Med-O-Lark when he was in high school and college. He went to camp when he was six years old, the youngest boy at Camp Winaco. "I can't remember not wanting to be a counselor," he said. "Counselors were the coolest things in the whole world. That's what I wanted to do." When I asked him what camp had taught him about leadership, he said that it taught him both leadership and "follower-ship," how to take one role and then another depending on the needs of the community. And what, I asked, was the most important thing he learned at camp?

> I guess it is to not be afraid to step outside of your comfort zone. Sometimes people are afraid to lead, because they've never been in that role before . . . risking falling on your face, risk looking like an idiot, or having people think you made a bad decision. That's the biggest leadership characteristic that camp gave me: a willingness to try.

ten

"CHILDSICK" AND HAPPY

CAMP DIRECTORS TELL ME that managing "childsickness"—parents' longing for their absent camper—is becoming a bigger problem for them than dealing with homesickness. They know how to support children suffering from the universal symptoms of homesickness, mild or more serious. What they do not know is how to handle the parents who yearn continually for contact with their children, who are complicit in smuggling cell phones into camp (kids turn in their old cell phones and keep their iPhones), who exacerbate their children's homesickness through constant contact, or who are checking their children's pictures every day and calling if they do not see a photo of their child smiling.

Judith Wright, the director of summer camps for the Movement for Reform Judaism in the United Kingdom, contacted me when she learned I was writing a book about camps. "Parents have," she wrote, "become more involved in the camping experience, and this is at the detriment of the experience. Mobile phones don't help! Parents seem to find it harder to let go even for the two weeks of summer camp." I called her and we talked about the challenges she faces in building a community of children when parents keep calling, thereby literally and psychologically pulling their children out of the community experience.

Even though it skirts the edge of stereotype, Judith told me the following story because it was iconic, funny, and universal. She received a call from a mother whose teenage son was on the Israel trip with a group of his peers; the mother demanded to be put in touch with her son. Judith reminded her that they had a no-phone-contact rule for the teen trips and went over all of the reasons for the policy. The mother acknowledged her points, but claimed that this was a very serious issue. Judy asked what it was. The mother said, "I've seen his photo and I can tell he's constipated." Judith tried not to laugh and then tried to reason with her, but the mother was adamant. She had to make contact with her son about this matter. Finally, Judy agreed to contact the leader of the trip who talked with the son, who reluctantly admitted that he was, indeed, constipated. So your mother does know you best. However, by the age of sixteen, a young adult traveling to Israel should be able to find some prunes or All-Bran cereal and not receive an emergency phone call from his mother to discuss his bowel movements. This isn't just a Jewish-mother story. All mothers know their children's bodies and worry about their health. You would be amazed by the worried calls and frantic instructions that camp nurses receive. The question for any parent is, Can you let go?

I laughed at Judith's story, but it makes me sad because I know that when the counselors look back on the boy's experience in Israel, they won't remember anything about his trip; all they will recall is the phone call from his mother. Her concerns will in some ways overshadow his independent experience of

Israel. *You do not want to be that mother.* I am imagining that if you picked up this book, you have already decided that you do not want to be that parent; that you intend to send your child away, or at least consider it, and you want to get it right. Here are seven suggestions to keep you from suffering too much from childsickness or intruding too much on your child's camp experiences.

1. Give your child the gift of letting him or her go

When I interviewed the humor columnist Dave Barry about his experiences as a camp counselor, he ended up telling me how much his daughter loved camp. "My daughter just went to camp at ten," he said. "It was like the best thing that ever happened to her in her life. . . . Now, that's all she talks about, and that's pretty upsetting because *we had nothing to do with it.*" As usual, Mr. Barry captures the problem succinctly. The hardest thing about camp is coming to philosophical terms with the reality that your child is going to have a lot of fun that you cannot see, you cannot photograph, and in which you cannot share. She will rise to challenges, make mistakes, sing and laugh and cry and have a crush on someone you will never meet. The only way you will learn about it will be if she tells you about it, and I guarantee that she will never tell you everything you would like to know.

Most important, however, she will discard some of her childhood self when she is away from you. Your child will return to you changed; something you have cherished will be gone; she will have shed a part of her baby self like a snake sheds a skin, without a thought. It will never fit her again and it will never come back. You will miss it. A mother said to me, when her eleven-year-old son returned home after his first summer at camp, "He had a wonderful summer, but things will never be the same again." He will feel stronger and you will feel a little bereft. When you send a child off to camp, the gift you are giving him or her is to let go. You have to be willing to sacrifice both that period of time with your child and, more important, be willing to let go of your importance in your child's life to make space for someone else and new experiences.

2. Prepare your child for homesickness

As I described in Chapters Three and Four, symptoms of homesickness, either mild or severe, are universal. It does not help your child to either hope or pretend that it will not happen. Almost all children experience some symptoms of homesickness; about one in five has significant symptoms, and one in fourteen has homesickness that does not remit and, in fact, grows more severe during a camp session. Cheerful predictions that everything will be fine after a few days at camp might be true for a majority of children; it will leave the severely homesick feeling betrayed. If you are sending a child away for a school overnight trip, a summer camp, or a semester abroad, you need to talk to him about possible homesickness and the strategies that he can use to manage it.

You also need to figure out whether you have a child who is at risk for severe homesickness. It is possible to predict whether a child will be extremely homesick by asking a number of questions.

Has your child had trouble with separations in the past?

Has he or she had trouble with sleepovers or school trips?

Does the child believe that he or she is going to be homesick?

Is your child saying negative things about camp? For
example: "Camp is going to suck. . . . I won't be good
at anything."

Has he or she been down or depressed in the months
leading up to camp?

If so, your child is likely to be at risk for serious homesickness.

Chris Thurber and his colleagues have developed a program
for helping children prepare for camp that parents can obtain on
DVD from the American Camp Association. Their research has
shown that if parents use the program with their children, they
can reduce homesickness by 50 percent. The keys to his program
are: involving the child in the decision, talking and strategizing,
using some cognitive therapy (for example, using a calendar to
measure time), and giving the child a chance to practice being
away from home under favorable circumstances. Three or four
successful overnights will give a child more confidence than any
amount of verbal reassurance.

3. Do not try to manage homesickness from a distance

Let's be honest: The cell phone has not helped the homesick
child at camp. More parental contact, especially illicit contact,
does not help the child. A phone call to parents is just as likely—
actually, more likely—to exacerbate the homesick feelings as it
is to calm them. What helps a homesick child is feeling that he
or she has some strategies for dealing with the feelings: getting
involved in activities, hanging out with friends, thinking about
distracting thoughts, talking to a trusted counselor. We all want
to comfort our children when they are in distress, so the temptation to try to manage your child's homesickness at a distance is
tremendous. The greater wisdom is to trust the camp authori-

ties. They are in the best position to know when and whether a child should be calling home.

That makes trust between parents and camp personnel essential, so my corollary to suggestion number three is: Don't send your child to camp unless you trust the people who run it. If you can imagine a camp director or village director sitting with and really comforting your child, and you can convey that trust to your son or daughter, you are doing well. If you cannot, your child will sense your uncertainty, and if you send the message, consciously or unconsciously, that the *only* person who can comfort your child is you, you might as well bring him or her home right away, because you have de-legitimized every other adult's attempts to comfort your offspring. Out of loyalty and love for you, your child will unconsciously reject others' efforts to help him or her.

If your child becomes seriously homesick, you should let the camp director or assistant director, the expert on the scene, be your guide. She or he will tell you when you are going to be needed, because sometimes a phone call is necessary. Perhaps the director has told your child, "If this doesn't get better, we'll both talk to your parents in a couple of days." That two-day wait might provide the child with the experience of being able to manage the homesickness on his or her own, making the call either unnecessary or a reward for patience and resilience.

What if you have an extremely homesick child who is in a situation that is not camp, something like an overseas class trip or a semester abroad? The first thing you need to do is find out whether or not your child has anyone with whom they can talk and urge him or her to reach out for support. Sometimes pride gets in the way and a child in misery just needs permission or a reminder to seek help. Sometimes, however, there is no help close at hand. I have friends whose son was in the Peace Corps in a tiny, poor village in a Spanish-speaking country. He had no one with whom he could speak English so, even though he was pretty fluent in Spanish, there was no one to whom he could tell his troubles. Even if he could have conveyed the nuances of his frustrations and longings in Spanish, he did not have anyone who shared his history or position. Despite his acute homesickness at a few points, he was determined to stay and make a success of it. His parents just had to sit on their end of the phone line and listen to him cry and absorb his helplessness. That's a lot of what parenting is about: bearing and acknowledging helplessness so that your child can find his or her resilience. In this case, the son recovered in a few days. In the meantime, of course, the parents had a lot of feelings to bear.

Whenever your child calls you full of anxiety, whether it is about camp or an upcoming college exam, don't just flood him or her with concern. Also, remember that the reflexive response of suggesting the obvious quick fix sends them the wrong message (a vote of no confidence), and with rare exception, if the quick fix were going to work, it would have worked already. Here are questions you can ask that help your child connect both with reality (concrete questions help) and with his or her own inner resilience. If a blunt no or yes response seems like a dead end, turn it around with a follow-up question.

For the camper:

Is there a counselor you like? (If the child says no, ask, How about the nurse?)

Does the counselor listen when you talk? Does it make you feel a bit better after you talk to him or her?

Are there any other children in your cabin who are homesick? (If the child says no, ask about children in other cabins. To whom do they talk?)

Has an older camper talked to you about homesickness? Perhaps you could ask the camp director whether there is a counselor there who was once homesick.

Are there many kids there who play soccer (or some other sport or activity) as well as you do?

Have you been crying all day? (The answer to this is almost always no, which makes the child feel stronger. At least she hasn't been crying all day!)

What is the worst part of the day? What's the best part?

If a child says anything about a better part of the day, or a positive aspect of an activity, don't immediately rev up like a cheerleader, chirping, "That's great! I am sure you'll have fun when you do it next time!" It is a bad policy to be a lot more cheerful than your child about his or her experience. You should be curious, empathic, and matter-of-fact: "Oh, I'm glad that there is something good. Will you have that again this week?" Throughout, you should convey that you are not overwhelmed by his or her panic, and that you have confidence that he or she will be able to soldier on. Don't require a quick turnaround; just convey hope for slow improvement. It is not so different talking to a nineteen-year-old in college than it is talking to an eleven-year-old at camp. You're trying to get your child to tap into his or her strengths and talk about his or her resources and strategies.

For the college student:

Are other people as worried about the exam as you?

Do you have a friend with whom you can study?

Have you been able to talk with your professor or R.A.?

Is there anyone there who is able to comfort you?

4. Do not make the "We'll take you home if you're unhappy" deal

If you make the "We'll take you home if you're really unhappy" deal with your child before he goes to camp, or suddenly offer it during a painful phone call, you undermine his chance for success. It is both ineffective parenting and bad psychology. It creates incentives for your child to feel miserable. If, on the other hand, you say, "We think you are going to be able to conquer your homesick feelings and make a go of it at camp," your child has the incentive to live up to your hopes, to please you and to feel stronger.

College-age students get homesick; high school students who have really looked forward to a semester abroad also get homesick. If you have a child who is miserable in college, you should not make the deal with him or her either, for the same reason. Perhaps you can visit, or you can invite your child to visit home, but unless you want to throw a year's tuition into the dumpster, you should ask him or her to stick it out for the year. Actually, you should have had that conversation before your child went off to college. No one is ever too old for the "What are you going to do if you get homesick?" conversation, or the "Are you really ready for college?" conversation.

The one exception to this general rule about not offering to bring children home is clinical depression or suicidal feeling. If your child is seriously depressed, you need to ask the question, "Have you thought of hurting yourself?" If the answer is yes or maybe, you must contact a roommate, campus security, or the administration and make sure someone is in regular contact with your child. You then should fly out or drive out, get him or her to the mental health services at the camp or college and decide whether treatment is needed, and go back home if you are not needed. I have heard of campers wailing, "I feel like I am going to die here." I have never heard of a camper actually injuring him- or herself in order to get home. Self-injury and depression in college students, however, is a trickier matter because they can withdraw from the world in dangerous ways, which is something campers, immersed in community, cannot do.

5. Help your children practice the skills they need before they leave

I was once consultant to an independent school in the Garden District of New Orleans late in August. When I entered the elevator of my hotel on a warm Tuesday morning at 7:30 A.M., I encountered a mother who already looked frantic and burdened. She was holding three textbooks, a large bottle of washing detergent, and a pair of size 13 running shoes that were clearly not hers. It was an armful. I asked why she was in New Orleans and she told me, "My son is a freshman at Tulane and I'm dropping him off." Then, without my asking a follow-up question, she complained anxiously, "And he's so disorganized and he doesn't know how to do his own laundry."

"How long have you been here?" I asked.

"We got here last night and I'm staying till Friday," she replied. "There's so much to do."

In my mind, you do not want to be that parent. You should not be a constant visitor to your freshman's dorm room during his first or second week there. You should not be in the basement laundry room teaching him—and it usually is a him—how to operate a washing machine. If you did not complete those lessons at home, you should leave it to his dorm mates or some kindly freshman girl to spend time in the laundry room with him. Or you should wait until his roommates object to the pile of smelly clothes around his bed, but you should not be teaching it during freshman orientation week.

There are two ways to teach children the skills they will need when they are away. One is by asking your child to help with cooking, laundry, cleaning, and many other chores around the house. Every child who goes to college should go off with a hammer, a screwdriver, and a wrench, and the experience of having used them. That said, not all useful skills are easily taught by parents. The second method of teaching your child necessary skills is to send them away from home for different kinds of trips before packing them off to camp: field trips, school overnight trips, sleepovers, a week at the grandparents every summer, or a trip abroad. As long as your child always travels with you, you are both deferring the moment when he or she learns to travel independently.

6. Use letters, postcards, and other slower forms of communication

Letters are uniquely powerful in the lives of campers and parents. Many parents have talked years later about their children's letters from camp; others have fetched them from a drawer to show me. For a child, the color of the stationery, the color of the ink, the handwriting, the smell of home (Do you remember ever smelling a letter?) are concrete manifestations of Mom or Dad. A camper can get them out to read and reread at rest time. Not all campers treasure their parents' letters; boys in particular misplace them. For many campers it is comfort enough to know that they have Mom's or Dad's letter stuck in the trunk. The notes are there, a comforting piece of home. I have had a camper show me a letter in his mother's handwriting with what he believed—and I agreed—were her tears smudging the script. He was touched by how much she missed and loved him. (I have also known campers writing extremely homesick letters to parents who have sprinkled a little water on their missives to fool their parents into believing they are sobbing uncontrollably. My guess is that some enterprising company will soon develop a DNA testing kit for campers' letters.)

Camps, which are always responsive to their customers, are now allowing parents to email responses to their children's letters so that the children get them more quickly. Other than our addiction to speed, what is the purpose of these rapid-fire communications? It is my understanding that the parents sent the child to camp to practice being independent; minute-by-minute contact with parents undermines the sense of separation. Call me old-fashioned, but why do communications have to get there so quickly? Some private camps tell me that the FedEx trucks have to back up to the office and unload what seems like tons of packages with snacks and other goodies for campers. And why do parents have to send so much stuff? Have we reached a stage where sending more and better care packages is a reflection of competitive parenting?

My advice: Stop the emails, just send one or two packages per summer and give yourself a break from checking the camp's online photos. Go buy some stamps and write a long letter or two or nineteen. Those letters will be more valuable to your child than any emails or packages. Furthermore, the time between sending and receiving a letter is a valuable opportunity for both parent and child to *think* about one another without having to do anything *with* or *for* each other. That reflection time will deepen your child's understanding of him- or herself, and it will increase the respect you have for one another. You will be proud that your child was able to be away from you, and your child will be proud that you managed without him or her. It will also strengthen the bonds of love between you. So many parents have reported that their campers return more loving and demonstrative than they were before they left.

Your child's letters to you, often maddeningly brief or cryptic, and sometimes coerced out of him or her by a counselor, will still be an important expression of love and connection, one that you can read and reread. They will make you happy: You will feel both childsick and happy. Even in the age of Skype and texting, the reality and rhythm of camp is best expressed in letters because the reality is that children need time away from their parents . . . and parents need time away from their children.

7. Take a vacation from parenting, have some fun and don't feel guilty about it!

It does not help your child's camp experience for you to feel anxious and miserable while he or she is away. You will, naturally, miss your children. At times you will feel their loss acutely. Psychologically and neurologically, childsickness is the parental equivalent of homesickness. The brain of a parent is wired to connect with her offspring. When they go away, your brain cells will be screaming, *Where is she? Where is he?* However, you cannot add value to your child's camp experience by suffering— even silently. Like your child, you *need* to grow up. Should you check the online camp album for photos of him or her? Only if you don't feel compelled to do so, and only if you'll be fine if your child isn't in the photos. Otherwise, step away from the Internet. I encourage you not to try to track your child's camp experience except through his or her letters. Enjoy being proud that you have raised a child who can go away, make new friends, learn new skills, and have a good time. You deserve a good deal of credit for supporting your child's independence and for letting go.

My friend John once observed that having children "makes your life and ruins your life, simultaneously." Parenting is one of the most demanding jobs that any of us will ever have, and there are precious few vacations from the responsibilities we have for our children. Sending a child to camp should free you to have some fun. Do all the things that are difficult to do when you have children: take a grown-up vacation, read a bunch of books, go to some foreign films, make love.

Your children will miss you when they are away. If they're struggling a bit with homesickness, then they'll have made some important developmental gains by the time they come home. Most likely they will be having a wonderful time or making progress in that direction. Why shouldn't you?

ACKNOWLEDGMENTS

When I started to write *Homesick and Happy,* my friend Steve Baskin laughingly warned me that there are three categories of people to avoid because they are likely to bore the pants off you: besotted lovers who want to talk about their new love, recent religious converts determined that you should also see the light, and camp folks. He was, of course, warning me about the tendency of former campers to rhapsodize about their beloved camps and every little meaningful thing that happened to them during their precious summers there. I appreciated his counsel, but the psychological power of camp was exactly what I was trying to understand. I found the willingness of current and former campers, counselors, and camp directors—people from the age of seven to seventy—to spend time teaching me about the meaning of camp in their lives both touching and extremely helpful.

There is no way I can thank all of them—all of you—because I talked to so many people, lots in formal interviews, many more in conversations at lunch, or on the ball field, or in a group staff training with fifty counselors in a room. Still others wrote to my website blog, others to my Facebook page. Sometimes I was surrounded by a group of nine- and ten-year-old girls all talking so fast I could hardly keep up, much less take down their names.

What I need everyone who talked with me to know is that I heard you and I learned from you. Many thanks.

Pete Hare combines great wisdom and an irresistible enthusiasm; it was he who pulled me back into the camp world after a thirty-year absence. His innocent invitation to do a staff training at Camp Keewaydin on Lake Dunmore proved to be the seed that sprouted into this book. The ever insightful and creative Scott Brody, the owner of Camps Kenwood and Evergreen, honored me by nominating me for the American Camp Association's Hedley S. Dimock Award and later nominated me for the board of the American Camp Association. My three years on the ACA board opened up the world of camps to me. Peg Smith's profound sense of mission inspired me; Art Wannlund embodies service leadership. I want to thank them and all of my fellow board members. I learned more from them than I was able to give back.

On our first meeting, Harriet Lowe, the editor of *Camping Magazine,* and I were trapped in her car in a snowstorm. By the time we finally got to the airport we were friends and she had convinced me that even though I was an outsider, I had something worthwhile to say about camping. Chris Thurber, PhD, brought me up to speed on the homesickness research and shared his great love of Camp Belknap with me. Maxson Jarecki, a member of Keewaydin's Section A 2010, took the initiative to contact me, offering to do the research for the "Passages" chapter as his senior project at the Dalton School. He did an extraordinary job of interviewing as well as filming many of the members of Section A and Section 1. Note to future employers: hire Maxson Jarecki when he graduates from college. Henry Holmes entrusted me with his personal journal from the Section A Bay trip. I am grateful for his faith and patience.

I want to thank fellow authors Dave Barry, Jeff Melvoin, Doug Stone, Mitch Zuckoff, and Catherine Steiner-Adair for sharing their love (or in the case of Doug, his dislike) of camps.

The following camp owners and directors invited me to their camps to do staff trainings, to conduct interviews, and volunteered to be interviewed: Susie and Steve Baskin, Camp Champions; Chris Burke, YMCA Camp Becket; Sandy Chivers, Camp Ojibway; Marc Cohen, Camp Hope; Shannon Donovan-Monti, YMCA Chimney Corners; Ellen Flight, Songadeewin of Keewaydin; Bruce Ingersoll, Keewaydin Temagami; Henry Kennedy and Charlie Richardson, Camp Kieve and the Kieve Leadership School; Ann Klotz and Seth Ohrbach, ETCS; Richard Lewis, Camp Wabun; Sherry and Harold "Mitch" Mitchell, Camp Downer; Laura and Mickey Morris, Buck's Rock Creative and Performing Arts Camp; Toby Dewey, Summer Arts at CSW; Yates Pharr, Falling Creek; Dane and Jaime Pickles, Camp Everwood; Kurt Podeszwa, Camp for All; Sandy and Missy Schenk, Green River Preserve; Jason Sebell, Camp Kenwood, and Alfred and E.C. Thompson, Camp Carolina.

When I was visiting Green River Preserve in the mountains of North Carolina, Sandy Schenk walked me into the dark woods so I could witness an unforgettable sight: thousands of blue ghost fireflies lighting up the forest floor. As unique as that experience was, however, there were moments of brilliant illumination in every interview I conducted and at every campfire I attended. I am grateful to all the directors, counselors, and campers at all the camps I visited for providing me with their insights. I hope I have done justice to them in the book.

My editor at Ballantine Books, Marnie Cochran, has been a blessing. She is smart, flexible, she recognizes a good story, and she reads what you send her *right away*. My trustworthy agent, Gail Ross, has helped me negotiate the shoals of publishing for fourteen years. She takes excellent care of me and keeps me out of trouble. My administrative assistant, Liz Diggins, runs my day-to-day life and calendar with humor and patience, even when I am maddeningly preoccupied with writing. My longtime research assistant, Lindsay G. Biewirth, is always there for me, ready to produce facts and verify claims in an instant. She worked on the bibliography of this book right up until hours before she gave birth to her beautiful daughter, Jane.

My friend and collaborator Teresa Barker's name does not appear on the front cover of this book, but the reader should understand that it is there in the hidden ink of inspired editing, conversation, critical mind, laughter, moral support, guidance, and organizational skills. We have worked on five books together over the last fifteen years and I feel as if I am just starting to learn all she has to teach me about writing.

Finally, I need to thank my wife, Theresa McNally, for her steadfast love and patience, for her discerning judgment, for her willingness to put down her own work to read the words of an insecure writer who needs to hear *right now* that what he is writing is on the right track. Theresa never attended overnight camp as a child but saw for herself the beneficial impact camps had on the growth and development of our children, Joanna and Will. And although she thought I was a little nuts to traipse off repeatedly to sleep in tents when I was in my sixties, isn't that the essence of marriage, to love someone even though you think they're crazy?

NOTES

Introduction: *A New York City Boy Goes Back to Camp*

xix   *In his book* Outliers: The Story of Success, *Malcolm Gladwell* Malcolm Gladwell, *Outliers* (New York: Little, Brown and Company, 2008).

xxi   *Hurricane Island Outward Bound School* "Outward Bound is a nonprofit educational organization and expedition school that serves people of all ages and backgrounds through active learning expeditions that inspire character development, self-discovery and service both in and out of the classroom." www.outwardbound.org.

xxiii   *In my book* The Pressured Child Michael Thompson and Teresa Barker, *The Pressured Child: Helping Your Child Find Success in School and Life* (New York: Ballantine Books, 2004). *including research by the American Camp Association* "The American Camp Association (formerly known as the American Camping Association) is a community of camp professionals who, for *100 years*, have joined together to share our knowledge and experience and to ensure the quality of camp programs." American Camp Association and Philliber Research Associates. "Directions: Youth Developmental Outcomes of the Camp Experience," 2005. www.acacamps.org.

One: *Off They Go*

8   *Rates of violent crime are at historic lows in the United States* David Von Drehile, "US Crime Rates Drop: Why Are There Fewer Murders," *Time,* February 22, 2010.

8   *Bill Polk* Personal interview with William Polk, former headmaster of the Groton School, 2010.

14   *Only at camp can they "be themselves"* American Camp Association and Philliber Research Associates, "Directions: Youth Developmental Outcomes of the Camp Experience," 2005.

16   *Research tells us that college-educated mothers* Tara Parker-Pope, "Surprisingly, Family Time Has Grown," *The New York Times,* April 5, 2010.

17   *William Damon, a professor of psychology at Stanford University* William Damon, *Greater Expectations: Overcoming the Culture of Indulgence in Our Homes* (New York: Free Press Paperbacks, 1995).

18   *Martin Seligman, the famed University of Pennsylvania psychologist* Martin Seligman, *The Optimistic Child: A Proven Program to Safeguard Children Against Depression and Build Lifelong Resilience* (New York: Free Press, 2002).

20   *Researchers in day care settings have observed* Michael Thompson, Catherine O'Neill Grace, and Lawrence Cohen, *Best Friends, Worst Enemies: Understanding the Social Lives of Children* (New York: Ballantine Books, 2001).

21   *Research shows that the fathers of teenage boys* R. W. Larson et al, "Changes in adolescents' daily interactions with their families from ages 10–18: Disengagement and transformation," *Developmental Psychology,* 32 (1996): 744–754.

22   *Ambitious parents with athletically talented children* Andre Agassi, *Open: An Autobiography* (New York: Random House, 2009).

23   *I recommend Fred Waitzkin's* Searching for Bobby Fisher Fred Wait-

zkin, *Searching for Bobby Fisher: Every Journey Begins with a Single Move* (New York: Penguin Books, 1984).

24 *In his book* The Second Family, *Ron Taffel* Ron Taffel and Melinda Blau, *The Second Family: Dealing with Peer Power, Pop Culture, the Wall of Silence and Other Challenges of Raising Today's Teens* (New York: St. Martin's Press, 2001).

25 *That Sigmund Freud called it the "family romance."* Sigmund Freud. *Totem and Taboo,* SE, New York: Moffat, Yard and Company, 1918: 1–161.

26 *CNN reported that half of the mothers* Stephanie Goldberg, "Parents Using Smartphone to Entertain Bored Kids," CNN Technology, April 26, 2010.

26 *When PBS released its iPad app in 2010* The Henry J. Kaiser Family Foundation, "Generation M2: Media in the Lives of 8- to 18- Year-Olds," January 2010.

26 *American children are spending fifty-three hours per week* The Henry J. Kaiser Family Foundation, "Generation M2."

27 *Equal amounts of time in front of lit-up screens.* The Henry J. Kaiser Family Foundation, "Generation M2."

29 *Forty years ago, 41 percent of children* National Center for Safe Routes to School, "US Travel Data Show Decline in Walking and Bicycling to School has Stabilized," April 8, 2010. www.saferoutespartnership.org/27892/450701.

29 *In his book* The Power of Play, *David Elkind* David Elkind, *The Power of Play: Learning What Comes Naturally* (Philadelphia, PA: Da Capo Press, 2007).

29 *Before 1995 mothers spent an average of about twelve hours* Parker-Pope, "Surprisingly, Family Time Has Grown."

29 *Educated fathers are also increasing the amount of time* Parker-Pope, "Surprisingly, Family Time Has Grown."

30   *With experts like Malcolm Gladwell, the author of* Outliers Gladwell, *Outliers.*

30   *In* Stand by Me, *the Rob Reiner movie* Rob Reiner, dir., *Stand by Me,* 1986.

31   *Hugo,* directed and produced by Martin Scorcese (Paramount Pictures, 2011). Based on the book *The Invention of Hugo Cabret* by Brian Selznick. (Scholastic Press 2007).

Two: *A Lost World of Family Time*

37   *American children spend an average of fifty-three hours per week* The Henry J. Kaiser Family Foundation, "Generation M2."

38   *According to surveys done by Pew Research and the Nielsen Company* Amanda Lanhart, "Teens, Cell Phones and Texting: Text Messaging Becomes Centerpiece Communication," Pew Internet & American Life Project, April 2010. http://pewresearch.org/pubs/1572/teens-cell-phones-text-messages.

41   *The average American family spends 45 percent* Sue Hensley and Annika Stensson, "Restaurant Industry Expected to Post Modest Sales Growth in 2009 as It Copes with the Weakest Economy in Decades," *National Restaurant Association's 2009 Restaurant Industry Forecast.* December 19, 2008. http://www.restaurant.org/pressroom/pressrelease/?id=1725.

41   *But even when dinners are prepared and eaten at home* Lisa Belkin, "Don't Turn Off the TV Week," *The New York Times,* April 21, 2009.

43   *But for the modern child from a small family* U.S. Census Bureau, Summary File 1 (SF 1) and Summary File 3 (SF 3). http://factfinder.census.gov/servlet/SAFFFacts.

48   *In her book* Children's Nature, *a history of the American summer camp* Leslie Paris, *Children's Nature: The Rise of the American Summer Camp* (New York and London: New York University Press, 2008).

49 *Catherine Steiner-Adair, a psychologist and school consultant* Catherine Steiner-Adair, *Full of Ourselves: A Wellness Program to Advance Girl Power, Health and Leadership* (New York: Teachers College Press, Columbia University, 2006).

51 *Shannon Donovan-Monti, the director of YMCA Chimney Corners for Girls* Personal interview with Shannon Donovan-Monti, director of YMCA Chimney Corners for Girls, July 2010.

52 *The grandfather of the director, Dick Lewis, had been one of the founders of Wabun* Personal interview with Richard Lewis, director of Camp Waban, May 2011.

53 *Johanna Liskowsky-Doak, whose friendship with her Camp Downer friends* Personal interview with Johanna Liskowsky-Doak, director of Camp Downer, December 2010.

56 *Bill Polk, the former headmaster of the Groton School* Personal interview with William Polk, former headmaster of the Groton School, September 2011.

Three: *A Fire in My Stomach*

62 *All summer and throughout the academic year* C. A. Thurber and J. C. Malinowski, *The Summer Camp Handbook* (Los Angeles: Perspective Publishing, 2000).

67 *The formal definition of homesickness* C. A. Thurber et al, "Homesickness in Preadolescent and Adolescent Girls: Risk Factors, Behavioral, Correlates and Sequelae," *Journal of Clinical Child Psychology* 2 (1999):185–96.

70 *Doug Stone, the coauthor of* Difficult Conversations Doug Stone et al, *Difficult Conversations: How to Discuss What Matters Most* (New York: Penguin Books, 2000). Personal interview, October 2011.

71 *All of the studies from 1943 to the present day* C. A. Thurber, "The Phenomenology of Homesickness in Boys," *Journal of Abnormal Child Psychology* 27 (1999):125–139.

75 *Only 7 percent, or one in fourteen campers* Thurber, "Homesickness in Preadolescent and Adolescent Girls," 185–196.

83 *There are children who cannot deal with certain aspects of camp* Stone, *Difficult Conversations*. Personal interview, October 2011.

84 *While the research finds that 7 percent of children suffer* C. A. Thurber and M. D. Sigman, "Preliminary Models of Risk and Protective Factors for Childhood Homesickness: Review and Empirical Synthesis," *Child Development* 69 (1998): 903–934.

Four: *Homesick and Happy*

92 *Chris Thurber also recommends* C. A. Thurber, "The Experience and Expression of Homesickness in Preadolescent and Adolescent Boys," *Child Development* 66 (1995): 1162–1178.

92 *Thurber's research suggests that campers* C. A. Thurber and J. R. Weisz, "'You Can Try or You Can Just Give Up': The Impact of Perceived Control and Coping Style on Childhood Homesickness," *Developmental Psychology* 33 (1997): 508 –517.

Five: *A Little Paradise*

107 *The director, Kurt Podeszwa, points to the outlets* Personal interview with Kurt Podeszwa, director of Camp for All, July 2011.

111 *Marc Cohen, the director of Camp Hope, also suggested that I use "caregivers"* Personal interview with Marc Cohen, camp director of Camp Hope, July 2011.

Six: *OMG, I Love You!*

130 *The four women—Johanna, Kelly, Amanda, and Cortney—arrived for dinner* Personal interviews, May 2011.

140 *Mitch, who combined a career as camp director* Personal interview with Mitch Zuckoff, August 2010.

144   *Pete Hare, the director of Camp Keewaydin on Lake Dunmore* Personal interview with Pete Hare, executive director of Keewaydin Foundation and camp director of Camp Keewaydin on Lake Dunmore, July and September 2010.

147   *In a charming collection of essays about summer camps called Sleep-away* Eric Simonoff, *Sleepaway: Writtings on Summer Camp* (New York: Penguin Group, 2005).

148   *Erik Erikson said that all conversation in adolescence is about identity* Erik H. Erikson, *Childhood and Society* (New York: Norton, 1950) 260.

Seven: *Passages*

159   *Even Bruce Ingersoll, now the director of Keewaydin Temagami* Personal interview with Bruce Ingersoll, director of Keewaydin Temagami, June and September 2010.

162   *Increasing numbers of college students in this country are reporting* C. Jenkins, "More College Students More Anxious, Depressed, Study Shows," *Daily Healthy Report,* February 17, 2011.

164   *Bret Stephenson, the author of* From Boys to Men Bret Stephenson, *From Boys to Men: Spiritual Rites of Passage in an Indulgent Age* (Rochester, VT: Park Street Press, 2006).

Eight: *"I Wish You Luck in Being Yourselves"*

180   *Those were the adjectives that David McDonald used* Richard Kalb, "Essay in Memory of Ernst Bulova" Retrieved on November 11, 2007. http://friendsofbucksrock.org.

184   *In order to better understand the arts colony experience* Personal interview with Toby Dewey, director of the Summer Arts Program at the Cambridge School in Weston, Massachusetts, August 2010.

Nine: *The Magic of Camp*

199   *Mitch Zuckoff, a professor of journalism at Boston University* Personal interview with Mitch Zuckoff, August 2010.

200   *Michal Sanger, an art teacher from Minnesota* Personal interview, October 2010.

204   *Yong Zhao, the presidential chair and associate dean of Global Education* Yong Zhao, *Catching Up or Leading the Way: American Education in the Age of Globalization* (Alexandria, VA: ASDC Publishing, 2009). http://zhaolearning.com/.

204   *Governments and authorities in every country work very hard* Yong, *Catching Up or Leading the Way.*

205   *Author Daniel Pink, in* A Whole New Mind Daniel Pink, *A Whole New Mind: Moving from the Information Age of the Conceptual Age* (New York: Riverhead Books, Penguin Group, 2005).

207   *Lance Ozier, author and educator, sees summer camp as* Lance Ozier, "Camps and Classrooms." *Camping,* March/April 2010.

207   *Pete Hare, a camp director and the son of a legendary* Personal interview with Peter Hare, director of Camp Keewaydin on Lake Dunmore, July and September 2010.

210   *The director of Spirit, Margie Anderson* Personal interview with Margie Anderson, director of Spirit, August 2011.

212   *Girl Scout Law* Girl Scouts of the USA, www.girlscouts.org.

213   New York Times columnist *David Brooks* David Brooks, "If It Feels Right . . ." *The New York Times,* September 12, 2011.

222   *The great American educator John Dewey* John Dewey, *Experience and Education* (New York: Kappa Delta Pi Publications, 1938).

223   *Scott Brody, the director of Camps Kenwood and Evergreen* Personal interview with Scott Brody, director of Camps Kenwood and Evergreen, October and December 2010.

224   *Children make great friends at camp* American Camp Association and Philliber Research Associates. "Directions: Youth Developmental Outcomes of the Camp Experience," 2005.

224   *Ellen Flight, the director of Camp Songadeewin of Keewaydin.* Personal interview with Ellen Flight, director of Camp Songadeewin of Keewaydin, September 2010.

225   *Many people who founded camps in the late 1800s* Leslie Paris, *Children's Nature: The Rise of the American Summer Camp* (New York and London: New York University Press, 2008).

225   *There have been dramatic decreases both in the amount of time* Richard Louv, *Last Child in the Woods: Saving Our Children from Nature Deficit Disorder* (New York: Algonquin Books, 2008).

225   *According to researchers at the University of Maryland* Louv, *Last Child in the Woods.*

225   *Of the mothers from the previous generation* Louv, *Last Child in the Woods* (New York: Algonquin Books, 2008).

228   *In 1929, Hedley S. Dimock and Charles E. Hendry published* Hedley Dimock and Charles E. Hendry, *Camping and Character: A Camp Experiment in Character Education* (New York: Kessinger Publishing, 2008).

228   *David Sedaris, the great American humorist, who is gay* David Sedaris, "I Like Guys," *Naked* (Canada: Little, Brown and Company, 1997).

229   *The average American child sees pornography* Safe Families: Statistics on Pornography, Sexual Addiction and Online Perpetrators and their Effects on Children. http://www.safefamilies.org/sfStats.php. Accessed September 2011.

234   *The longtime humor columnist for the* Miami Herald, *Dave Barry* Personal interview with David Barry, September 2010.

Ten: *"Childsick" and Happy*

238   *Judith Wright, the director of summer camps for the Movement for Reform Judaism* Personal interview with Judith Wright, director of Summer Camps for the Movement for Reform Judaism in the UK, December 2010.

240   *When I interviewed the humor columnist Dave Barry.* Personal interview with David Barry, September 2010.

242   *Chris Thurber and his colleagues have developed a program* Chris Thurber, *The Secret Ingredients of Summer Camp Success: How to Have the Most Fun with the Least Homesickness,* DVD-CD (Martinsville, IN: American Camp Association, 2006).

BIBLIOGRAPHY

Books

Adler, Thomas. *Campingly Yours*. Chandler, AZ: Five Star Publications, Inc., 2009.

Agassi, Andre. *Open: An Autobiography*. New York: Random House, 2009.

Back, Brian. *The Keewaydin Way: The Story of the World's Oldest Canoe-Trip Camp*. Salisbury, VT: Roy Waters Scholarship Fund, 2004.

Damon, William. *Greater Expectations: Overcoming the Culture of Indulgence in Our Homes*. New York: Free Press Paperbacks, 1995.

Dewey, John. *Experience and Education*. New York: Kappa Delta Pi Publications, 1938.

Dimock, Hedley and Charles E. Hendry. *Camping and Character: A Camp Experiment in Character Education*. New York: Kessinger Publishing, 2008.

Elkind, David. *The Hurried Child: Growing Up Too Fast Too Soon*. Cambridge, MA: Da Capo Press, 2001.

———. *The Power of Play: Learning What Comes Naturally*. Philadelphia, PA: Da Capo Press, 2007.

Erikson, Erik H. *Childhood and Society*. New York: Norton, 1950.

Fenn, Abbott T. *The Story of Keewaydin: 50 Years at Dunmore: 1910–1959*. Keewaydin Camp, Inc., 1959.

Freud, Sigmund. *Totem and Taboo*, SE, 1–161. New York: Moffat, Yard and Company, 1918.

Gladwell, Malcolm. *Outliers*. New York: Little, Brown and Company, 2008.

Kahn, Laurie Susan. *Sleepaway: The Girls of Summer and the Camps They Love*. New York: Workman Publishing, 2003.

Kolb, David. *Experiential Learning: Experience as the Source of Learning and Development*. Englewood Cliffs, NJ: Prentice-Hall, 1984.

Kessler, David A. *The End of Overeating: Taking Control of the Insatiable American Appetite*. New York: Rodale Press, 2009.

Kessler, Lauren. *My Teenage Werewolf: A Mother, a Daughter, a Journey Through the Thicket of Adolescence*. New York: Penguin Group, 2010.

Lewin, Kurt. *Field Theory in Social Science*. New York: Harper Collins, 1951.

Louv, Richard. *Last Child in the Woods: Saving Our Children from Nature Deficit Disorder*. New York: Algonquin Books, 2008.

Marano, Estroff Hara. *A Nation of Wimps: The High Cost of Invasive Parenting*. New York: Random House, 2008.

Marson, Philip. *A Teacher Speaks: A Personal History of Forty Years in the Classroom with a Program to Solve the Deepening Crisis in American Education*. New York: David McKay Company, Inc., 1960.

McPhee, John. *Coming into the Country*. New York: Farrar, Straus and Giroux, 1991.

———. *The Survival of the Bark Canoe*. New York: Farrar, Straus and Giroux, 1975.

Miller, Susan A. *Growing Girls: The Natural Origins of Girls' Organizations in America*. New Brunswick, NJ: Rutgers University Press, 2007.

Mowat, Farley. *Born Naked*. New York: Houghton Mifflin Company, 1993.

Paris, Leslie. *Children's Nature: The Rise of the American Summer Camp*. New York and London: New York University Press, 2008.

Rapkin, Mickey. *Theater Geek*. New York: Simon & Schuster, 2008.

Reed, T. L., and R. L. Grabill. *Camp Pemigewassett: The First 100 Years*. Privately published, Wentworth, NJ, Camp Pemigewassett, 2008.

Rowling, J. K. *Harry Potter and the Deathly Hallows*. New York: Arthur A. Levine Books, 2009.

Sedaris, David. "I Like Guys" in *Naked*. Canada: Little, Brown and Company, 1997.

Seligman, Martin E. P. *The Optimistic Child: A Proven Program to Safe-

guard Children Against Depression and Build Lifelong Resilience. New York: Harper Perennial, 1995.

————. *Authentic Happiness: Using the New Positive Psychology to Realize Your Potential for Lasting Fulfillment.* New York: Free Press, 2002.

Selznick, Brian. *The Invention of Hugo Cabret.* New York: Scholastic Press, 2007.

Skenazy, Lenore. *Free-Range Kids: How to Raise Safe, Self-Reliant Children (Without Going Nuts with Worry).* San Francisco: Jossey-Bass, 2009.

Simonoff, Eric. *Sleepaway: Writings on Summer Camp.* New York: Penguin Group, 2005.

Steiner-Adair, Catherine. *Full of Ourselves: A Wellness Program to Advance Girl Power, Health and Leadership.* New York: Teachers College Press, Columbia University, 2006.

Stephenson, Bret. *From Boys to Men: Spiritual Rites of Passage in an Indulgent Age.* Rochester, VT: Park Street Press, 2006.

Stone, Doug, Bruce Patton, Sheila Heen, and Roger Fisher. *Difficult Conversations: How to Discuss What Matters Most.* New York: Penguin Books, 2000.

Stone, Kas. *Paddling and Hiking the Georgian Bay Coast.* Ontario, Canada: Boston Mills Press, 2008.

Taffel, Ron, and Melinda Blau. *The Second Family: Dealing with Peer Power, Pop Culture, the Wall of Silence and Other Challenges of Raising Today's Teens.* New York: St. Martin's Press, 2001.

Thompson, Michael, Catherine O'Neill Grace, and Lawrence Cohen. *Best Friends, Worst Enemies: Understanding the Social Lives of Children.* New York: Ballantine Books, 2001.

Thompson, Michael, and Dan Kindlon. *Raising Cain: Protecting the Emotional Life of Boys.* New York: Ballantine Books, 2000.

Thompson, Michael, and Teresa Barker. *The Pressured Child: Helping Your Child Find Success in School and Life.* New York: Ballantine Books, 2004.

Thurber, Christopher A., and Jon C. Malinowski. *The Summer Camp Handbook: Everything You Need to Find, Choose and Get Ready for Overnight Camp—and Skip the Homesickness.* Los Angeles: Perspective Publishing, 2000.

Tulley, Gever, and Julie Spiegler. *Fifty Dangerous Things (You Should Let Your Children Do)*. Montara, CA: Tinkering Unlimited, 2009.

Van Slyck, Abigail A. *A Manufactured Wilderness: Summer Camps and the Shaping of American Youth, 1890–1960*. Minneapolis, MN: University of Minnesota Press, 2006.

Vorenberg, Mike. *Faithful and True: 100 Years at Keewaydin on Dunmore: 1910–2009*. Salisbury, VT: The Keewaydin Foundation, 2009.

Waitzkin, Fred. *Searching for Bobby Fisher: Every Journey Begins with a Single Move*. New York: Penguin Books, 1984.

Weidensaul, Scott. *Return to Wild America: A Yearlong Search for the Continent's Natural Soul*. New York: North Point Press, 2005.

White, E. B. *Stuart Little*. New York: HarperCollins, 1945.

———. *Essays of E. B. White*. New York: HarperPerennial, 1977.

Zhao, Yong. *Catching Up or Leading the Way: American Education in the Age of Globalization*. Alexandria, VA: ASDC Publishing, 2009.

Articles

American Camp Association and Philliber Research Associates. "Directions: Youth Developmental Outcomes of the Camp Experience," 2005.

Belkin, Lisa. "Don't Turn Off the TV Week." *The New York Times*, April 21, 2009. www.nytimes.com.

Bialeschki, M. D., K. A. Henderson, and P. A. James. "The Camp Experience: An ACA Perspective on Developmental Outcomes for Youth." *Taproot: A Publication of the Coalition for Education in the Outdoors*.

———. "Camp Experiences and Developmental Outcomes for Youth." *Child and Adolescent Psychiatric Clinics of North America* 16 (2007): 769–788.

Bialeschki, Deborah M.D., et al. "Happy but Sad: Outcomes at Morry's Camp." *Camping Magazine*, January/February, 2002.

Brooks, David. "If It Feels Right . . ." *The New York Times*, September 12, 2011.

Coleman, M. "The Experiential Classroom: Camp." *Camping Magazine*, March/April 2010.

Cooper, H., et al. "The Effects of Summer Vacation on Achievement Test Scores: A Narrative and Meta-Analytic Review." *Review of Educational Research* 66 (1996): 227–268.

Goldberg, Stephanie. "Parents Using Smartphone to Entertain Bored Kids." *CNN Technology*, April 26, 2010.

The Henry J. Kaiser Family Foundation. "Generation M2: Media in the Lives of 8- to 18-Year-Olds." January 2010.

Henderson, K. A., M. D. Bialeschki, and P. A. James. "Overview of Camp Research." *Child and Adolescent Psychiatric Clinics of North America* 16 (2007): 755–767.

Henderson, K. A., et al. "Restaurant Industry Expected to Post Modest Sales Growth in 2009 as It Copes with the Weakest Economy in Decades," Sue Hensley and Annika Stensson, assts. *National Restaurant Association's 2009 Restaurant Industry Forecast*. December 19, 2008. www.restaurant.org/pressroom/pressrelease/?id=1725.

Jenkins, C. "More College Students More Anxious, Depressed, Study Shows." *Daily Healthy Report*, February 17, 2011.

Kalb, Richard. "Essay in Memory of Ernst Bulova." Friends of Buck's Rock. Retrieved on November 11, 2007. http://friendsofbucksrock.org.

Lanhart, Amanda. "Teens, Cell Phones and Texting: Text Messaging Becomes Centerpiece Communication." *Pew Internet & American Life Project*. April 2010. http://pewresearch.org/pubs/1572/teens-cell-phones-text-messages.

Larson, R. W., et al. (1996). "Changes in Adolescents' Daily Interactions with Their Families from Ages 10–18: Disengagement and Transformation." *Developmental Psychology* 32(1996): 744–754.

Muchnick, B,, and Penny Bryan. "Positive Learning." *Camping Magazine*, May/June 2010.

National Center for Health Statistics. "Women Are Having More Children, New Report Shows Teen Births Continue to Decline." Referencing *Births: Final Data for 2000* NVSR, vol. 50, no. 5 104 (PHS) 2002–1120, February 12, 2002.

National Center for Safe Routes to School. "US Travel Data Show Decline in Walking and Bicycling to School has Stabilized." April 8, 2010. http://www.saferoutespartnership.org/27892/450701.

Ozier, Lance. "Summer School and Summer Camp." *Camping Magazine,* March/April 2010.

———. "Camps and Classrooms." *Camping Magazine,* November/ December 2009.

———. "Morry's Camp Education Symposium Follow-up Report." http:// www.projectmorry.org/pages/education/pdf/symposium_follow_up _2006 . . .

Parker-Pope, Tara. "Surprisingly, Family Time Has Grown." *The New York Times,* April 5, 2010.

Safe Families. "Statistics on Pornography, Sexual Addiction and Online Perpetrators and their Effects on Children." www.safefamilies.org/ sfStats.php.

Schank, Roger C. "What we learn when we learn by doing." *Technical Report 60.* Evanston, IL: Northwestern University's Institute for the Learning Sciences. October 1994.

Scheuler, Leslie, and Michelle Gambone. "Deepening Knowledge of the Variables: Youth Development Findings from Group Camps." Search Institute's *Insights and Evidence* 4(1)(2007): 1–11.

Stephenson, Bret. "Rites of Passage." *Adolescent Mind,* December 20, 2008. Accessed on October 5, 2011, http://www.adolescentmind.com/ rites_of_passage1.htm.

Thurber, Christopher. "Children's Coping with Homesickness: Phenomenology and Intervention." In: van Tilburg MAL, Vingerhoets AJJM, eds. *Psychological Aspects of Geographical Moves: Homesickness and Acculturation Stress.* Tilburg, Netherlands: Tilburg University Press (1997):143–163.

———. "The phenomenology of homesickness in boys." *Journal of Abnormal Child Psychology* 27 (1999):125–139.

———. "Creating Healthy Camp Experiences." *Pediatrics* 127 (2011): 794–799.

———. "The Experience and Expression of Homesickness in Preadolescent and Adolescent Boys." *Child Development* 66 (1995):1162–1178.

Thurber, Christopher, and M. D. Sigman. "Preliminary Models of Risk and Protective Factors for Childhood Homesickness: Review and Empirical Synthesis." *Child Development* 69 (1998):903–934.

Thurber, Christopher, and Edward Walton. "Preventing and Treating Homesickness." *Pediatrics* 119 (2007): 192–201.

Thurber, Christopher, and J. R. Weisz. "'You Can Try or You Can Just Give Up': The Impact of Perceived Control and Coping Style on Childhood Homesickness." *Developmental Psychology* 33 (1997):508–517.

Thurber, Christopher, D. R. Patterson, et al. "Homesickness and Children's Adjustment to Hospitalization: Toward a Preliminary Model," *Children's Health Care* 36(1)(2007):1–28.

Thurber, Christopher, M. D. Sigman, et al. "Homesickness in Preadolescent and Adolescent Girls: Risk Factors, Behavioral Correlates, and Sequelae." *Journal of Clinical Psychology* 28 (1999): 185–196.

U.S. Census Bureau, Summary File 1 (SF 1) and Summary File 3 (SF 3) http://factfinder.census.gov/servlet/SAFFFacts.

Von Drehile, David. "US Crime Rates Drop: Why Are There Fewer Murders?" *Time,* February 22, 2010.

DVDs and Movies

Hugo. Martin Scorsese. 2012. Based on the book *The Invention of Hugo Cabret.* Brian Selznick, New York: Scholastic Press, 2007.

The Secret Ingredients of Summer Camp Success: How to Have the Most Fun With the Least Homesickness. Christopher Thurber, creator. American Camp Association. 2006.

Self-Esteem Through the Camp Experience: A Research Forum. Healthy Learning. 2010.

Stand by Me. Rob Reiner, director. 1986.

Websites

American Camp Association

www.acacamps.org.

CAMP, an American Camp Association resource for families

www.acacamps.org/parents

Girl Scouts of the USA

www.girlscouts.org

Outward Bound
www.outwardbound.org

People

CHRIS THURBER

"CampSpirit is the online home of Dr. Christopher Thurber, a board-certified clinical psychologist, author, consultant, and father. A graduate of Harvard University, Chris cofounded Expert Online Training, a revolutionary set of Web-based educational tools for camp staff and health care professionals. He also hosts ACA's homesickness prevention DVD -CD set and coauthored the bestselling *Summer Camp Handbook*. Chris is widely published in the academic and popular press and has more than thirty years of camp experience. He is a longstanding member of the ACA's Research Committee. All of Chris's personal and professional work is guided by the principles of leadership-by-example and interpersonal development."

LANCE OZIER

"Lance Ozier, Ed.M., is education coordinator at Project Morry and an instructor in teacher education at The City College of New York and Teachers College, Columbia University. In addition to *Camping Magazine,* Ozier's writing has appeared in the *Journal of Democracy and Education,* and the Daybooks for Critical Reading and Writing."

Personal Interviews and Camp Directors

Anderson, Margie, director of Spirit. Interviewed August 2011.

Barry, David, columnist for the *Miami Herald*. Interviewed September 2010.

Brody, Scott, director of Camps Kenwood and Evergreen. Interviewed October and December 2010.

Cohen, Marc, director of Camp Hope. Interviewed July 2011.

Dewey, Toby, director of the Summer Arts Program at the Cambridge School in Weston, Massachusetts. Interviewed August 2010.

Donovan-Monti, Shannon, director of YMCA Chimney Corners for Girls. Interviewed July 2010.

Flight, Ellen, director of Camp Songadeewin. Interviewed July and September 2010.

Hare, Peter, director of Camp Keewaydin on Lake Dunmore. Interviewed July and September 2010.

Ingersoll, Bruce, director of Keewaydin Temagami. Interviewed July and September 2010.

Lewis, Richard, director of Camp Waban. Interviewed May 2011.

Liskowsky-Doak, Johanna, director of Camp Downer. Interviewed December 2010.

Podeszwa, Kurt, director of Camp for All. Interviewed July 2011.

Polk, William, former head of Groton School, 2010. Interviewed September 2011.

Sager, Michal, art teacher, Minnesota. Interviewed October 2010.

Wright, Judith, director of Summer Camps for the Movement for Reform Judaism in the UK. Interviewed December 2010.

Zuckoff, Mitch, professor of journalism, Boston University and author of *Lost in Shangri-La*. Interviewed August 2010.

ABOUT THE AUTHOR

MICHAEL THOMPSON, PhD, is a clinical psychologist, lecturer, consultant, and former seventh-grade teacher. He conducts workshops across the United States and internationally on social cruelty, children's friendships, and boys' development. With Dan Kindlon, PhD, he co-authored the *New York Times* bestseller *Raising Cain: Protecting the Emotional Life of Boys,* which was adapted into an acclaimed documentary shown on PBS. With Teresa H. Barker, he co-authored *The Pressured Child: Helping Your Child Find Success in School and Life; Speaking of Boys: Answers to the Most-Asked Questions About Raising Sons,* and *It's a Boy!: Your Son's Development from Birth to Age 18.* With Catherine O'Neill Grace and Lawrence J. Cohen, PhD, he co-authored *Best Friends, Worst Enemies: Understanding the Social Lives of Children* and *Mom, They're Teasing Me: Helping Your Child Solve Social Problems.* A former board member of the American Camp Association, Dr. Thompson is married and the father of two. He lives in Arlington, Massachusetts, and can be reached at http.michaelthompson-phd.com.

ABOUT THE TYPE

This book was set in Sabon, a typeface designed by the well-known German typographer Jan Tschichold (1902–74). Sabon's design is based on the original letterforms of Claude Garamond and was created specifically to be used for three sources: foundry type for hand composition, Linotype, and Monotype. Tschichold named his typeface for the famous Franfurt typefounder Jacques Sabon, who died in 1580.